**Mayflov
Christian
Resources**

Old Testament
Manual

Copyright © 2001 Mayflower Christian Books

British Library Cataloguing in Publication Data. A catalogue record for this book is available from the British Library.

Published by Mayflower Christian Books,
114 Spring Road, Southampton SO19 2QB.

Typeset by Mayflower Christian Books.

ISBN: 0 907821 11 1

Contents

Foreword

Why develop an Old Testament Manual?

Thank you for purchasing the Old Testament Manual. We hope it will be of great benefit.

We were aware that many UK primary school teachers wanted material that faithfully reflected traditional Christian teaching as found in the Bible. As a result we developed the Mayflower Christian Resources New Testament Manual, which was well received. Many teachers have since asked us to produce an Old Testament version.

The Old Testament is full of moral and spiritual guidance that is still of great relevance to children today. The Old Testament addresses vital issues: Where does life come from? Is there a difference between human beings and other living things?; Why is the world like it is? How does God expect us to live? How do we see God working in the world today? It is full of fascinating characters such as Noah, Moses, Joseph and Daniel, who loved and obeyed God.

The Old Testament is also the preparation for the New. It records God's establishment and dealings with the nation of Israel in preparation for the coming of the Saviour - Jesus Christ. The Bible tells us that his coming into the world and subsequent life death and resurrection are the fulfilment of Old Testament promise and prophecy.

Our intention has been to present the Bible's record of these things clearly, simply and accurately through the Lesson Outlines, Teacher's Notes and other materials.

We hope that through this resource many will become more familiar with the character and purposes of God as revealed in the Old Testament and benefit from its wealth of moral and spiritual guidance.

Frances Fountain
Writer of Christian resources for children and Sunday school teacher

Ruth Goodridge
Professional artist and illustrator of Christian books and resources

Linda Smalley
Qualified schoolteacher and writer of Christian resources for children

Mark Stocker
Qualified schoolteacher and a Christian church minister

Mayflower Christian Books

the publishing branch of

MAYFLOWER CHRISTIAN BOOKSHOP CHARITABLE TRUST
114, Spring Road, Sholing, Southampton, SO19 2QB

Teacher's Introduction

Each lesson in this Manual has:

- A **Lesson Outline** with a List of Relevant Passages from the Bible, *Themes*, *Aims*, *Resources* list and Suggested *Other Ideas and Activities*;

- **Teacher's Notes** which give the teacher a *Summary* of the story's main points, an introduction or *Point of Contact*, an outline of the story and events, an *Illustration* to help highlight the main point, and a *Things to Learn* statement which states what the children should learn from the story;

- **Suggested 'Discuss' Questions** which the teacher might like to use for review, in informal discussion as the children are at work, or with the whole class;

- An **Optional Children's Story Sheet.** This can be used so that the children read the basic story, rather than having the teacher tell the story to them;

- A **Puzzle Page** which can be used to highlight and consolidate the main points in the story;

- An **Activity Sheet** and sometimes a **Picture** which can be used as an extra resource or to highlight a main part of the story. *Please note: generally every **Activity Sheet** needs scissors, glue (or stapler) and coloured pencils. Sometimes it is necessary to photocopy an **Activity Sheet** in 2 (contrasting) colours.

Differentiation

With any single Puzzle Page activities do vary in the level of ability required of the children. Teachers may choose to differentiate as to which activities they set for certain children. They may also, at certain times, like to give the word answers on the board as a help with crosswords and other activities.

Maps

These are included at the back and cover some of the areas mentioned in the Manual.

Health & Safety

Care should be taken when cutting or piercing of paper is required with some Activity Pages, and with the use of paint or adhesives and any other possible allergy triggering substances. Teachers are referred to their Health and Safety Guidelines.

Copyright

Lesson Themes

Section and Lesson	Themes
Beginnings	
Creation	Power, Wonder, Design
Adam & Eve	Creation of Man & Woman, Temptation, Sin, Salvation
Noah & the Flood	Courage, Obedience, Judgment, Deliverance
Abraham - The Man Who Trusted God	God's Promises, Trust, God's Faithfulness
Jacob - The Man God Changed	Deceit, Kindness, Mercy
Joseph's Coat & Dreams	Favouritism, Jealousy, Hatred
Joseph - From Prison to Power	Hardship, Patience, Unselfishness, Change
Joseph Forgives His Brothers	Being Sorry, Forgiveness, Reconciliation
Moses	
Moses' Birth & Call	God's Plan, Preparation
Pharaoh & The Plagues	Stubbornness, God's Power
The Passover	Slavery and Freedom, Judgment & Deliverance
Crossing the Red Sea	God's Power, Praise, Deliverance
The Israelites in the Wilderness	God's Provision and Goodness, Complaining
The Ten Commandments	Law, Order, Right & Wrong
The Tabernacle & The Golden Calf	Idols, Forgiveness, Worship
Israel in The Land	
Joshua & the Walls of Jericho	Faith, Obedience, Trust
Ruth - The Girl Who Put God First	Choices, Unselfishness, Reward
Samuel Listens to God	Prayer, Obedience
David & Goliath	Danger, Trust, Bravery
David - The Man Who Loved His Enemy	Jealousy, Loving Your Enemies
Solomon - The Wise King	Riches, Wisdom, Putting God First
Decline, Exile & Return	
Jonah - Preacher on the Run	God's Presence, God's Forgiveness
Elijah on Mount Carmel	God's Character, God's Power, Prayer
Daniel in the Lion's Den	Good Behaviour, Doing What Is Right, Standing Firm
Esther Saves Her People	Taking Opportunities, Gifts & Talents
Nehemiah Rebuilds Jerusalem	Hard Work, Perseverance, God's Plan

Lesson Aims

Section and Lesson	Aims
Beginnings	
Creation	To teach the Bible's account of the creation of the universe and all that is in it.
	To encourage reflection upon the wonder of God's design in creation.
Adam & Eve	To consider the Bible's teaching that men & women are made by God.
	To recount the Bible's account of the entry of sin into the world.
	To show God's kind provision for Adam & Eve after they had disobeyed.
Noah & the Flood	To teach the Biblical account of Noah and the flood.
	To highlight the attitude of being willing to stand alone.
	To illustrate what the Bible teaches about the character of God.
Abraham - The Man Who Trusted God	To teach the Bible's account of the life of Abraham.
	To see Abraham as an illustration of faith and trust in God.
	To show that the Bible teaches that God always keeps his promises.
	To teach that Abraham is considered to be the founder of the Jewish nation.
Jacob - The Man God Changed	To recount the life of Jacob.
	To consider deceit and its consequences.
	To illustrate God's mercy to Jacob despite his failings and dishonesty.
Joseph's Coat and Dreams	To teach the events in the early life of Joseph.
	To consider the subject of jealousy and its consequences.
	To encourage children not to be jealous of others.
Joseph - From Prison to Power	To describe Joseph's transition from prison to power.
	To consider Joseph's exceptional behaviour.
	To show that the Bible teaches Christians how to respond to opposition and difficulty.
Joseph Forgives His Brothers	To teach the Bible's account of Joseph being reconciled to his brothers.
	To consider the need to say sorry when we have hurt others.
	To show what is the Bible's teaching on forgiveness.

Lesson Aims (continued)

Moses	
Moses' Birth & Call	To teach the Biblical account of the birth and call of Moses. To consider preparation for future work and vocation. To teach that God will help and protect those who are willing to serve him and work for him.
Pharaoh & The Plagues	To teach the Biblical account of Moses and the plagues on Egypt. To show God's power over all creation - the planets, animals, the weather, etc. To consider stubbornness and its consequences.
The Passover	To describe the Bible's account of the first Passover. To teach the children that the Passover is still celebrated by Jews today. To highlight the New Testament's teaching regarding the Passover.
Crossing the Red Sea	To teach the Bible's account of how the Israelites crossed the Red Sea, but Pharaoh and his army was drowned.
The Israelites in the Wilderness	To teach the children about the Israelites' journey across the wilderness. To consider God's provision for people today. To encourage the children to be grateful/thankful for their daily food and not complain.
The Ten Commandments	To make the children aware of the Ten Commandments. To show that God has made the difference between right and wrong very clear. To show that the commandments are relevant to people's lives today.
The Tabernacle & The Golden Calf	To teach the Bible's account of the Israelites and the golden calf. To describe the role and arrangement of the tabernacle. To consider what the Bible teaches regarding forgiveness.
Israel in The Land Joshua & the Walls of Jericho	To teach the Bible's account of Joshua's conquest of the city of Jericho. To consider why Joshua was such a courageous leader. To reflect on the faith and courage of Christians.

Lesson Aims (continued)

Ruth - The Girl Who Put God First	To teach the Biblical account of Ruth.
	To consider how unselfish Ruth was and how God rewarded her unselfishness.
	To consider the choices we make in life.
Samuel Listens to God	To teach the Biblical account of the birth and call of the prophet Samuel.
	To consider prayer and its role in the life of a Christian.
	To consider how Christians obey God today.
David & Goliath	To teach the story of David and Goliath.
	To show how God helps those who trust him.
David - The Man Who Loved His Enemy	To relate the Bible's story of how David was persecuted by Saul before he became King.
	To teach that we should have a loving attitude toward those who hate us.
Solomon - The Wise King	To describe the wealth and wisdom of King Solomon.
	To reflect on the importance of wisdom.
	To show where wisdom can be found.
Decline, Exile & Return Jonah - Preacher on the Run	To teach the Biblical account of Jonah and the fish.
	To show that the Bible teaches that God is everywhere.
	To illustrate God's kindness and willingness to forgive.
Elijah on Mount Carmel	To recount the story of Elijah on Mount Carmel.
	To teach that the Bible shows there is only one God who is living and powerful.
	To show that the Bible teaches that God answers prayer.
Daniel in the Lion's Den	To tell the Biblical account of Daniel in the lions den.
	To highlight the importance of good behaviour.
	To show that we should not be afraid to stand firm for what we know is right.
Esther Saves Her People	To teach how God protected the Jewish nation through Esther.
	To consider how we should make the most of God given opportunities and abilities.
Nehemiah Rebuilds Jerusalem	To teach the Biblical account of the rebuilding of the walls of Jerusalem under Nehemiah.
	To emphasise the value of perseverance.
	To consider the role of Jerusalem with regard to God's promise to send Jesus into the world.

Creation

Genesis 1 - 2: 3

Themes	Power, Wonder, Design

Aims	To teach the Bible's account of the creation of the universe and all that is in it. To encourage reflection upon the wonder of God's design in creation.

Resources	Bibles, Children's Story Sheet, Puzzle Page, Activity Sheets. (For a book which has large and beautiful illustrations of what the world may have been like when created see 'The Loving Creator" by Carine Mackenzie, published by Christian Focus Publications - ISBN 0 906 731 054 available from most Christian Bookshops.)

Other Ideas & Activities

1. Activity Sheets – follow instructions on Sheets.
2. Display – "God saw that it was good." Discuss why the creation was good. Every child makes an animal, tree or flower to put on class display.
3. Research wonderful things in creation & evidence of purpose and design: - e.g. how a plant is pollinated and reproduces (a spectacular example is the bee orchid); the migration of birds (like the Arctic tern) over long distances; the individuality of each snowflake; the vastness of the universe; the complexity of a human cell.
4. Show slides/posters of a diverse range of creatures/plants/natural landscapes.
5. Compose a piece of music using the idea of chaos to order.
6. Listen to opening of Haydn's "Creation" and discuss – could be linked to looking at the first few verses of Psalm 19.
7. Look at the hymn "All things bright and beautiful" – read, sing , discuss.
8. How many birds or flowers or trees or animals can you think of? List them. Use books to find out about others and include them in your list. Give your work the title, "God made all these birds (or flowers...etc)". This could also be put with the class display (see activity 2 above).

Teacher's Notes

Summary: God is the great creator of the world. At first he made an empty, dark, bare sphere. Then, the Bible says, for six days he made something new on each day, beginning with light and ending with people. All the wonderful living things we see around us, have been made and designed by God. God is so powerful, he only needed to say what he wanted and immediately it appeared. On the seventh day God rested.

Point of Contact
The Diversity of Life
- Do you have a favourite animal, tree or flower?
- Which animal is the largest/smallest?
- Is there an animal you particularly don't like?

God Is Eternal

The Bible teaches that God was here even before he made the world (Psa. 90:2) God never had a beginning and will never have an end. He is alive now and will always be alive forever and ever. An insect may only live for a few days, a plant or flower for a few weeks, a cat or dog may live for ten years or more. People can live to be over 100 years old and some trees can live for over a thousand years, but eventually everyone and everything must die, except God.

God Planned the World

When God decided to make the earth, he thought out how to make a perfect world for people to live in. Before he began, there was absolutely nothing here, so first of all he made the earth. It was very big, with no proper shape and it was completely empty (Gen. 1:2). There were no rivers or hills, no birds or animals and no people. There wasn't even any light. The earth was black and dark with water all over the surface.

God Created Light

The world was covered by thick blackness. God said, "Let there be light', and immediately the light appeared. God showed his power. He just spoke and the light appeared. God saw that the light was good. God then separated the light from the darkness to make day and night. This made up one whole day – the first day.

The Second Day

God made the sky. The sky divided the water that was on the earth from the water vapour above the earth. The sky was like a lovely blue curtain, (Ps.104:2). God also made the air. He knew that all the birds, animals and people would need air to breathe when He made them.

Dry Land

On the third day, God gave us the dry land by gathering all the water on the earth into particular places. Now there were hills and valleys, seas, rivers and lakes. God also made things grow on the bare earth - grass, trees, fruit and vegetables. God made thousands of different plants and flowers, of all different sizes, shapes, colours and smells – lilies, orchids, cherry trees, apple trees, daffodils, bluebells - all of them colourful and beautiful. The Bible says that God saw that it was good.

The Fourth Day

God made the sun, moon and stars to provide light and to give us days, seasons and years. At night we can look up at the moon and stars. God made them shine less brightly so that we can see their beauty and yet still be able to sleep.

Fish and Birds

It was now the fifth day. God called into being birds and fish. God didn't just make one kind of fish and bird, he made a vast variety of shapes, sizes and colours, from a tiny goldfish to an enormous whale. God put the fish in the seas, lakes and rivers. God also made all the birds, from a little robin to a huge eagle (which has wings 3 metres wide). He gave them wings to fly in the sky and the ability to perch and rest in the trees. God looked at everything he made and he was very pleased. He saw that it was good.

The Last Day of Creation
On the sixth day, God made many different animals to live in the world. From the large elephant to the tiny ant. God said, "Let the earth bring forth all the animals". And immediately they all appeared. Lions, sheep, cattle, pigs, horses, butterflies, giraffes, moths, bats, all the many thousands of different animals, insects and reptiles were brought into being with all their different colours, shapes and sizes. The Bible says that God is so powerful that he created all these things just with his word.

However, God saved his most important creation until last. He said, "Let us make man in our own image." God created Adam and Eve, the first man and the first woman.

He put them into a world where they had everything they needed. They had the light of the day in which to work, and the darkness of night in which to sleep. They had fresh air to breathe, and the sun to keep them warm. Fruit and vegetables grew in abundance so they had plenty of good food to eat. They could see and enjoy all the beautiful things around them. God told Adam and Eve to take care of the world they were in and to have children and fill the earth with people.

The Bible says, "Then God saw everything that he had made and indeed it was very good."

The Seventh Day
On this day the Bible says that God rested. This wasn't because he was tired (Ps 121: 4). God took time to consider and enjoy all that he had created. Many Christians still keep one day in seven as a day of rest, when they can worship God and thank him for all he has given us.

Illustration: Evidence Of Design
Suppose you visited someone who had made a superb model railway. It was perfect in every detail – every seat in the trains, lights in the tunnels, and even the tiny tickets in the ticket office. As you stood amazed, admiring the skill, you might ask, "But who made this?" How surprised you would be if someone answered you that it all came together on its own and just happened.

So, as we look at this wonderful world with all its amazing detail and beauty, the Bible says it could not have come about by accident. There is someone behind all we see who planned and designed this world and made all that is in it.

Things to learn:
- The Bible says that God made the universe and everything in it in six days.
- The order of creation in Genesis is:
  1. Heavens, earth, light & darkness
  2. Clouds & water
  3. Land, sea, trees & flowers
  4. Sun, moon & stars
  5. Fish & birds
  6. Animals & man
- The creation shows the greatness of God. He designed and planned all the wonderful things in the world.
- On the seventh day he rested.

Discuss
- What does the world around you tell you about God?
- What can you make?
- What can't you make?
- What does create mean?
- What things will men and women never be able to make?

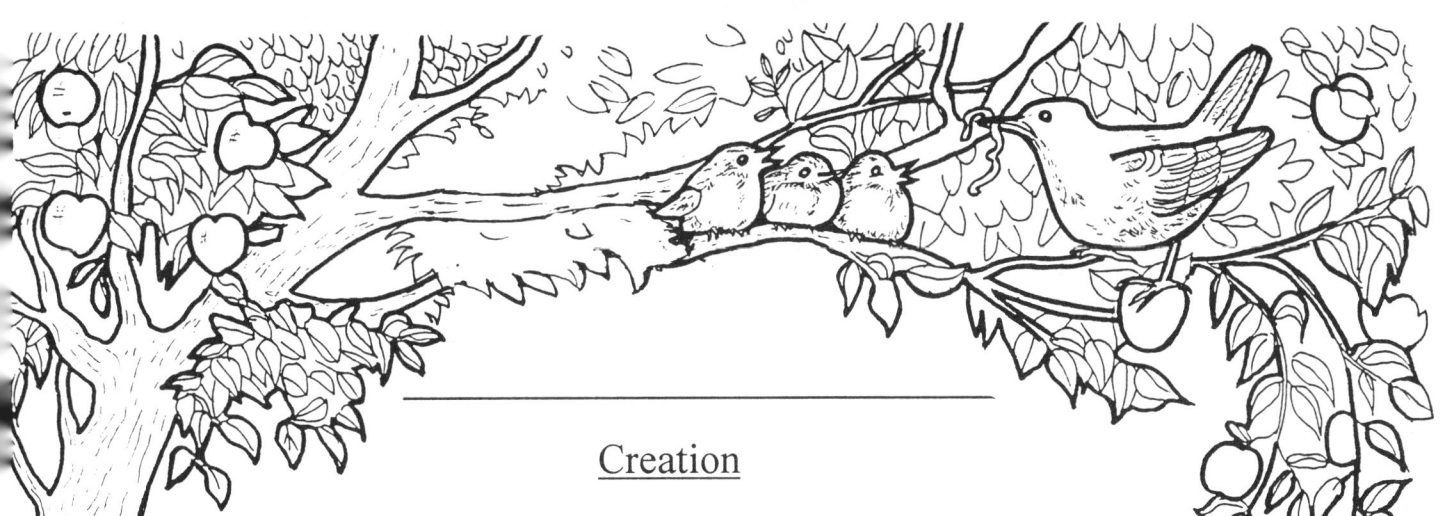

Creation

God made everything. In the beginning there was nothing except God. The earth was empty and dark

On the first day, God said, "Let there be light". Immediately there was light. God saw that the light was good. He separated the light from the darkness to make day and night.

On the second day, God made the sky and the air that we breathe.

On the third day, God made the land. Now there were hills, mountains, rivers and seas. God made things to grow on the earth – grass, trees, plants, flowers, fruits and vegetables. God saw that all he had made was very good.

On the fourth day, God made the sun, moon and stars to give light, and divide the time into days, seasons and years.

On the fifth day, God made the fish and all the creatures which live in the seas and rivers. Then he made all the birds.

On the sixth day, God made all the animals; from the tiny insect to large elephants and giraffes. God just spoke and all these things were made.

Then God made the first man and woman – Adam and Eve.

The Bible says, "Then God saw everything that he had made and indeed it was very good." On the seventh day, God rested.

Name.. Date............................

CREATION

God made the world...

..and everything in it.

Find 10 things that God created in the grid.

h	s	s	r	a	t	s
u	o	d	s	o	r	l
m	o	k	r	e	o	a
a	y	o	w	i	s	r
n	o	o	m	u	b	i
s	l	o	n	o	o	r
f	i	s	h	s	e	a

sky flowers sun birds anim
humans sea fish moon sta

Write the first letter of each picture in the numbered boxes - to make a verse.

1. 2. 3. 4. 5. 6. 7.

8. 9. 10. 11. 12. 13. 14.

☐☐☐   ☐☐☐☐   "☐☐☐   ☐☐☐☐☐   ☐☐
3 6 10   12 14 1 10   2 5 9   9 11 5 8 5   13 5

☐☐☐☐☐"   ☐☐☐   ☐☐☐☐☐   ☐☐☐
2 1 3 11 9   14 4 10   9 11 5 8 5   7 14 12

☐☐☐☐☐ . Genesis ch.1v3
2 1 3 11 9

Can you remember what God called the darkness ?
What did He call the light ?

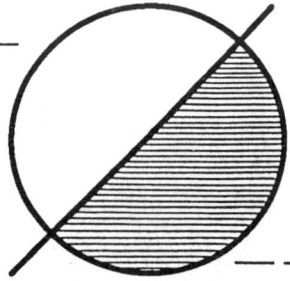

_ _ _ _

_ _ _ _

Here are two words from our story that describe God. Can you put in your own words what they mean ?

Creator_____

_____

Eternal_____

_____

How God made the World

CREATION – ACTIVITY SHEET

1. Cut out the puzzle pieces.
2. Stick them in the right order to the page, starting with the centre circle.
3. Number the days in each circle.

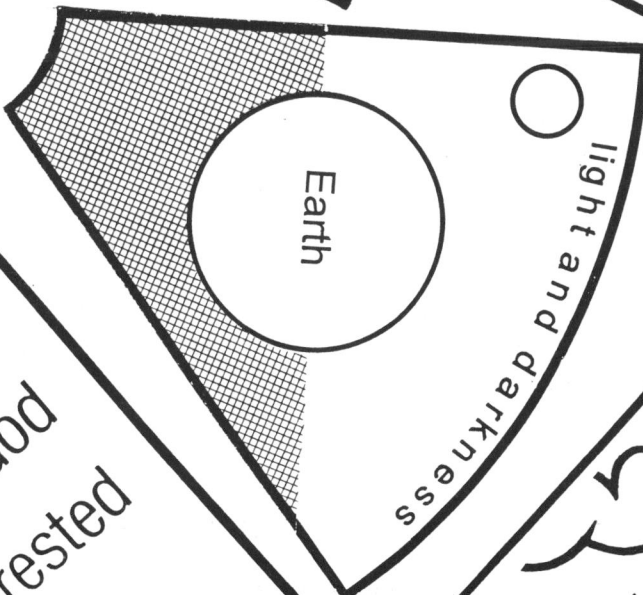

animals and man

sun, moon and stars

trees, earth and sea

fish and birds

God made everything in 6 days

Earth

light and darkness

clouds and water

Genesis 1

On the 7th day God rested

Thankyou God
for
everything.

Adam & Eve

Genesis 2:4 - 3:24

Themes	The Creation of Man & Woman, Temptation, Sin, Salvation

Aims	To consider the Bible's teaching that men & women are made by God.
	To recount the Bible's account of the entry of sin into the world.
	To show God's kindness to Adam & Eve after they had disobeyed.

Resources	Bibles, Children's Story Sheet, Puzzle Page, Activity Sheets.

Other Ideas & Activities
1. Activity Sheets – photocopy tree on green paper.
2. Make a list of things we can do which animals are not able to do: e.g. know, appreciate and worship God; reading, writing, talking; emotions and feelings, making discoveries, inventions.
3. Discuss what life was like for Adam and Eve in the Garden of Eden. How would it be different to our world/lives today? Discuss the Bible's teaching that sin/disobedience to God has resulted in these changes.
4. Read Revelation 21:1-7. Use this passage to make a list of what will be in heaven and what will not. How does this compare with our lives here?

Teacher's Notes

Summary: The Bible says that God made men and women, boys and girls to be like himself. We are different to the animals. He has given us a conscience, a soul and understanding. Adam and Eve disobeyed God and ate of the tree of the knowledge of good and evil. This spoilt their relationship with God. It also brought sin, suffering, decay and death into the world. Although they had disobeyed God, God was kind to them. He promised them that, one day, Jesus would come and save Adam and Eve and many others from all the things sin has done.

Point of Contact
A Fallen World
- Why is it that people lie, cheat and steal?
- Why are there such things as thorns, weeds, illness and death?
- Can you imagine what it would be like to live in a place where there would not be any of these things?
- What would you call a place like that?

The Creation of Man and Woman
The Bible says that God created all that exists in this world and universe in six days. On the sixth day God created his best and most important creation. Just like all of the animals, Adam and Eve were made from the dust of the ground. In many ways people

were similar to the animals. However, in many ways they are very different. Here are just three ways.

(1) Conscience
The Bible says that like God, men and women have a clear understanding of the difference between right and wrong. When we do something that is wrong, our conscience raises an alarm so that we feel guilty or uncomfortable. Animals, however, don't feel guilty if they do wrong things. You may get very cross with it, but you can't make your cat sorry for killing a bird. You can't expect your dog to feel guilty for chasing the neighbour's cat, or a fox for catching and killing a rabbit. However, the Bible says that men and women are different to animals, in that they know in their heart, because they have a conscience, when they have done something bad (Rom. 2:14,15).

(2) Soul
When God created humans he not only gave them a conscience but he also gave them a soul (Gen. 2:7). God did not give animals a soul. Our soul is the invisible part of us that can know and appreciate God. God put Adam and Eve in a lovely place called the Garden of Eden. Here he would do something he never did with any of the other living things he had created. Here he met with Adam and Eve and talked with them as friends. God was able to do this with them because Adam and Eve had a soul. Every human being is born with a soul.

(3) Understanding
God also gave Adam and Eve powerful minds. This meant that men & women would be able to understand languages, read and write, compose music, play instruments, think and reason very powerfully. We remember and think about what has happened in the past and try to anticipate what we think will happen in the future. We can look at ourselves and think about our place in the world and how we stand in relation to others.

Different
These things show that men and women are very different to animals. Though they have some things in common, there are many special abilities people have which shows how different they are. They were made to know God and enjoy being God's friend.

Paradise
The Garden of Eden was a wonderful place. Many beautiful trees grew there and provided them with more than enough food to eat. Sparkling rivers of clean water passed through the garden watering the land and trees. Adam and Eve enjoyed their pleasant and peaceful surroundings. Adam and Eve had everything they could want to make them happy. They enjoyed being with each other and spending time with their friend and provider, God. They admired the beauty of the garden and enjoyed caring for the place he had put them in. They were in a perfect place.

The Tree of the Knowledge of Good and Evil
God told Adam and Eve that they could eat as much fruit as they needed from any tree of the garden, except one. God said, "Of every tree of the garden you may freely eat, but of the tree of the knowledge of good and evil you shall not eat, for in the day you eat of it you shall surely die." God loved Adam and Eve and had provided so wonderfully for them. He wanted them to love and obey him in return. They could show their gratitude and love by doing this one thing which he asked.

Temptation!
One day Eve was alone in the garden. Suddenly a snake spoke to her. He asked Eve why God would not allow her and her husband Adam to eat of every tree in the garden. He was trying to make Eve believe that God was being mean in not letting them eat of the tree of knowledge. It was clear as he spoke that this snake was being used by God's enemy, the Devil (Rev. 12:9). He wanted Adam and Eve to disobey God and sin.

Eve listened to the snake and began to think that God was not being fair. "We may eat of the fruit of the trees in the garden, but of the fruit of the tree which is in the midst of the garden, God has said, 'You shall not eat it, nor shall you touch it, lest you die.' " This answer didn't really show how generous and kind God had been to them.

"You will not surely die," said the Devil. God doesn't want you to eat it because he knows that when you do, you will be as wise as he is. Eve believed the Devil's lie.

Sin!
Eve looked at the tree of the knowledge of good and evil. How beautiful the fruit looked! How pleasant it must taste! How good it will be to be as wise as God! Eve gave in. Eve picked some fruit and ate. She gave some to Adam and though he knew it was wrong, he also ate the fruit.

A Terrible Shock!
After they had eaten Adam and Eve soon realised that the Devil had lied to them. They had gained the knowledge of what it means to do wrong, and now they also had a terrible feeling of guilt. They knew they had done wrong and that God would not be pleased with them.

Fear and Hiding
Suddenly Adam and Eve heard God walking in the garden. They ran and hid. God called to them. They came trembling into his presence.

"Have you eaten of the tree of which I commanded you that you should not eat?" asked God. Adam blamed Eve. "The woman you gave to be with me, she gave me of the tree, and I ate," said Adam. Eve blamed the snake. "The serpent deceived me and I ate," said Eve.

The Consequences
God told Adam and Eve that they could no longer live in the beautiful Garden of Eden and have God's friendship and presence with them, as they once did. Their relationship with God was spoilt. From now on life would be hard. The ground would produce thorns, weeds and thistles, making it much harder for Adam to grow the food he needed to live.

Adam and Eve's children and descendants would sin as well. They would do many wrong things, such as lying, stealing and murder. Worst of all, man and woman, created by God to live forever, would now eventually die. The Bible tells us (Rom. 8: 20,21) that, as a result of Adam and Eve's sin in the garden - what is called "the Fall" - disease, sickness, decay, pain, sorrow, ageing, hatred, jealousy and all manner of wrongdoing, have now become part of this world's everyday existence.

God's Kind Promise

Even though Adam and Eve had disobeyed God, he still showed them great kindness and mercy. He told them that one day, Jesus would be born and eventually die on the cross (1John 3:8b). He would put right all the damage that the Devil had done. He would save Adam and Eve and many others from the terrible effects of sin.

Illustration: A Conscience At Work

A young boy was warned by his parents never to climb up into the loft on his own. One day, while they were out, he climbed up in order to get something. Unfortunately he slipped and his foot pushed the ceiling board down! Now he was so worried that his parents would find out that he had disobeyed them

He quickly got some nails and a hammer and pinned the ceiling board back up. He then had to get some paint and filler, fill the crack and then paint over it. To make sure that the paint would dry before they got home, he had to stand on a stool drying it with a hair drier for over an hour. His parents were none the wiser. The boy was pleased that he had got away with it.

However, as time went on, the boy started to feel concerned that he had deceived his parents and not obeyed them as he should. He felt troubled and ashamed. Eventually, he went to them and confessed all that he had done. His parents said they were disappointed that he had not told them before, but that they were glad he had now confessed to his wrong doing. They forgave him and told him never to deceive them again. The boy promised he wouldn't! He didn't like the feelings he had had from a troubled conscience!

Things to learn:

- In the beginning God made men and women, and everything he had created, perfect.
- He made men and women different to animals, giving them a conscience, a soul and understanding.
- Adam and Eve disobeyed God and sin came into the world.
- The Bible says this is why there is evil, suffering and death.
- God promised Adam and Eve that Jesus would eventually come as Saviour.

Discuss

- How are people different to animals?
- Can an animal sin?
- What is our conscience?
- How do you know you have one?

Adam and Eve

God made everything. On the sixth day he made Adam, the first man. God made Adam from the dust on the ground. Adam was different to everything God had made before.

God gave Adam a conscience, which meant that he could tell the difference between right and wrong. God also gave Adam a soul, and a mind, which could think and understand. God made a wife for Adam called Eve.

Adam and Eve lived in the Garden of Eden. This was a beautiful place and they were very happy there. Adam and Eve had everything they wanted. God told Adam and Eve that there was one thing they must not do. They must never eat the fruit from the tree of the knowledge of good and evil.

One day when Eve was alone, a snake spoke to her. He told her that it wouldn't matter if she ate the fruit from the tree of the knowledge of good and evil. Eve believed the snake and forgot what God had said. She picked some fruit from the tree and ate it. She gave some to Adam to eat. Immediately Adam and Eve knew they had done wrong and knew that God would not be pleased with them.

Then Adam and Eve heard God walking in the garden. They were afraid and ran away to hide. God called them to come to him. Adam and Eve came to God, afraid of what he might say. When God asked Adam whether he had eaten the fruit of the tree of knowledge of good and evil, Adam blamed Eve. Eve blamed the snake. But God knew what had happened.

God told Adam and Eve that they could no longer stay in the Garden of Eden. Adam would now have to work hard to grow his own food.

God promised Adam and Eve that one day Jesus would be born into the world. He would put right the damage which Adam and Eve had done.

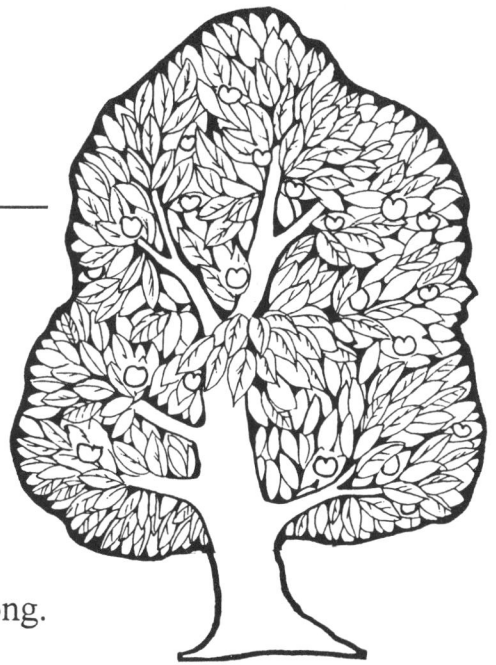

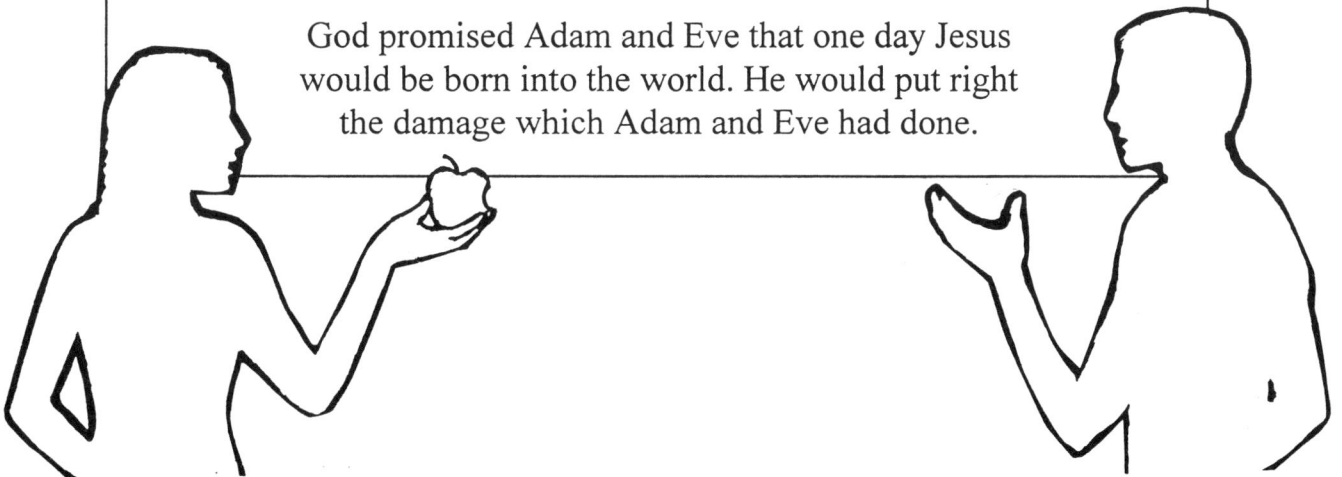

Name.. Date......................

ADAM AND EVE

Cross out the wrong words.
Adam and Eve lived in the garden of
Gethsemane / Eden. They **were /
weren't** allowed to eat any of the fruit,
especially / except that of the tree of
the knowledge of good and evil.
The devil came to **Adam / Eve** disguised
as a **snake / fox** and tempted her to
break God's rule. **Before / after** Eve had
eaten the fruit, she gave some to Adam
and he ate it **as well / instead.**
They both **thought / knew** they had
done wrong and were **glad / ashamed.**

....

**Can you match the puzzle pieces to make
a Bible verse ? Write it in the spaces.**

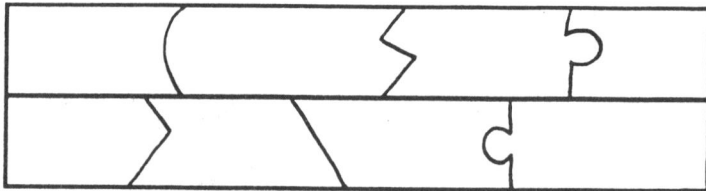

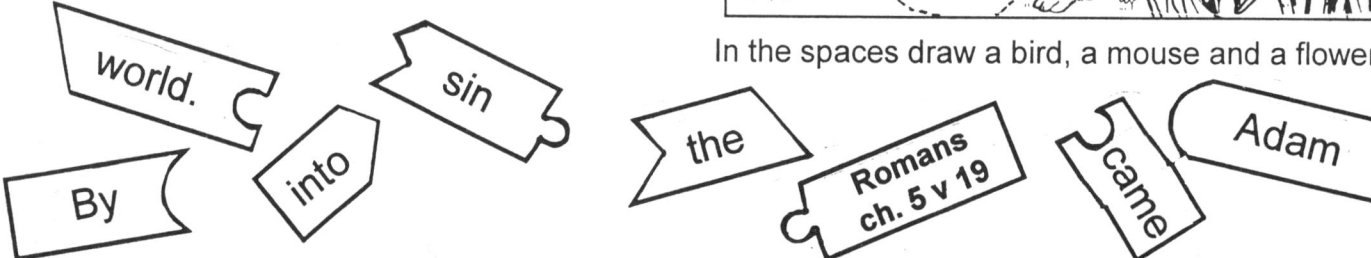

In the spaces draw a bird, a mouse and a flower

world.   sin

By   into

the   Romans ch. 5 v 19   came   Adam

**Colour in the things which *only*
humans and *not* animals,
have or can do.**

5 senses   soul   read   heart   skin   hair

conscience   eyes   brain   compose music   write

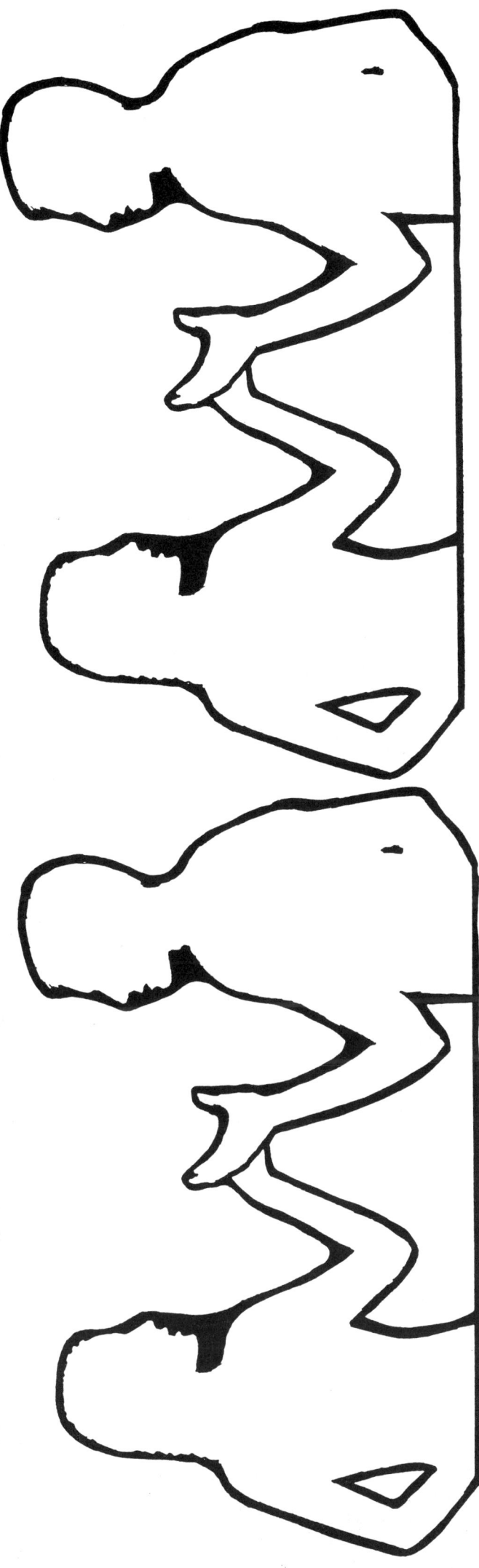

ADAM & EVE – ACTIVITY SHEET
Cut out Adam and Eve and stick
or staple at the base of the tree.
Design some fruit to go in
Adam's hand and also stick
some on the tree.

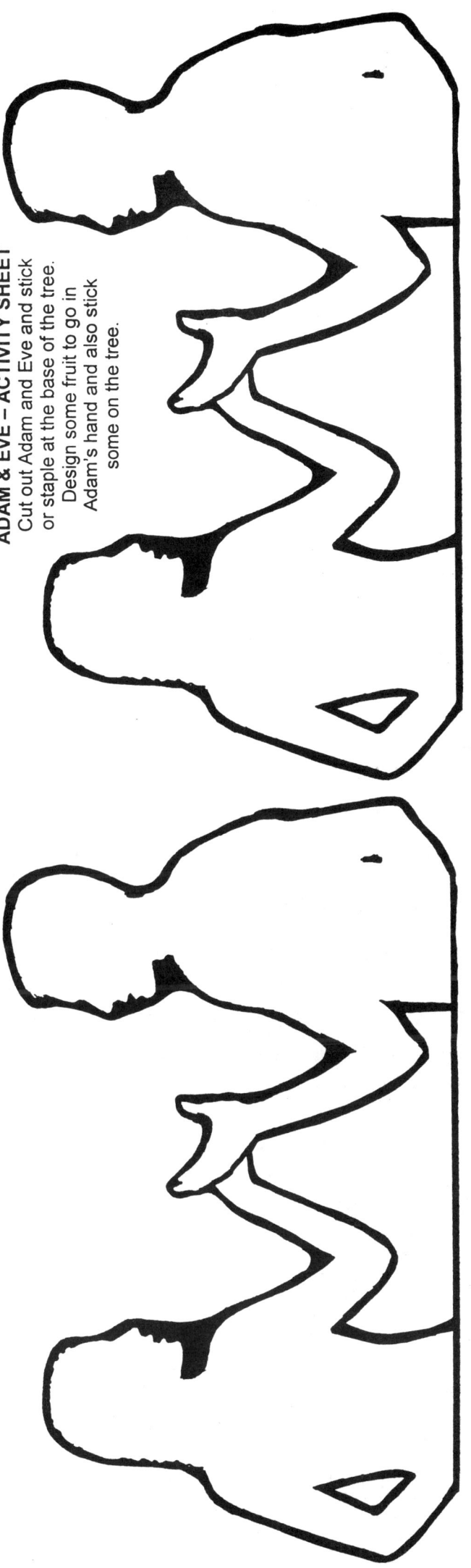

Adam and Eve disobeyed God by eating
the fruit.

Gen. ch.3

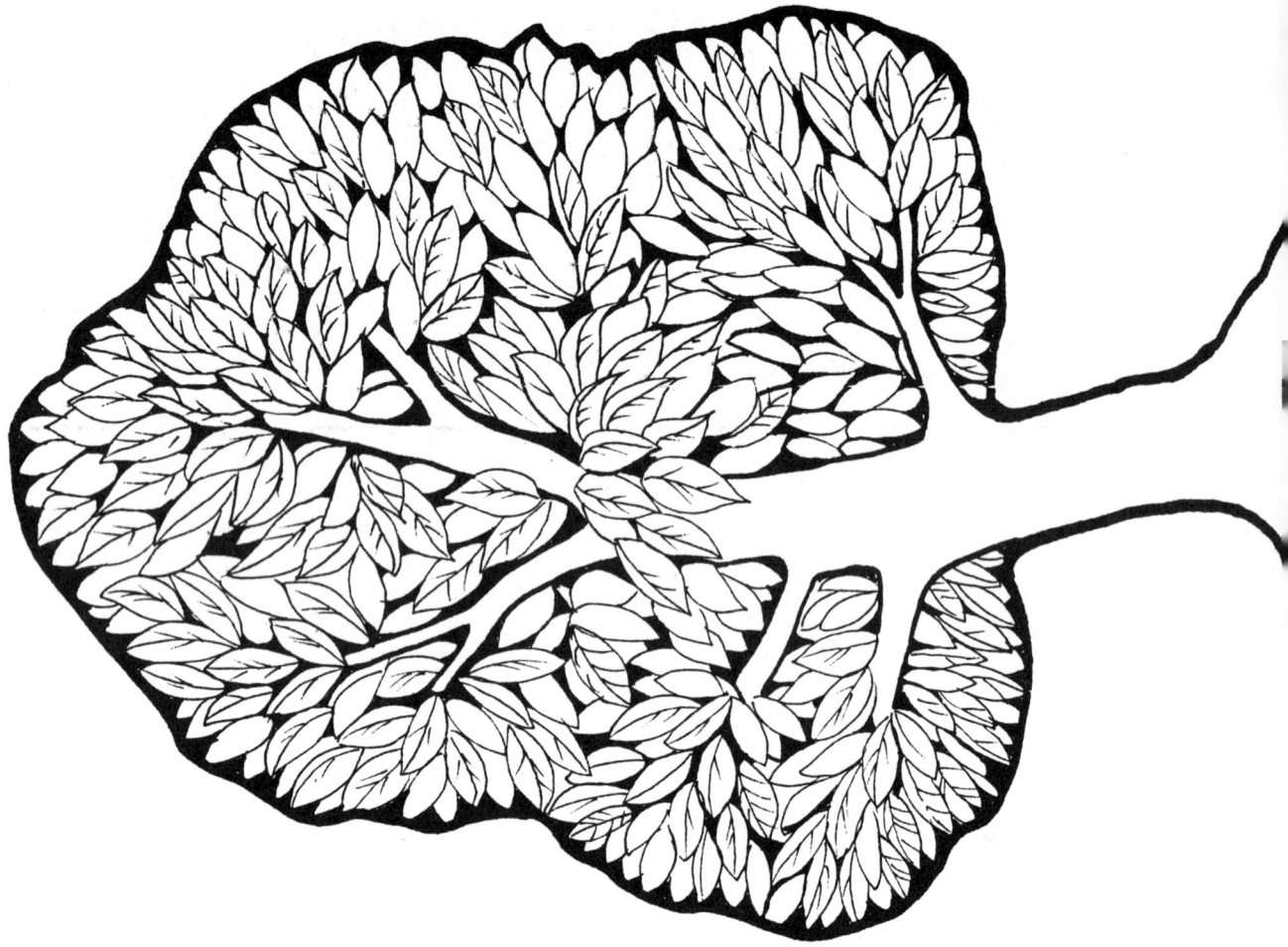

Adam and Eve disobeyed God by eating
the fruit.

Gen. ch.3

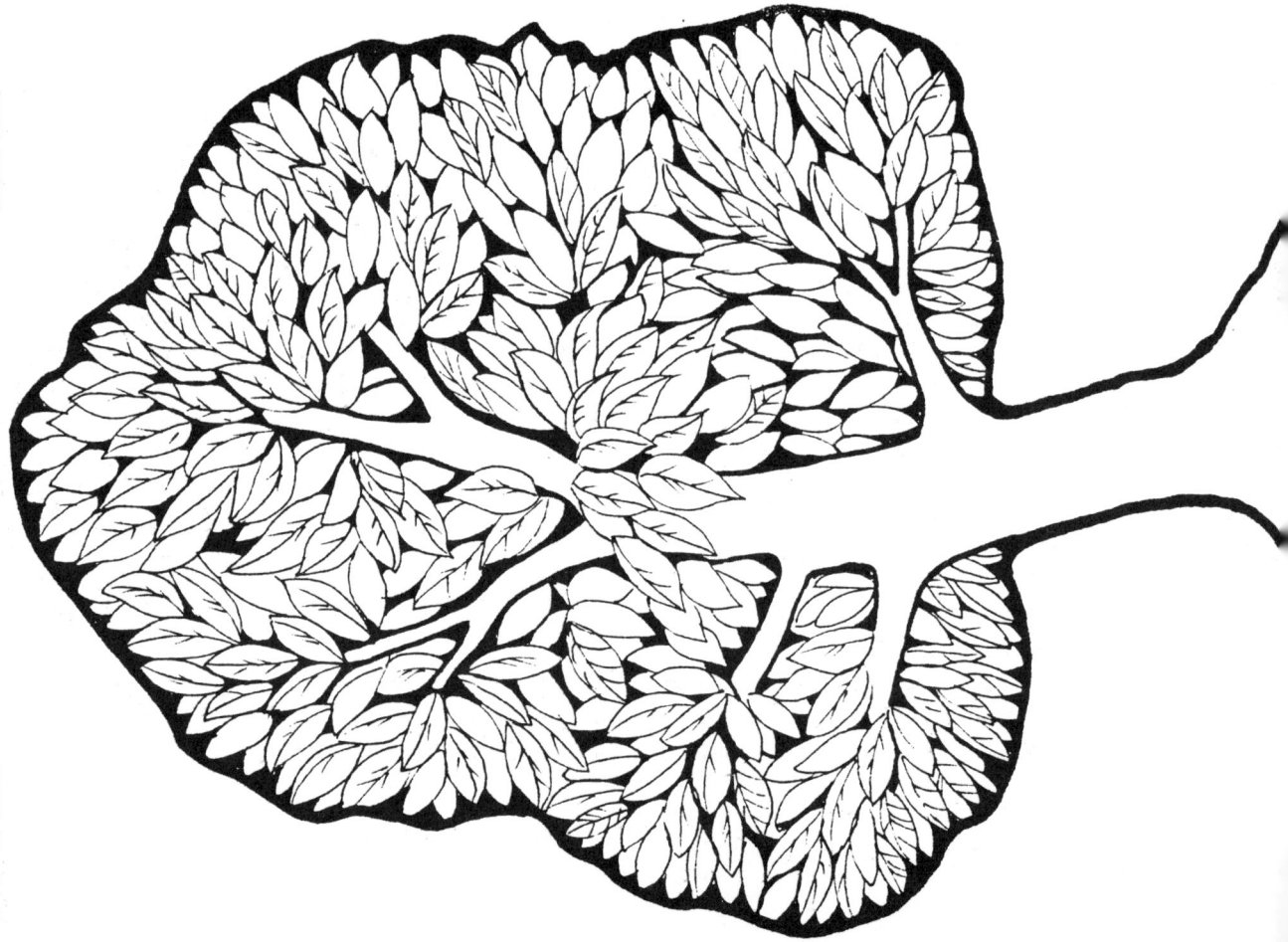

Noah and the Flood

Genesis 6:1 - 9:17

Themes	Courage, Obedience, Judgement, Deliverance

Aims	To teach the Biblical account of Noah and the flood.
	To highlight the attitude of being willing to stand alone.
	To illustrate what the Bible teaches about the character of God.

Resources	Bibles, Children's Story Sheet, Puzzle Page, Activity Sheets.

Other Ideas & Activities

1. Activity Sheets – photocopy ark on brown/grey paper/card.
2. Draw a rainbow and name the colours in order. Then make up an acrostic of - ROYGBIV - to remember the colours.
3. Make a class collage of after the flood, including ark, animals, rainbow.
4. Discuss what cubits were (measurement from elbow to top of middle finger - roughly 45cm). Using the dimensions given in the notes, work out the length, width, height (and even the volume?) of the ark in metres and cubic metres.
5. Design your own ark. Consider the size it would have to be and how many different rooms it would have to have. Remember that food storage would be needed and different animals would have to be separated. This could link to work on habitats.
6. Find the location of Mount Ararat in an Atlas, and then draw a map of its location.
7. Look at news reports on floods around the world. Find out more about their effects and the devastation they bring.
8. There is a lot of geological evidence for the flood which could be mentioned. This evidence can be found in books such as "Bone of Contention" by Sylvia Baker, published by Evangelical Press, available from most Christian Bookshops.

Teacher's Notes

Summary: The people God had created had forgotten him. One man, called Noah, was different. He loved God and wanted to please him. God told Noah that he was going to flood the whole earth and destroy everyone except Noah and his family. He told him to build a large boat called an ark and take two of every animal into it. Noah trusted God and was obedient. Though people laughed at Noah, he continued to build the ark. When it was finished God sent rain and a great flood on the earth. Everything which lived on the land died. Noah had obeyed God and God had been true to his word. He had protected Noah and his family and saved them from the flood. God has promised never to flood the earth again.

Point of Contact
Being Different

- Have you ever felt that you were the odd one out?
- How did you feel?
- Is it easier if your parents/teachers support you and encourage you?

An Evil World
God had created the world and all the things that were in it. Adam and Eve, the first man and woman, had sons and daughters. By this time, many people had been born and were living on the earth. But the sad thing is that the people in the world, that God had created, had forgotten him. They were selfish and thought only about themselves, and never about God. They did many evil things. God was angry and sad.

Noah
God saw one man who was different. His name was Noah. He loved God and wanted to please him. God told Noah that he was going to flood the whole earth and destroy everyone except Noah and his family.

A Great Ship
He told Noah to build a large boat called an ark. The Bible tells us that God gave Noah the exact measurements. The ark was to be 300 cubits long, 50 cubits wide and 30 cubits high. (The volume of the ark would exceed that of 400 double decker buses.) It would have 3 floors, a window in the top and a door at the side.

On His Own
Noah believed all God had said and so he began building the ark. The Bible tells us (2Peter 2:5) that Noah spoke to the people around him. He warned them of the coming flood and of their need to make preparation for it so they would not be destroyed. However, no one believed Noah. There had never been a flood before. They probably laughed at him and thought he was mad. They carried on just as they had done, ignoring God and doing many wicked things. Noah trusted God and was still obedient. He continued to build the ark, following the plan which God had given him. Then at last, one day, it was finished.

Animals
God told Noah to take his family and all the animals and birds who lived on the land, into the ark with him. Nearly all of the animals came to him in pairs (a male and a female). The Bible tells us that the animals came quietly and obediently to Noah and entered the ark (Gen. 7:7-9). Noah must have taken enough food on board to feed them all. God then told Noah to go inside the ark with all his family - his wife, his three sons, Shem, Ham and Japheth, and their wives. When they were all safely in the ark the Bible says that God shut the door.

The Great Flood
It began to rain as it had never rained before. The skies were black. The clouds burst and water poured down. The rivers and lakes overflowed, whilst the sea bed was moved, spilling the seas' waters all over the land. Houses, trees and eventually hills and all the mountains were covered. Everything which lived on the land - men and women, and all the land animals and creatures, died. The rain continued for forty days and forty nights.

A Great Wind
After five months had passed God sent a wind over the earth which began to dry up the water. After ten months Noah looked out of his window and could see the tops of the mountains. Eventually the ark came to rest on top of a mountain called Ararat.

A Raven and A Dove
Another forty days passed. Noah decided he would see if the ground was nearly dry. He opened the window and sent out a hardy bird - a raven. The bird must have been able to find somewhere to stand and also find food, because it didn't return to Noah.

Noah then sent out a more delicate bird - a dove. But the dove returned to the ark because it could not find any tree to rest in or any food to eat. Seven days later he sent the dove again. This time it came back with an olive leaf in its beak. Trees and bushes were now growing!

After another seven days Noah sent the dove again, but this time it did not return. It had obviously found food and was happy to remain outside. Noah now knew that soon he and his family would be able to leave the ark and live on the land once more.

Back to the Land
God told Noah it was time for him to leave the ark. He, his family and all the animals went out onto the land. It must have felt good for Noah and his family to walk on the earth once more. The animals and birds too, must have been glad to be free, having been in the ark for so long.

Thanksgiving
The first thing that Noah did when he left the ark was to build an altar and offer a sacrifice. God had been true to his word. He thanked God that he had protected him and his family and saved them from the flood.

Rainbow
God gave Noah a special promise that he would never again flood the whole earth. He said, "While the earth remains, seed time and harvest, and cold and heat, and winter and summer, and day and night, shall not cease" (Gen. 8:22). God put the rainbow in the sky as a sign of his promise.

Illustration: Willing To Stand Alone
Eric Liddell was a Christian chosen to run for the English team in the 1924 Paris Olympic Games. He was widely expected to win gold in the 100 yards sprint (as it was in those days). Liddell found out that the final of this race was to be run on a Sunday. He was a Christian who believed that Sunday was God's day. He believed it was to be kept special, in obedience to the fourth commandment. As a result he refused to race.

Many people were upset because he refused to run. The papers of his day wrote articles which criticised him and the stand he had taken. They even called him a traitor. However, Eric believed he must obey God and put him first and not worry about the criticism of others. He was willing to stand alone.

Eventually Eric was asked to run in the 400 yards on a different day. He agreed, although his times at this distance were not that good. He received great acclaim when, having entered a race for which he was completely untrained, he finished a clear five metres ahead of the favourite, in first place! He had one gold for England. But more than that Eric had stood firm, obeyed God and stood alone. God helped him. God was faithful. The Bible says, "He who honours me I will honour."

Eric went on to be a missionary in China and Japan. It was here that he eventually died.

(* "Eric Liddell, God's Athlete" by Catherine Swift - Heroes of the Cross series, published by Marshall-Pickering, ISBN 0 551 01354 0 - available from most Christian Bookshops.)

Things to learn:

- God was angry when he saw how wicked the people of the world had become.
- Noah was told by God to build an ark.
- He continued to build the ark even though people laughed at him.
- God sent a flood to cover the whole world.
- Noah was obedient, trusted God and was kept safe in the ark.

Discuss

- The Bible says that God is in control and has power over everything. How is this shown by the story of Noah and the flood?
- If you knew something was right, but you were the only one who thought that way, would you be willing to stand alone for what is right?
- What do you think of when you see a rainbow?
- Do you think God will ever break his promise?

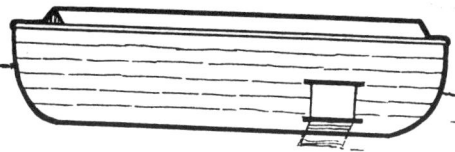

Noah and the Flood

The people of the world had forgotten God. They only thought of themselves. God was angry and sad.

Noah was different. He loved God and wanted to please him. God told Noah he was going to flood the earth. He told Noah to build an ark. The people laughed at Noah building the ark. Noah told them that God was going to flood the earth, but they did not believe him.

When Noah had finished the ark, God told him to go inside with his wife, his three sons and their wives. God also told Noah to take into the ark a pair of every kind of living creature. The animals came quietly and obediently to the ark. When everyone was safe in the ark, God shut the door.

Soon it began to rain. The water poured out of the sky. The rivers and seas overflowed and covered the land, trees, hills and even the mountains. Everything left on the earth died. It rained for forty days and forty nights. Noah and his family must have been glad that God was looking after them.

After many days, God sent a wind, which began to dry up the water. When ten months had passed, Noah could see the tops of the mountains appearing. The ark stopped floating and rested on the top of a mountain called Ararat. Noah decided to find out if the ground was dry. He opened the window and let out a raven. The raven did not come back to the ark, so it must have found some food. Then Noah sent out a dove. The dove soon came back to Noah, as it could not find any trees or food. Seven days later, Noah sent out the dove again. This time it came back with an olive leaf in its beak. It had found some trees!

Then God told Noah it was time for everyone to leave the ark. Noah opened the door for all the animals and birds. How glad they must have felt to be free again. Noah and his family were glad too. The first thing that Noah did was to thank God for keeping them all safe. God promised Noah that he would never flood the whole earth again. The sign of the promise was a rainbow in the sky.

Name...   Date.............................

NOAH AND THE FLOOD

**Can you unscramble the words
and fit them into the story.**

kar

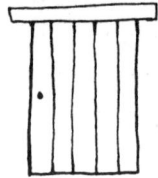
aerth

oord

God told Noah to bring his _ _ _ _ _ _ into the ark
because it would soon be time for the _ _ _ _ to
start. A male and female of every kind of _ _ _ _ _ _
came into the ark as well, and God shut the _ _ _ _
behind them. The rain started, _ _ _ _ _ _ came
gushing out of the ground and soon the whole
_ _ _ _ _ was covered. This continued for forty
days and forty nights. All the animals and people
not in the _ _ _ drowned. Only _ _ _ _ and his
family were safe because they had believed God
and had gone into the ark.

iran

haoN

aterw

minala

yilfam

Fill in the crossword.

1.What could
Noah see the
tops of in
the tenth month ?

2. On what
mountain did the ark
come to rest as the
flood went down ?

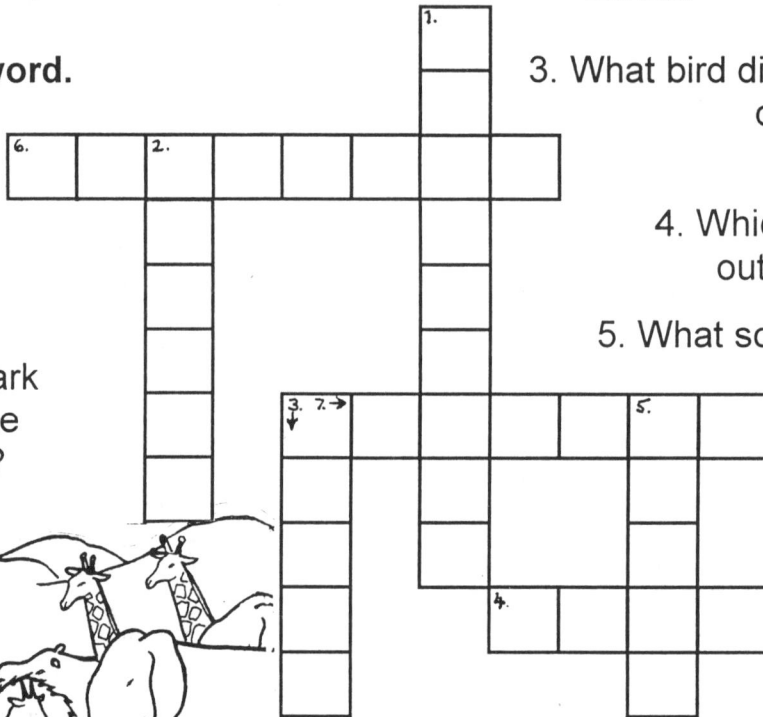

3. What bird did Noah send out fort
days later, that did no
come back

4. Which bird did Noah sen
out that did come back

5. What sort of leaf did it bring

6.How did Noa
fee
towards God

7. What was th
sign God gav
to show he wi
never again floo
the earth

The rainbow is a

promise that..........

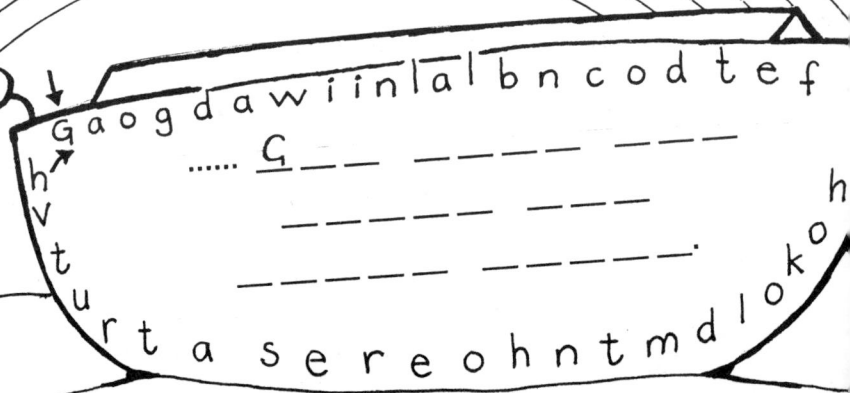

Take every other letter to find the answer.

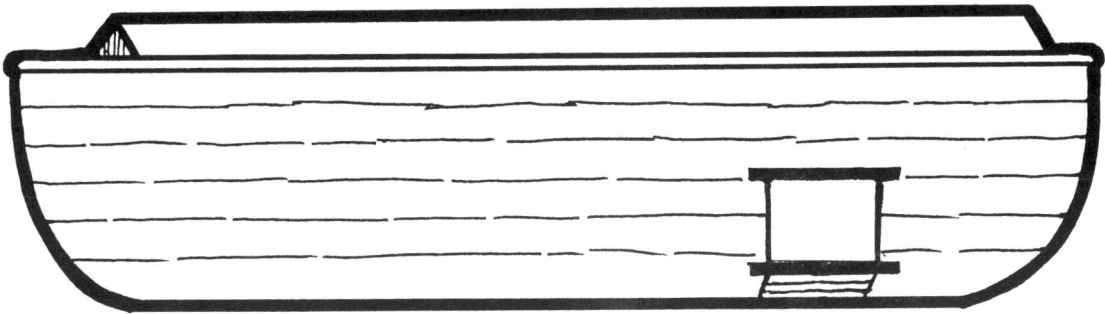

NOAH & THE FLOOD – ACTIVITY SHEET

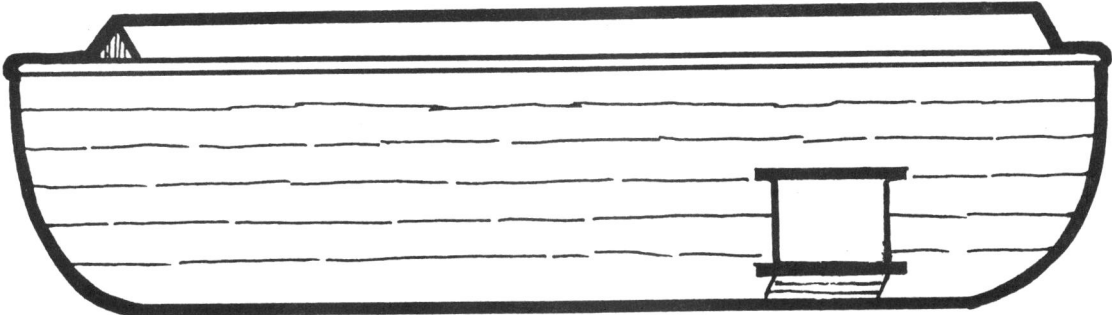

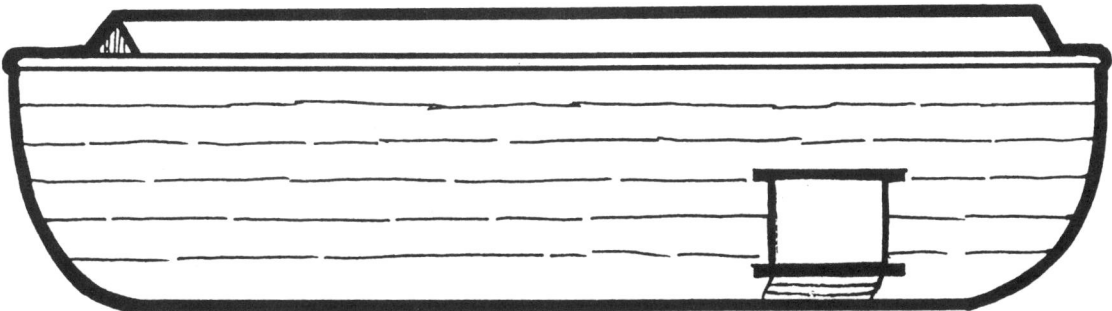

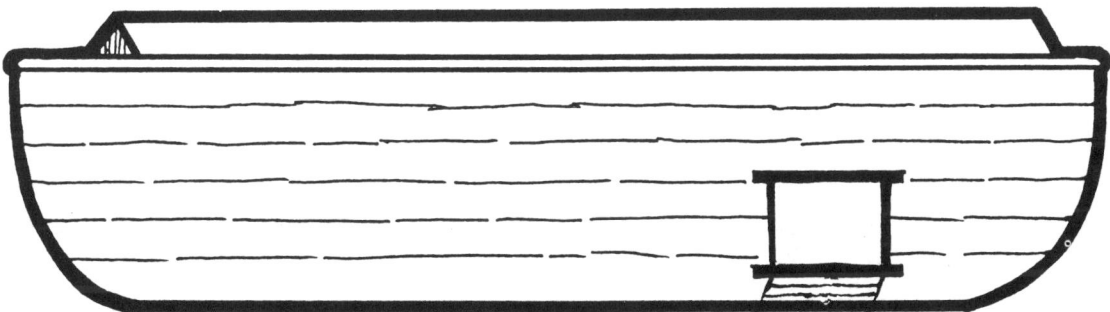

Cut out ark and stick along dotted line on 'animal' picture. Line up the procession with the door.

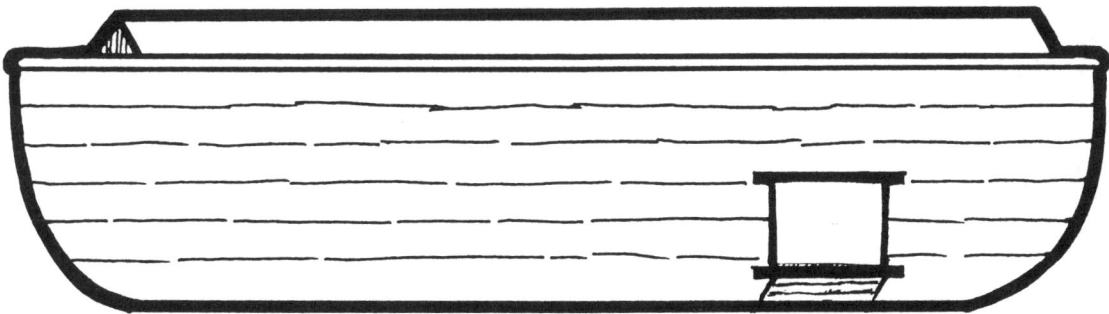

Noah, his family and all the animals went into the ark. God closed the door behind them.

Gen. ch. 7

NOAH & THE FLOOD – ACTIVITY SHEET

Noah, his family and all the animals went into the ark. God closed the door behind them.

Gen. ch. 7

Abraham – The Man Who Trusted God

Genesis 11:27 - 21:7

Themes	God's Promises, Trust, God's Faithfulness

Aims	To teach the Bible's account of the life of Abraham.
	To see Abraham as an illustration of faith and trust in God.
	To show that the Bible teaches that God always keeps his promises.
	To teach that Abraham is considered to be the founder of the Jewish nation.

Resources	Bibles, Children's Story Sheet, Puzzle Page, Activity Sheet, Map.

Other Ideas & Activities

1. Activity Sheet – stick on black/dark paper/card; needs silver stars.
2. Look on a map at the route Abraham took to Canaan. Make a copy and label, Ur, Babylon, the River Euphrates, Haran, Canaan, Shechem, the Mediterranean Sea. Use arrows to show Abraham's journey. Work out the approximate distance Abraham must have travelled from Ur to Shechem. Remember his limited means of transport and the difficulties that would have been faced along the way.
3. Years ago people did not believe that Ur existed and that the story of Abraham wasn't true. However in the 1930s the remains of the city of Ur was discovered. It is now a well explored archaeological site. Find out more about it or pay a visit to the British Museum. Find out about the city, its people, their way of life and the famous ziggurat.
4. Using a dictionary and the story, can you write a definition of the word 'faith'? What is specific about the Christian faith?
5. Discuss "going to new places" and the feelings associated with this, e.g. starting school, moving house, changing classes, etc.

Teacher's Notes

Summary: Abraham is called the friend of God (James 2:23). He obeyed God and left his good home in Ur. God was faithful and kept his promises. He led Abraham to the land of Canaan, which he had given to him. God also promised that one day Abraham's descendants would become a great nation and live in this country. After a wait of about 25 years, the baby God had promised was born to Abraham and Sarah. Abraham believed what God had said and obeyed him. He knew he could trust God. He is the founder of the Jewish nation.

Point of Contact
Going To An Unknown Place
Imagine you and your family had to leave home without knowing where you are going.
- How would you feel?
- What would you take with you?
- What would you miss most?

Ur
Abraham and his wife Sarah lived in a city called Ur. At this time it was one of the largest cities in the world. The people there were rich and had lots of possessions. The people of Ur worshipped their own gods. They built temples and bowed down to the statues of their hand-made gods.

Abraham and Sarah
Abraham and Sarah did not go to the temples to worship the gods which the people of Ur had made. They believed there was one true and living God who had made the stars, planets, and the earth and all that is in it. Abraham was a very rich man. He had many servants, herds and flocks, as well as silver and gold. He and Sarah had a very comfortable life in Ur.

Go To Another Country
One day God spoke to Abraham and told him to go to another country. God did not tell Abraham where to go, but he promised that he would show him the way. He promised that the new land would belong to Abraham, his children and grandchildren. He said that he would make his descendants a great nation. Abraham must have been puzzled about this. He and Sarah had no children and now they were both old. Abraham was about 75 and Sarah 65. God promised them that they would one day have a child.

Abraham Obeys
Abraham did not refuse but obeyed God straight away. He loved God and wanted to be obedient to him. He believed that God would keep his word and that he could trust him. The Bible calls this faith.

Abraham and Sarah packed their belongings and made arrangements for the journey. They took many servants, animals and provisions and began travelling northwards from Ur alongside the river Euphrates. At night they would probably stop and sleep in tents. After crossing the river and travelling west they stayed in Haran for a short while and then continued on their journey a further 300 miles to a town called Shechem (show map).

The Promised Land
At last they had now arrived in the new country of Canaan (now called Israel), that God had promised to Abraham. Now they had a new home where they could put up their tents and settle down. Abraham and Sarah must have been happy that God had shown them the way. Here Abraham built an altar to thank God. For many years Abraham and his family lived in Canaan, enjoying the beautiful land God had given them.

Where Is The Baby?

Now Abraham and Sarah waited for the baby God had promised to give them. Many years passed and still no baby came. They must have wondered whether God had forgotten to keep his word.

Many times God reminded Abraham that he would have children, grandchildren and great grandchildren, who would eventually become a large nation. One night God spoke to Abraham and said, "Now look up at the sky and see if you can count the stars." Of course there were too many to count. God said that one day there would be so many people in Abraham's family that you would not be able to count them, just like the stars. The Bible says that Abraham had great faith. He believed and trusted that God would keep his word, even though it seemed impossible, because of their age.

Three Visitors

On a hot day Abraham was sitting in the doorway of his tent. He looked up and noticed three men coming towards him. He ran up to them and welcomed them. He invited them to rest and have something to eat. Although these visitors looked like men, two of them were angels and one of them was God. When they were having the meal God asked Abraham, "Where is Sarah your wife?" Abraham replied, "Here in the tent." Then God told Abraham that in a year's time Sarah would have a baby boy. Sarah was listening behind the tent door and heard this conversation. She laughed at the thought of an old woman like her having a baby. She was now 90 years old and Abraham nearly 100.

God Knew

God knew that Sarah was laughing. He said to Abraham, "Why does Sarah laugh at the thought of having a baby in her old age?" Sarah was afraid and told a lie. She said, "I did not laugh!" But God knew and said, "You did laugh." How foolish Sarah was to think that she could lie to God. Soon after this the visitors left.

Isaac

About a year later Abraham and Sarah had a baby boy called Isaac, just as God had promised. Despite their old age, God had kept his word. God had shown to Abraham and Sarah that he is the promise keeping God who can be trusted. How happy Sarah was to have her own baby at last. She must have felt ashamed that she had ever doubted God's promises.

The Founding Of A Nation

God promised Abraham that one day his family would become a great nation and live in the land of Canaan. When Isaac grew up he had a son called Jacob. Jacob had 12 sons. The family grew and grew until their descendants were as numerous "as the stars in the sky". They were called the nation of Israel. God had kept his promise to Abraham.

Israel Today

The descendants of Abraham are now called Israelis or Jews. They still live in Canaan, which is now called Palestine. The Jews know that Abraham is the founder of the nation of Israel.

Illustration: The Faith of the Pilgrim Fathers

The Pilgrim Fathers (as they were called) were a group of Christians who believed God was guiding them to go to the 'New World' (which today is known as the United States of America). After sailing almost four thousand miles across the Atlantic Ocean, in a ship called the Mayflower, they arrived on the east coast of America.

To begin with life was very hard for the pilgrims and some died because of illness. However difficult things were they still trusted in God. Together they set up a government and after a year they had built a settlement. The harvest that year was good, so they had a special celebration to give thanks to God for helping them and providing for them.

Today if you visit America you will find that they still celebrate Thanksgiving Day on the fourth Thursday in November. They remember the faith of the first pilgrims to come to America, and how God provided for them. These few pilgrims became the founders of the USA.

In a similar way Abraham was guided to go to the land of Canaan. Here a great nation came into being. The Jews look back to Abraham as their founder, just as the Americans look back to the Christians who first came to their land.

Things to learn:
- Abraham was a man of great faith.
- God made many promises to Abraham.
- Abraham trusted God and obeyed him.
- God kept all the promises he made to Abraham.
- Abraham is the founder of the nation of Israel.
- God always keeps his promises. He is completely trustworthy.

Discuss
- How does the life of Abraham show that God can be trusted?
- What does it mean to trust someone?
- Who do we trust to keep their word?
- How do you know you can trust them?

Abraham - The Man Who Trusted God

Abraham and his wife Sarah lived in Ur. They loved and worshipped God. Abraham was a very rich man. He had lots of servants, animals and a very comfortable home.

One day God told Abraham that he must leave Ur. God promised Abraham that he would show him the way to a new country, which would belong to him and his family. Abraham and Sarah must have wondered what God meant, as they had no children of their own. But they trusted God and knew that he always kept his promises.

Abraham and Sarah packed their belongings and began their long journey. At last they arrived in the new country of Canaan, the land God had promised to Abraham.

Now Abraham and Sarah waited for the baby God had promised to give them. Many years passed and still no baby came. They must have wondered whether God had forgotten to keep his promise.

On a hot day Abraham was sitting in the doorway of his tent. He looked up and noticed three men coming towards him. He invited them to rest and have something to eat. Although these visitors looked like men two of them were angels and one of them was God.

While they were having the meal, God asked Abraham where Sarah was. Abraham said that she was in the tent. God told Abraham that in a year's time Sarah would have a baby boy. Sarah was listening behind the tent door. She laughed at the thought of an old woman like her having a baby!

God asked Sarah why she was laughing. Sarah was afraid and told a lie. She said, "I did not laugh!" But God knew and said, "You did laugh." How foolish Sarah was to think that she could lie to God. Soon after this the visitors left.

About a year later Abraham and Sarah had a baby boy called Isaac, just as God had promised. Abraham became the father of the nation of Israel.

ABRAHAM - THE MAN WHO TRUSTED GOD

Fill in the spaces with the words below.

Abraham's wife was called __ __ __ __ __. They lived in the land of __ __ until __ __
spoke to Abraham and told him to leave there and go to __ __ __ __ __ __. God
promised to bless __ __ __ __ __ __ __ and make his descendants a great
__ __ __ __ __ __ . Abraham __ __ __ __ __ __ God.

ABRAHAM   NATION   GOD   UR   SARAH   OBEYED   CANAA

Join up these phrases with arrows to make sentences.
The first one has been done to show you what to do.

Abraham was sitting....   ....Sarah had a....   ....of God's promise
Three men....   ....reminded Abraham.....   ....and have something to ea
He invited them....   ....came to visit....   ....at the hottest time of da
The visitors....   ....to rest under a tree....   ....baby boy called Isaa
Several months later....   ....in his tent door....   ....and he ran to greet the

(See if you can fill in the spaces with the letters in the stars

God said to Abraham... "Look now toward
heaven and count the __ __ __ __ __ __
if you are able to number them...
so shall you

d __ __ __ __ __ __ __ __ __

be'

Join the dots to make a te

ABRAHAM – ACTIVITY SHEET

Cut out picture along thick black line.
Stick 'night sky' square of dark
paper/card behind Abraham's
tent. Stick stars onto this.

God said he would give to
Abraham as many descendants
as stars in the sky.

Gen. ch.15

God said he would give to
Abraham as many descendants
as stars in the sky.

Gen. ch.15

God said he would give to
Abraham as many descendants
as stars in the sky.

Gen. ch.15

Jacob - The Man God Changed

Genesis 25 - 33

Themes	Deceit, Kindness, Mercy

Aims	To recount the life of Jacob. To consider deceit and its consequences. To illustrate God's mercy to Jacob despite his failings and dishonesty.

Resources	Bibles, Children's Story Sheet, Puzzle Pages, Activity Sheet, Map.

Other Ideas & Activities
1. Activity Sheet - stick on black/dark paper/card.
2. Draw a ladder and on each rung put a word which describes Jacob's character, showing how he changed throughout his life, from "Jacob" at the bottom to "Israel" at the top. The bottom rungs could have "deceiving", "lying" going through to "sorry" and "scared" and then up to "trusting" and "honest".
3. Discuss why people use disguises (e.g. fun, entertainment, not to be recognised, to do something bad) using available materials. Do others recognise you? Use the costumes to make a short play about someone who used a disguise to fool others.
4. Write a short story about someone who was deceitful. The story could show how 'one thing can lead to another'. The story could show how a whole series of deceptions were produced by one initial deceit, and how the person involved got further into 'deep water' as time went on.
5. Choose the names of imaginary twins and describe how different they were in personality and behaviour.

Teacher's Notes

Summary: Jacob played a nasty trick on his old blind father. He deceived him so that he could obtain something he badly wanted. His brother Esau was angry, because he had stolen the blessing. Jacob had to escape. Jacob lost everything because he had lied. On the journey to his uncle's home he had a special dream, where he saw a ladder to heaven. God forgave Jacob and promised to help him. Jacob learned to trust in God for all his needs. God changed Jacob from being someone who would deceive others to get his way, to being someone who would depend on God and do things honestly. God changed Jacob's name to Israel. God forgave Jacob's sin and changed his life. The Bible tells us that he is willing and ready to forgive those who are sorry.

Point of Contact
Twins
- Do you know any twins?
- Did they like the same things?
- Do they look like each other?

- Have you ever found it hard to tell them apart?

Isaac's Children

Abraham's son Isaac married Rebekah. After a long wait of twenty years Rebekah gave birth to two boys, Esau and Jacob. Even though they were twins they looked and behaved very differently.

Esau

When Esau was born his parents noticed that he was red and covered in hair. So they called him "Esau" which means "hairy". Esau was an outdoor boy and when he grew up he became a hunter. He would go into the woods, fields and mountains and shoot wild animals with his bow and arrow. Isaac liked Esau because of the animals and birds he caught and prepared for the dinner table.

Jacob

Jacob had very smooth skin. He was a quiet person who would spend his time indoors and looking after the animals in the fields and pens near the home. His mother Rebekah liked Jacob more than Esau.

The Birthright

Esau was the firstborn of the two twins and therefore had what is called the 'birthright'. This meant Esau, as the oldest, had certain privileges that Jacob didn't. After his father, Esau was considered the head of the family. Jacob had to look up to Esau as the older brother.

One day Esau returned from hunting in the fields. When he came home he was very tired and hungry. Jacob had cooked a stew. Esau said to Jacob, "I am so hungry! Please give me some of that stew!" Jacob saw that here was a great opportunity! He replied, "Give me your birthright and I will give you some stew".

Esau was so hungry and cared so little about being the oldest, that he agreed. Esau gave his birthright to Jacob just to have some stew!

Jacob's name means "deceiver". (It was already clear that he was someone who would use all sorts of tricks and craftiness to get his way.)

The Blessing

Several years later Isaac realised it would not be very long before he died. He was now very old and blind. He decided he would give his eldest son Esau his special blessing. He would ask God to specially bless Esau and care for him and keep him safe. He would pass onto Esau the promises God had made to him.

Isaac called Esau. "Please go into the fields and hunt for an animal. Come home and cook it for my dinner. After we've eaten I will bless you before I die." Neither Isaac, nor Esau realised that Rebekah was listening outside the tent door.

Rebekah's Plan

Rebekah ran to Jacob. "Quickly," she said, "Your Father is about to give Esau his special blessing! You must go to him and take some food and get the blessing before Esau does." "But how can I?" said Jacob. "Though my father is old and blind, when he feels my arms and smells me he will realise I don't feel or smell like Esau, and I will be found out." But Rebekah had a clever plan. She attached goatskins to his arms and dressed him in Esau's clothes.

In Isaac's Tent
Jacob approached Isaac. "My father, " he called. "Who are you my son?" asked Isaac. "I am Esau your firstborn," lied Jacob. Isaac was confused. How had he got the food so quickly? Jacob lied, telling Isaac that God had helped him find it.

Isaac called and said, "Please come near, that I may feel you, my son, whether you are really my son Esau or not." Jacob went near his blind father. His father touched his arms and felt the goatskins. Jacob said, "The voice is the voice of Jacob, but the hands are those of Esau."

"Bring me the meal you have made," said Isaac. Jacob brought the meal his mother had made for him. She had made it in exactly the same way as Esau did. Having enjoyed the meal Isaac decided it was time to bless his son. "Come near now and kiss me," said Isaac. Jacob had also put on Esau's clothes, which his mother had given to him. As Jacob leant over Isaac, Issac smelt the smell of Esau.

Sure now that Jacob was his son Esau, Isaac gave him his special blessing. "May God bless you and make you rich in crops and animals. May you live long and happily and may the family obey you and your brothers serve you."

Esau's Sorrow
Jacob had only just left Isaac when Esau returned from his hunting. He cooked the meat and took the dinner to his father Esau asking him for his blessing. Isaac had a great shock when he realized that this was the real Esau! Isaac trembled and said, "I have already eaten a meal and blessed the one who brought it." Esau realised what Jacob had done. Angrily he said to himself, "When Isaac is dead I will kill Jacob!" Rebekah heard of Esau's plans.

Escape!
Worried that Jacob would soon be killed, Rebekah sent Jacob away to stay at the home of his uncle Laban. Jacob left his parent's home to walk the 300 miles to his uncle's. He was now alone, with no one to talk to. Jacob had time to think about his lying and deceit, and where it had brought him. As a result of his deceit he had been forced to leave his father, mother and his friends. Would he ever see them again?

The Ladder to Heaven
When Jacob reached Bethel he looked for a place to sleep. All he could find was a stone for a pillow. That night God spoke to Jacob through a very vivid dream. He saw a tall ladder reaching from the earth all the way up to heaven. Angels were going up and down on the ladder. Then God stood at the top of the ladder and spoke to Jacob telling him of his plans for him in the future. God showed his love and kindness to Jacob, who did not deserve to be forgiven. God promised that he would never leave Jacob.

The Need to Look to God
God was showing Jacob that he must not try and get things by deceit and lying. He must trust in the God who is willing to bless him. The ladder shows that God is willing to send

his help and kindness down from heaven to those people who look up to him for help. Christ says in John 1:51 that he is the true ladder - the true way by which God can bless and help men and women, boys and girls.

When Jacob awoke he was amazed at what he had seen and that the Lord was ready to forgive him. He made a promise that he would look to God to help him in the days ahead. To remind himself of the place, he made a pillar of stones. He included in it the stone he had used for a pillow.

Many Years Later
Jacob was away from home for many years. He worked for his uncle Laban, and became very wealthy. Jacob had two wives called Leah and Rachel, daughters of his uncle Laban. He also had many children. God was kind to Jacob. Rather than doing things on his own, Jacob learned to trust in God.

A New Name
To show how Jacob had changed, God gave him a new name. He would no longer be called "Jacob", which means "deceiver", but "Israel", which means "one who is a prince with God." Many years later Jacob returned to Bethel and there he thanked God for looking after him. How kind God had been to him, to forgive him the many wrong things he had done, and to keep him safe all these years.

Illustration: God Changing Someone
Alves Reis was once the world's most notorious counterfeiters. He cheated people by using forged money. He managed to cheat some very rich men out of millions of pounds. However, one day he realised how bad he had been and asked Jesus to forgive him. He became a completely changed man and wanted to live so that he could always do what pleased God.
(* The story of Alves Reis can be found in 'Men of Destiny' - by P. Masters, published by the Wakeman Trust, ISBN 1 870855 03 5 - available from most Christian Bookshops.)

Things to learn:
- Jacob deceived his brother Esau and his father Isaac.
- Dishonesty and cheating are always wrong in God's eyes.
- God showed Jacob mercy and kindness even though he did not deserve it.
- Jacob had to learn to trust in God.
- God is willing to forgive and help anyone who is truly sorry.

Discuss
- Have you ever deceived anyone to get your own way, or to get out of trouble?
- Were you found out?
- What happened?
- How did you feel?
- Did you learn not to deceive again?
- Have you ever received something you don't deserve?

Jacob - The Man God Changed

Isaac and Rebekah had twin boys called Jacob and Esau. Esau grew up to be a hunter. He had rough, hairy skin. Jacob looked after sheep and the goats. He was a quiet boy and had smooth skin.

Esau was the older twin and would therefore get a birthright when his father Isaac died. One day Esau came home and was very hungry. Jacob had cooked a meal and Esau asked him for some food. Jacob wanted Esau's birthright. He said that Esau could only have some food if Esau gave him his birthright. Esau was so hungry that he agreed.

A few years later Isaac, their father, knew he would soon die. He wanted to give Esau a special blessing, so he called Esau and asked him to hunt an animal and cook it for his dinner. Then he would bless Esau.

Meanwhile, Rebekah, his mother, went to find Jacob. She wanted Jacob to get his fathers' blessing instead of Esau. So Rebekah put goatskins on Jacob's arms and dressed him in Esau's clothes. This made him feel and smell like Esau. Then Rebekah gave Jacob some food to take in to Isaac.

Jacob went in to his father who was now old and blind. Isaac asked him, "Who are you, my son?" Jacob lied. "I am Esau", he said. Isaac thought that the voice sounded like Jacob but the skin felt like Esau. After eating the meal, Isaac gave Jacob his special blessing.

Esau was angry with Jacob for stealing the blessing, so Rebekah told Jacob to go and stay with his Uncle Laban. On the way he stopped one night to rest. He used a smooth stone for his pillow. As he slept he dreamed that he saw a ladder reaching up to heaven. God spoke to Jacob and promised that he would always be with him and help him.

Jacob stayed with his Uncle Laban for many years. He had two wives, Rachel and Leah, and also many children. God changed Jacob's name to Israel.

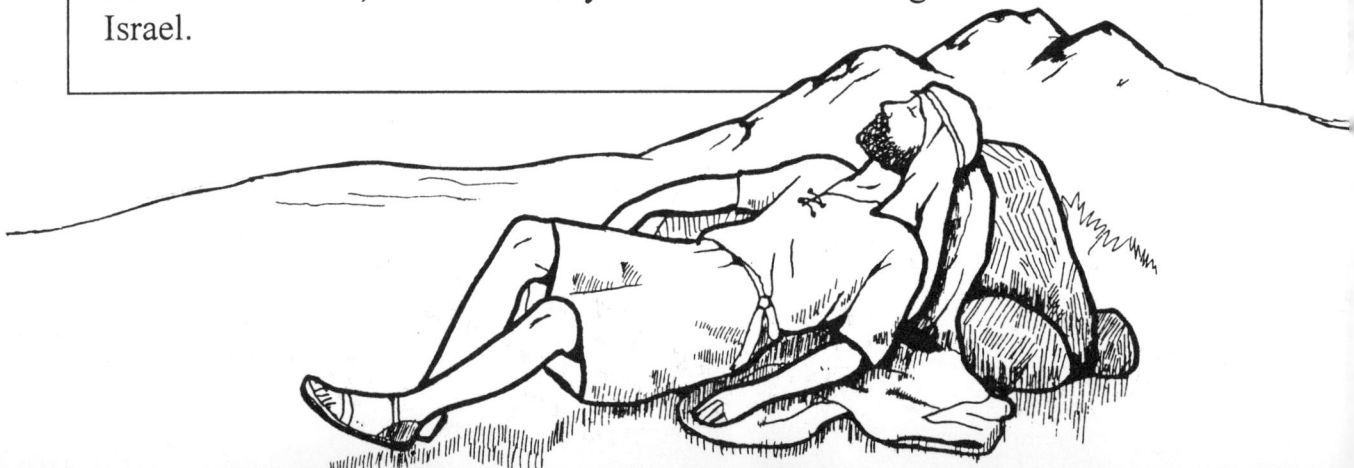

JACOB - THE MAN GOD CHANGED

Circle the right answer.

Rebekah gave birth to...................a son...............twin sons.................a daughter.

Jacob liked to............................stay indoors..........go out walking............play sport.

Esau liked to..............................sing......................wrestle....................hunt.

Jacob tricked..............................Esau...................Rebekah.................Isaac.

Jacob took his brother's.................camel.................favourite spear..........blessing.

This made Esau very.....................glad.....................angry........................sorry.

Rebekah sent Jacob away to live with his....brother...........uncle.................cousin.

On the way Jacob had a.................dream..................fall........................surprise.

God changed Jacob's name to.......Abraham...............Israel.......................Esau.

Write below two things that Jacob did to deceive Isaac.

....

....

....

Write below two lies that Jacob told.

....

....

....

☆	G	a	o	t	h	o	u
r	o	d	k	n	t	s	g
u	t	l	c	e	a	h	h
e	v	o	f	v	m	e	d
d	r	q	i	e	n	d	e
J	a	c	o	b	o	i	d
e	v	r	e	s	e	d	n
i	t	k	r	a	m	t	o

Beginning at the star follow the maze to find out about Jacob. Write the letters below.

_ _ _   _ _ _ _ _

_ _ _ _ _ _   _ _ _

_ _ _ _ _ _   _ _

_ _ _   _ _ _

_ _ _ _ _ _ _ _

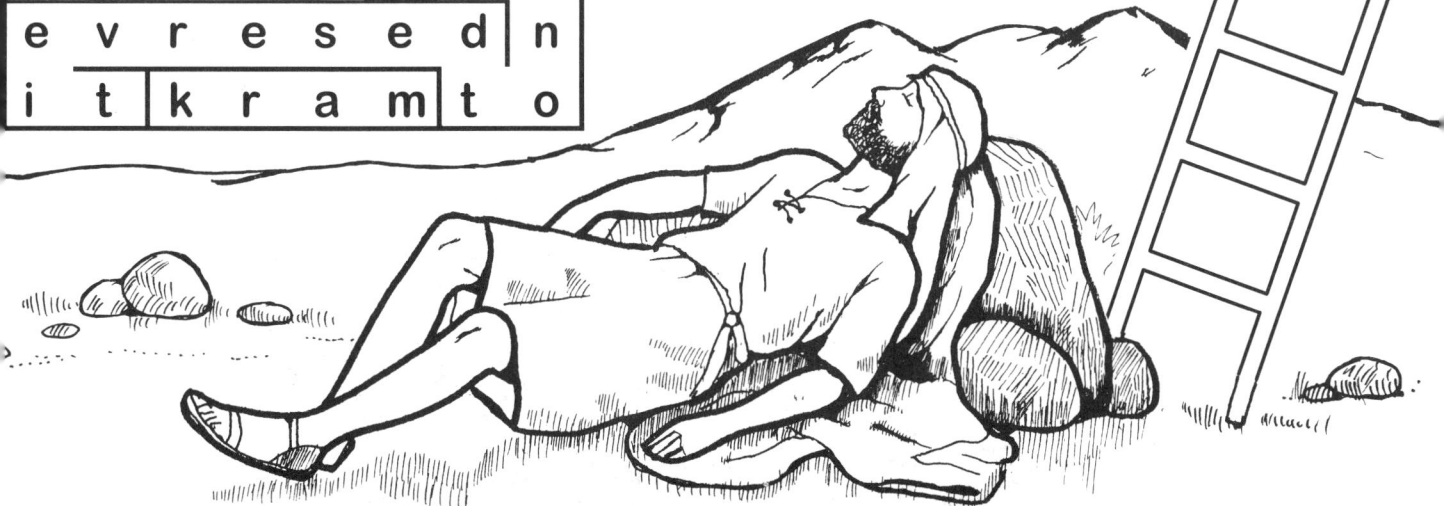

Ladder 2 uprights & 5 rungs

Ladder 2 uprights & 5 rungs

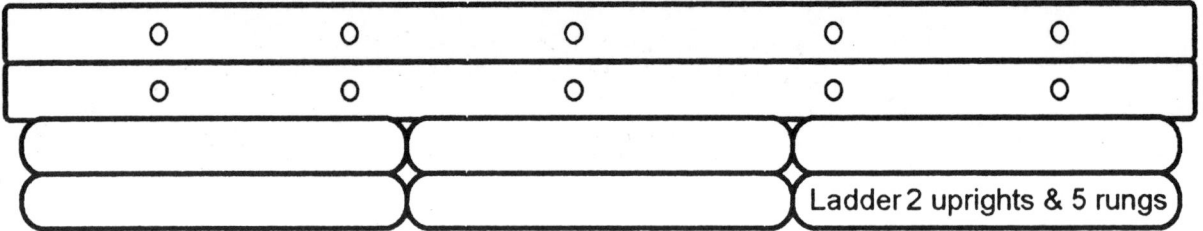

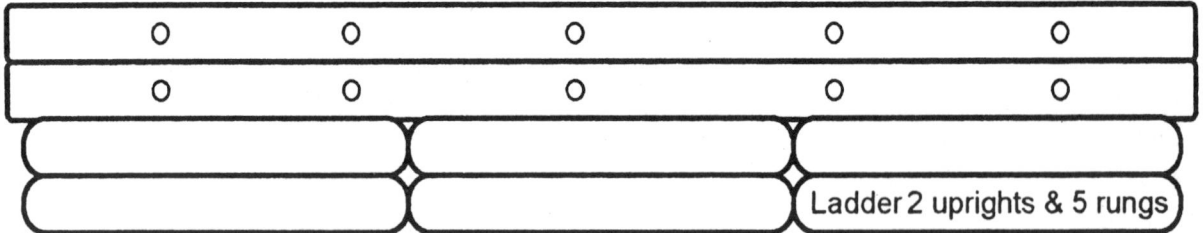

God spoke to Jacob through a dream.   Gen. ch.28

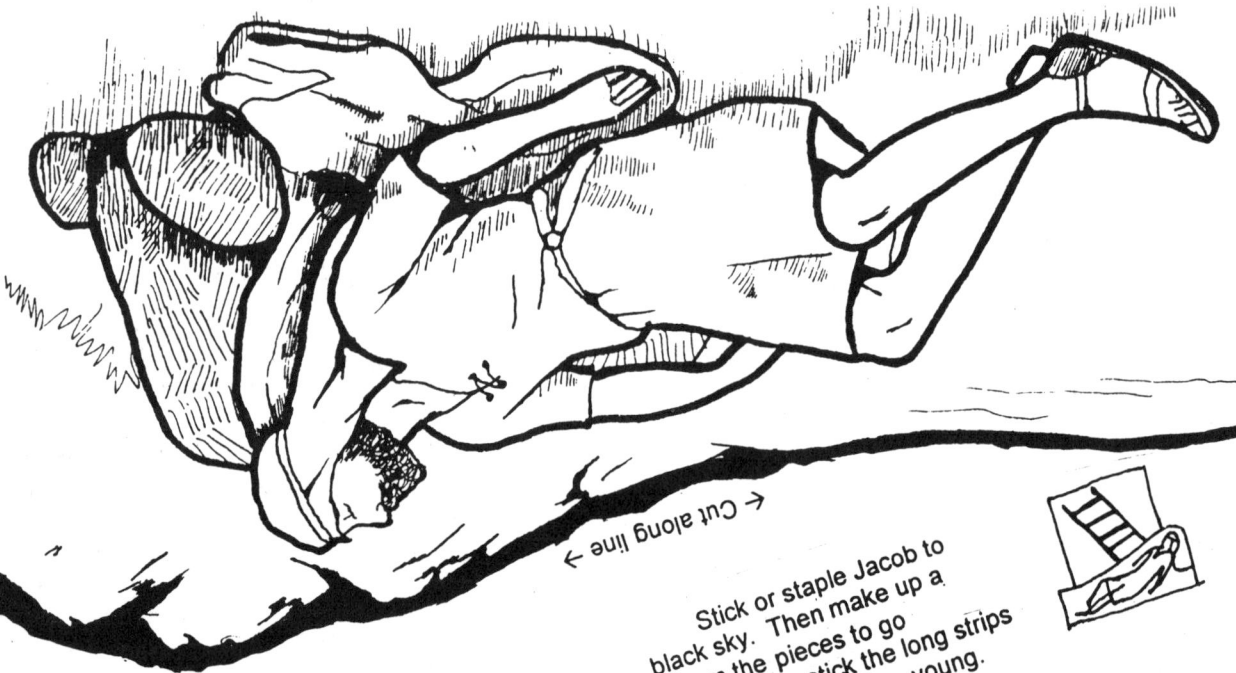

← Cut along line →

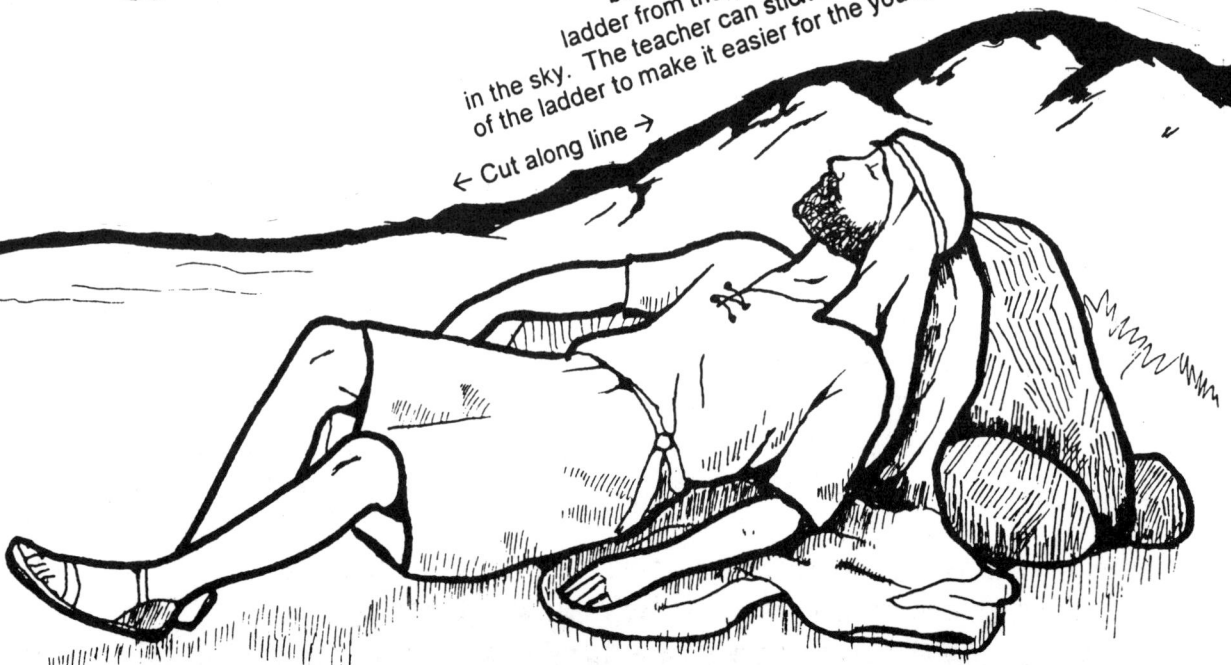

Stick or staple Jacob to black sky. Then make up a ladder from the pieces to go in the sky. The teacher can stick the long strips of the ladder to make it easier for the young.

← Cut along line →

God spoke to Jacob through a dream.   Gen. ch.28

Name... Date.......................

ABRAHAM'S FAMILY GROWS

the stars so shall your descendants be... how could you count them... the sand on the seashore...

S _ _ _ _ _

A _ _ _ _

D _ _ _ _

D _ _

L _ _ _ _

J _ _ _ _

Z _ _ _ _ _ _

R _ _ _ _

G _ _

N _ _ _ _ _ _

I _ _ _ _

J _ _ _ _

B _ _ _ _ _ _ _

start

Follow the letters around the tree to find out what God promised to Abraham.

"
_ _ _ _ _ _ _ _
_ _ _ _ _ _ _ _
_ _ _ _ _ _ _ _
_ _ _ _ _ _ _ _
_ _ _ _ _ ....
_ _ _ _ _ _ _ _ _
_ _ _ _ _ "
_ _ _."   Genesis ch.15 v 5

Esau

J _ _ _ _

I _ _ _ _

A _ _ _ _ _

Asher
Zebulun
Joseph
Jacob
Levi
Naphtali
Isaac
Benjamin
Issachar
Judah
Abraham
Dinah
Dan
Gad
Reuben
Simeon

Write in the names on this family tree.

Cross out the wrong words.

1. God promised Abel / Abraham that one day he would have a very great family.
2. Abraham and Sarah had a son called Isaac, when they were quite young / very old.
3. Isaac had twin sons called Jacob and Esau / Joseph and Benjamin.
4. God gave Jacob twelve / ten sons and one daughter.
5. One of his sons was sold as a king / slave in Egypt, his name was Joseph.
6. Joseph saved his whole family from starving when there was a famine because he was in charge of the water / food.
7. Jacob and all his family came down to Egypt to live / visit.
8. God blessed Jacob's family and they multiplied greatly / but they all died out.
9. A cruel / kind king came on the throne and made all the Israelites into slaves / very rich.
10. God promised that after 400 years had passed he would take them back to the land He had promised them called Bethlehem / Canaan.
11. One day many years later a **very special person** would be born into Abraham's family and through Him all the world would be blessed. His name was **J _ _ _ _**.

Joseph's Coat and Dreams

Genesis 37

Themes	Favouritism, Jealousy, Hatred

Aims	To teach the events in the early life of Joseph. To consider the subject of jealousy and its consequences. To encourage children not to be jealous of others.

Resources	Bibles, Children's Story Sheet, Puzzle Page, Activity Sheets.

Other Ideas & Activities

1. Activity Sheets need brightly coloured material, 4 x 6 cm.
2. Ask the children to design a coat of many colours. This could be a collage activity.
3. Draw round a child on the floor (lying on a large sheet of paper). Draw in the large outline of a coat at the top of the shape. Children then cut up pieces of coloured paper and stick all over coat - class collage activity.
4. Make a display of Joseph in a coat of many colours. Include other brothers in display with various speech bubbles showing what they were thinking and contemplating.
5. A discussion about bullying: Why do people bully others? What do we think of people who bully? What should we do if we see someone being bullied or we are bullied ourselves? Should bullying be allowed? Compile a "Bullying Code", where rules are written and advice given as to how the children should behave towards each other and what they should do when they witness or suffer from bullying. Produce as a booklet for school or class use.

Teacher's Notes

Summary: Joseph was Jacob's favourite son. The brothers were jealous when he was given a beautiful coat of many colours. They became angry when they heard his dreams. They planned to murder him but instead they sold him to traders going to Egypt. Jacob was broken hearted because he believed his son had been killed. All this happened because of the terrible jealousy the brothers had towards Joseph. Jealousy can spoil relationships. It is something we should be aware of and seek to overcome.

Point of Contact

Favouritism

- Is it right for parents to have a favourite in the family?
- What do the other children think about it?
- Suppose the favourite child was given a special gift?
- How might the other brothers and sisters react?

A Favourite

Jacob was a farmer who had twelve sons. Joseph was born when Jacob was an old man and he became his father's favourite. Joseph would often stay with his father while his older brothers went out to work in the fields. However, one day when Joseph was with his brothers they behaved very badly. (We don't know what they did. They may have used bad language or been cruel to the animals.) Joseph was right not to tell his brothers off, but instead he felt that he had to tell his father. The brothers were angry that Joseph had told on them. Right from the beginning, Joseph's brothers could behave badly, but Joseph sought to do what pleased God.

A Special Coat

One day Jacob did a very foolish thing. He made Joseph a beautiful coat with many colours in it. It was probably woven with a special design, with silver and gold threads. It was most probably like one worn by a king. Joseph's brothers did not admire him in his new coat but became exceedingly jealous. Why should Joseph receive this gift when they only had rough old coats? It must have been hard for Joseph as it was not his fault that his father favoured him.

Special Dreams

One night when Joseph was seventeen, he had some special dreams from God. The next morning Joseph told them to his family. In the first dream Joseph saw twelve bundles of corn bow down to him. In the second dream, the sun, moon and eleven stars all bowed down to him. Joseph knew that the dreams meant that one day his family would all bow down before him. The brothers were very angry and their father Jacob was not pleased. He said, "Shall your mother and brothers and I indeed bow down before you?" Joseph may have made a mistake in telling his family his dreams. He did not mean to look as if he was proud or making himself appear to be a very important person.

The Search

In the dry season shepherds often had to travel from place to place, finding grass for their sheep. Once when Joseph's brothers were away from home Jacob became anxious to know if all was well. He asked Joseph to go and see if his brothers were alright. Joseph was obedient and willing to go. He travelled northwards but was unable to find them. Then he met a stranger who was able to tell Joseph where his brothers were. Eventually Joseph could see them in the distance.

Kill Him!

When the brothers saw Joseph in the distance they joked and said, "Look, here comes the dreamer." Their jealousy had turned to hatred and they began to plan how they could get rid of Joseph. At first they thought of killing Joseph and putting his body in a deep pit. "Then we will see what becomes of his dreams", they said. One of the brothers called Reuben was not as cruel as the others and did not like the idea. He suggested they threw Joseph into a pit and just leave him there. The brothers liked this idea, believing that Joseph would just die of starvation.

As Joseph approached, maybe expecting a welcome, the brothers grabbed him, tore off his beautiful coat of many colours, and threw him into the deep pit from which it was impossible to escape. He called out to his brothers to have pity on him (Gen. 42:21), but they just ignored him and carried on eating their meal. It shows how hard they had become. They so hated him, that they weren't in the least bit sorry for him.

To Egypt

Just at that moment some Midianite traders passed by. They were on their way to Egypt with spices and other goods. Judah, one of Joseph's brothers said, "Let us sell Joseph to these traders." The brothers liked the idea. So Joseph was pulled out of the pit and sold to the Midianites for twenty pieces of silver. Joseph was taken away by strangers to a country he had never seen, to live with people whose customs and language he did not understand. It must have been hard for Joseph to be taken far away from his home and his father's love. Although Joseph was in great trouble the Bible tells us that God was with Joseph looking after him and keeping him safe (Acts 7:9).

Broken Hearted

The brothers returned to Jacob. On their way home they killed a goat and dipped Joseph's special coat in its blood. They showed the coat to their father Jacob who recognised it and said, "A wild animal has killed him. Without doubt Joseph was torn to pieces." The old father cried bitterly and wondered how he would live without his favourite son Joseph. Even though his family tried, they could not comfort him. How evil the brothers were to bring all this sorrow on their father.

Illustration: Overcoming Jealousy

A family gathered to open their presents on Christmas day morning. As everyone pulled off the paper, Rachel was upset. Though she had been given some lovely presents, she felt that her sister's were better than her own. This really upset her mother who had tried so hard to make sure that all had similar things and equal quantities. Rachel ran upstairs in tears.

Her sister tried to comfort her, telling her that she could share her presents if she wanted. She even offered to let Rachel have some of them. But Rachel refused to accept anything. It looked as if the whole day was going to be spoiled.

Gradually Rachel had a change of mind. She realised that what was meant to be a happy family day was being ruined by her jealousy. She had made her mother and sister sad. She even started to dislike her self for behaving in the way she had. How could she be so self centred, and spoil every one else's day? Any way, as she started to look at her gifts more closely she realised just what lovely things she had been given, and how much care her mother had shown. To think she had treated her mother so badly! The problem was not with Rachel's presents, but with Rachel's attitude.

Rachel realised she had so much to be thankful for! Not only did she have some lovely gifts, but above all the concern and care of her parents and sister. How could she be jealous! She went back downstairs feeling very ashamed. Here she apologised to all and thanked her mother for her kindness.

Things to learn:

- Joseph was Jacob's favourite son.
- Joseph's brothers were jealous of him and sold him as a slave.
- We should not be jealous of others.

Discuss

- Have you ever been jealous of anyone?
- What makes you 'jealous'?
- How can we avoid being jealous? (Perhaps one answer is to try and be positive - think of all the good things you have and be thankful for what you've got. Try and make the most of these things.)
- Does jealousy always lead to hatred?
- Do you think Joseph's brothers thought they would ever be found out? (The Bible says, ".......be sure your sins will find you out", Numbers 32:23.) They thought they'd made sure Joseph's dreams would never come true.

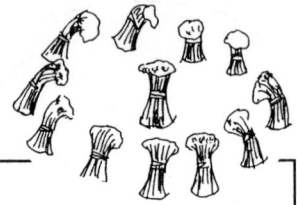

Joseph's Coat and Dreams

Jacob had twelve sons. Joseph was Jacob's favourite. He gave Joseph a lovely coat made with many colours. Joseph's brothers were very jealous.

One night Joseph had a dream. In the morning he told his family his dream. He said that he had seen twelve bundles of corn bow down to him. Then he had seen the sun, moon and eleven stars bow down to him. Joseph's brothers were angry. They must have thought he was being proud.

One day when Joseph's brothers were looking after their sheep, their father asked Joseph to take some food to them. When his brothers saw Joseph coming, they began to think how they could get rid of Joseph.

When Joseph came near them, his brothers tore off his coat and threw him into a deep hole. It was impossible for Joseph to get out. He called out to his brothers to let him out, but they took no notice.

It was not long before some people came by. They were on their way to Egypt to sell things. The brothers decided to sell Joseph to these people, as a slave. So they pulled Joseph out of the hole and sold him to the people for twenty pieces of silver.

Joseph must have wondered what would happen to him now. The Bible tells us that God was looking after Joseph and keeping him safe. Joseph trusted God.

Meanwhile, Joseph's brothers went home to Jacob their father. On the way home they killed a goat and dipped Joseph's coat in the blood. They lied to Jacob and told him that Joseph had been killed by a wild animal. Jacob was very sad to have lost his favourite son, Joseph. He believed that Joseph was dead.

JOSEPH'S COAT AND DREAMS

oin the dots then colour
ection by looking
the code mark.

..........Red

..........Green

.........Blue

...........Yellow

.........Orange

1. Who gave this special coat to Joseph? J __ __ __ __
2. Why did he give it to him ?
   H __   I __ __ __ __
   h __ __
3. How did this make his brothers feel ?
   T __ __ __   h __ __ __ __
   J __ __ __ __ __
4. What did they call him ?
   D __ __ __ __ __ __ __
5. What did they do to him ?
   T __ __ __   s __ __ __
   h __ __

True or False ?

Put a ☺ against the true sentences and a ☹ against the false ones.

Joseph had eleven brothers. ☺

Joseph's brothers loved him. ☺

Joseph had two dreams. ☺

Joseph's brothers were jealous. ☺

Joseph's brothers wanted to help him ☺

They sold Joseph to traders. ☺

They told their father the truth. ☺

God was with Joseph. ☺

Joseph's father said this to him:-

⚸⚶⌘LL ✠✋○♎ ≋✋♦⚶⫯♎ ⌘●♋ ☐

♌●♋ ✠✋○♎ ♎♎✋♦⚶♎✡ ☐●♋✋✋♋ ♎✋W

♋✋W● ♎✋✛✋♎♎✋ ✠✋○

Can you 'translate' these words with this code ?

a	n	i	r	h	t	o	m	u	y	s	b	f	e
⌘	●	☐	♎	❖	♦	✋	≋	○	✠	☆	Ω	⚙	♋

_ _ _ _ _   _ _ _ _   _ _ _ _   _   _ _ _   _ _ _ _

_ _ _ _ _ _   _ _ _ _ _   _ _ _ _   _ _ _ _   _ _ _ _ _

Gen.ch.37 v 10

The brothers brought Joseph's coat to their Father pretending they
had found it.   Gen. ch.37

Cut out a coat
shape
and stick
here. Red felt-tip
for blood.   S3.2

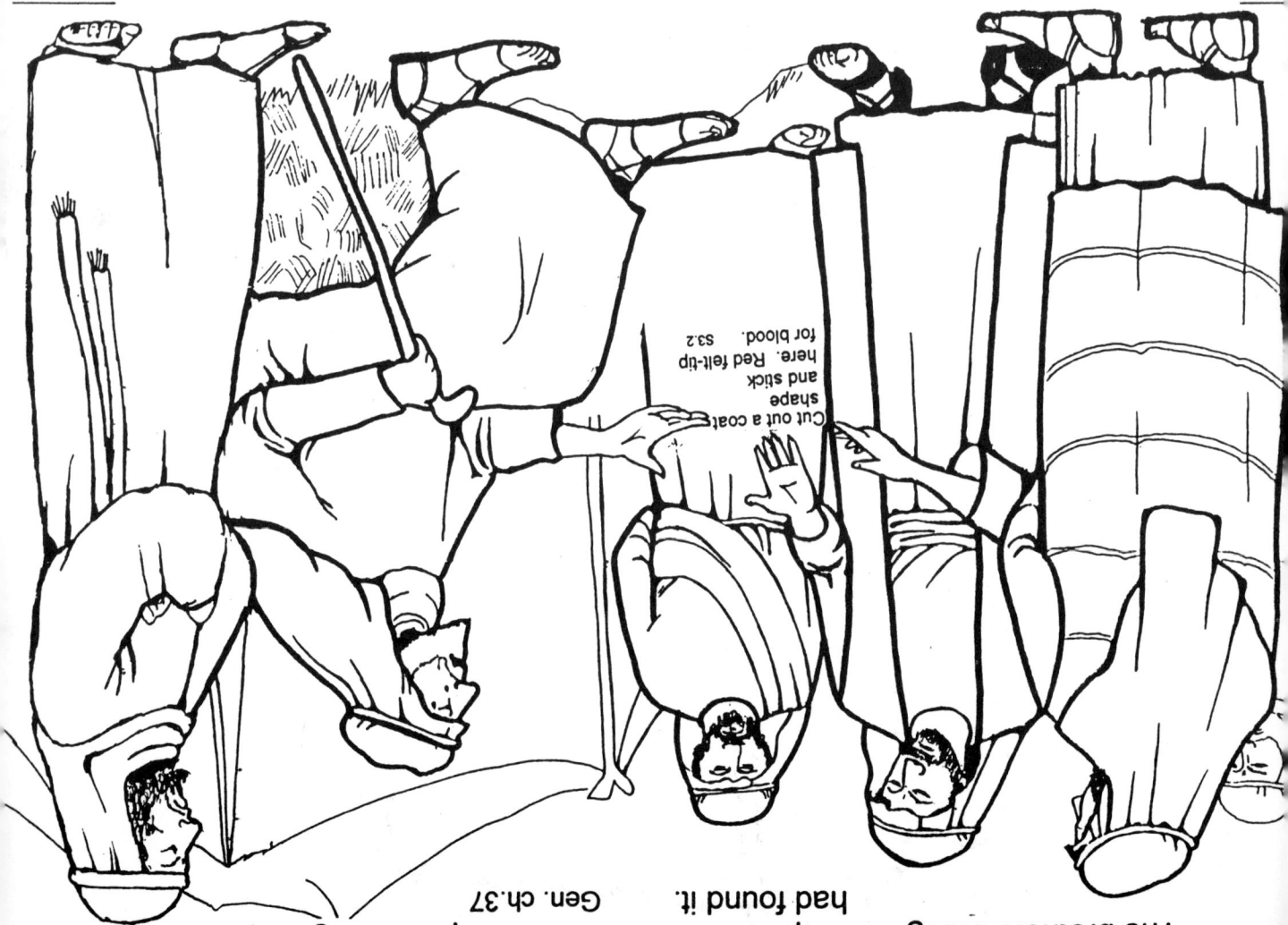

The brothers brought Joseph's coat to their Father pretending they
had found it.   Gen. ch.37

Cut out a coat
shape
and stick
here. Red felt-tip
for blood.   S3.2

JOSEPH'S COAT AND DREAMS – ACTIVITY SHEET

Design a coat using bright colours and patterns.

Joseph - From Prison to Power

Genesis 39, 40 and 41

Themes	Hardship, Patience, Unselfishness, Change

Aims	To describe Joseph's transition from prison to power. To consider Joseph's exceptional behaviour. To show that the Bible teaches Christians how to respond to opposition and difficulty.

Resources	Bibles, Children's Story Sheet, Puzzle Page, Activity Sheet.

Other Ideas & Activities

1. Activity Sheet needs, for prison & palace, suitable pens to draw in chains of iron and gold. Pictures could be decorated with suitable materials e.g. glitter.
2. Look up the word "conscientious". Write down all the ways in which Joseph was conscientious.
3. Write a character profile for Joseph. Write one for yourself listing positive and negative aspects. Compare and then highlight, by underlining with colours, those parts you most admire in Joseph, and those you would like to develop/improve upon.
4. How would each of the following have described Joseph's character -Potiphar; Potiphar's wife; the jailor; the butler; the baker; Pharaoh? Discuss with a friend and write down your answers to share with the class.
5. Write a story about changes of circumstances. This could tell of a change like Joseph's or it could be the reverse. It might be a story about change caused by such events as moving house, the arrival of a relative or new family member, or a change of schools, or something more dramatic!

Teacher's Notes

Summary: Joseph was sold as a slave to Potiphar and became the chief servant in his house. He was wrongly sent to prison when Potiphar's wife lied about him. Joseph could have complained and been miserable, but even in prison he made himself useful in helping the jailor, who soon came to trust Joseph. He was also concerned for the other prisoners. He was able to predict what would happen to Pharaoh's butler and baker by interpreting their dreams. Joseph had been in prison for several years, but he still had faith in God. When Pharaoh had dreams only Joseph could tell him their meaning. As a result Pharaoh made Joseph ruler over Egypt. Christians seek to obey the Bible and please God in all they do, and however difficult the situation may be.

Point of Contact
Patience
- Are you always patient?
- Are you always patient with others?
- When is it difficult to be patient?
- Have you ever had to wait for something for a long time?
- How did you feel as the weeks or months passed by?

For the background to this lesson see "Joseph's Coat and Dreams".

Sold As A Slave
When Joseph arrived in Egypt he was taken to a market place and sold as a slave. It was a terrible experience for Joseph to be taken from his father and his home, but the Bible says that God was watching over him and taking care of him. Joseph was bought by a man called Potiphar, an important officer in Pharaoh's army. Though a slave, Joseph wasn't miserable, but worked hard. It wasn't long before Potiphar realised what a good worker Joseph was. He could see he could be trusted. He made him the chief servant over his entire household.

Potiphar's Wife
Potiphar's wife was jealous of Joseph. One day Potiphar returned home to his wife, who lied to him that Joseph had treated her badly. Potiphar believed her lies and so had Joseph put into prison.

Prison!
At this time prisons were cold, dark dungeons beneath the palace of the King. Prisoners were only given bread and water to eat and drink. Their ankles would be in chains to stop them escaping.

Joseph could have felt very sorry for himself and become bitter, but instead he made himself useful and helped the jailor. Soon the jailor began to see that Joseph was capable and trustworthy and put him in charge of all the prisoners. The prison must have been a happier place with Joseph around. Even though life was hard for Joseph, he trusted God and was obedient to him.

Butler & Baker
One day two new prisoners arrived. They had both been working in the Palace but Pharaoh had been angry with them and sent them to prison. One night they both had vivid dreams. The next morning Joseph could see that they were troubled and so he asked them what was the matter. Joseph was kind and thoughtful and wanted to help them.

God helped Joseph to tell the men what their dreams meant. Joseph told the butler that in three days he would be back in the palace giving Pharaoh his wine, but Pharaoh would have the baker hanged.

All Joseph said came true. The butler returned to Pharaoh's court, but the baker was executed. Before the butler left the prison, Joseph asked him a special favour. "Please," he said, "tell Pharaoh about me and get me out of this prison." Unfortunately for Joseph, the butler forgot all about him. He had to stay in prison a further two years. However, Joseph still continued to trust God and be patient.

Pharaoh Dreams!
One night Pharaoh dreamt that he saw seven fat cows coming out of a river. Seven thin cows followed, who then ate up the fat cows. Then he saw seven fat ears of corn eaten by seven thin ears. He was greatly troubled by these vivid dreams. He asked the wise men and magicians in his court to tell him the meaning, but they could not do it. It was then that the butler remembered the man Joseph who had told the meaning of his dreams when he was in prison.

In Pharaoh's Court
So Joseph was called for. Having washed, shaved and put on new clothes, Joseph entered into the presence of Pharaoh.

"Can you tell me what my dreams mean?" he asked.
"It is God who will show me," replied Joseph.

Having told Joseph his dreams, Pharaoh waited to hear the reply. Joseph spoke: "God is showing you what will happen in the future. The seven fat cows and fat ears of corn means there will be seven years of plenty in Egypt. The thin cows and ears of corn show that this will be followed by seven years of famine. The King must choose a wise man who can arrange for food to be stored in the years of plenty so that there will be enough food to eat when the seven famine years come."

Ruler Over Egypt
Pharaoh was amazed. "God has shown you these things and you are wise," he said.

He turned to his servants. "Can we find such a one as this, a man in whom is the spirit of God?". Although Pharaoh was still king he made Joseph ruler over all of Egypt. He was like the Prime Minister of his country. The King gave Joseph his own ring with his seal in it, which meant that Joseph was able to make laws and other important decisions which everyone in the land would have to obey.

A Great Change
Pharaoh gave Joseph expensive clothes and a gold chain to wear around his neck. He had a chariot to ride through the streets in and all that saw him had to bow before him. Pharaoh also gave him his daughter as a wife.

The change for Joseph must have seemed incredible. That morning he had woken in prison. By the end of the day he was ruler over all Egypt! A dark prison, little food, rags to wear and a chain around his ankle, had now all been replaced by all the things a rich man would have.

The Bible says that through all his difficult experiences Joseph had been patient and trusted in God. Joseph knew that it was God who had helped him and brought him through.

When Jesus was unfairly treated, he continued to be patient and caring, and more concerned for others than himself. Even when they are treated unkindly, Christians still seek to be kind, and more concerned for others than themselves.

Illustration: Kind And Helpful, Even When Badly Treated

Georgi Vins was a Christian minister in Russia. Because he preached about Jesus he was put in prison in Russia for eight years. He did not deserve to be treated like this because he had done nothing wrong. He was in a prison where he had to share a cell with 50 others. It was bitterly cold and the food was very poor. He was forced to work very hard with the other prisoners. He became ill with heart trouble and almost died.

However, while in prison Georgi showed love and kindness to the prison officers. He befriended other prisoners and helped them. Like Joseph, God gave him help to have faith, show kindness to others and be patient.

Christians all over the world prayed for him and eventually he was suddenly released. He was put on a plane to Moscow and then on to the USA. Like Joseph, in one day he was taken from prison and suffering and given his freedom.

(*The story of Georgi Vins can be found in 'Three Generations of Suffering: An Autobiography' - by Georgi Vins, published by Hodder & Stoughton, ISBN 0 340 20417 6 - available from most Christian Bookshops.)

Things to learn:
- Joseph served faithfully in Potiphar's house.
- Even in prison Joseph behaved well and helped others.
- Having interpreted Pharaoh's dreams he was made ruler of Egypt.
- Joseph could behave like this because he trusted in God.
- Christians find God helps them to love those who hate them.

Discuss
- How do you feel when you are unfairly treated?
- Do you complain about little things?
- What can we learn from Joseph's behaviour?

Joseph - From Prison to Power

When Joseph arrived in Egypt he was sold as a slave. Joseph was bought by Potiphar, an important officer in Pharaoh's army. Potiphar saw that Joseph was a good worker and he made him his chief servant.

One day Potiphar returned home to his wife, who lied to him that Joseph had treated her badly. Potiphar believed her lies and had Joseph put in prison.

Joseph used his time in prison to help the jailor. Soon the jailor saw that Joseph was trustworthy and put him in charge of all the prisoners.

One day Pharaoh's butler and baker arrived in the prison. Pharaoh had got angry. One night they both had dreams. God helped Joseph to tell the men the meaning of their dreams. Joseph told the butler that in three days he would be back in the palace giving Pharaoh his food, but the baker would be executed.

All Joseph had said came true. Joseph asked the butler to ask Pharaoh to get him out of prison. But the butler forgot all about him. Joseph had to stay in prison for two more years. Joseph still continued to trust God and be patient.

One night Pharaoh dreamed that he saw seven fat cows which were eaten up by seven thin cows. Then he saw seven fat ears of corn eaten by seven thin ears. He asked if anyone could tell him the meaning of the dreams. The butler remembered Joseph. Joseph was called for. Having washed, shaved and put on new clothes, he came before Pharaoh.

Joseph told Pharaoh the meaning of his dreams. He said that the seven fat cows and fat ears of corn meant there would be seven years of food in Egypt. The thin cows and ears of corn showed that this would be followed by seven years of famine. Pharaoh was amazed. Although Pharaoh was still king he made Joseph ruler over all of Egypt.

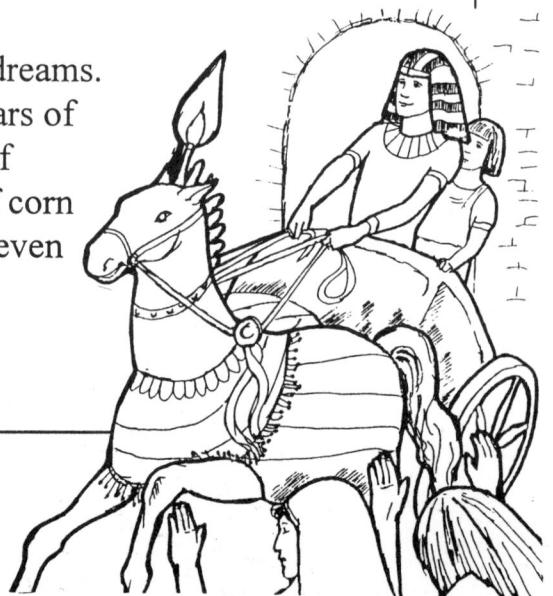

JOSEPH - FROM PRISON TO POWER

Cross out the wrong words........

Pharaoh had a dream only the **butler / Joseph** could tell him what it meant. So Joseph was **taken out of** / **left in prison.** He was cleaned up and given new clothes.   The dream Pharaoh had was about 7 **sheep /cows.**   Pharaoh also saw some **ears of corn / flowers** in his dream. **Joseph knew the meaning of the dream all by himself** / **God gave Joseph the meaning of the dream.** It meant **7 /2** good years of plenty and then 7 bad years of **war** *I* **famine.**

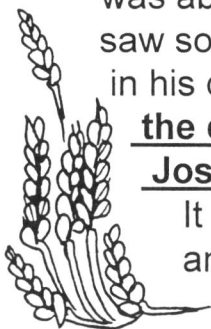

Find out what Pharaoh said to his servants about Joseph, by writing down the first letter of each object.

_ _ _ _ _ _ _ _ _ _ _ _ _ _ _ _ _ _ _

_ _ _ _ _ _ _ _ _ _ _ _ _ _ , _ _ _ _

_ _ _ _ _ _ _ _ _ _ _ _ _ _ _ _ _

Genesis 41. v 38.

Joseph's life changed a great deal.   Can you fill in the missing words ?

The butler f _ _ _ _ _ _ him, but Pharaoh
s _ _ _ _ f _ _ Joseph. He was taken out of
a p _ _ _ _ _ _, and put in a p _ _ _ _ _ _.
He was d _ _ _ _ _, but he s _ _ _ _ _ _.
He changed from r _ _ _ _, to r _ _ _ _ _ _.
He was a p _ _ _ _ _ _ _ _ _, but he was
made a P _ _ _ _ _   M _ _ _ _ _ _ _ _.
His feet were in i _ _ _ _ chains, but
Pharaoh gave him a g _ _ _ _ chain.

Prime Minister   dirty   riches   prisoner   forgot

gold   palace   shaved   iron   prison

ent for   rags

God took Joseph from prison
from chains of iron ...
and from rags ...
to the palace,
to chains of gold,
to riches.

Gen. ch.41

Joseph Forgives His Brothers

Genesis 42 - 50

Themes	Being Sorry, Forgiveness, Reconciliation

Aims	To teach the Bible's account of Joseph being reconciled to his brothers. To consider the need to say sorry when we have hurt others. To show what is the Bible's teaching on forgiveness.

Resources	Bibles, Children's Story Sheet, Puzzle Page, Activity Sheet.

Other Ideas & Activities
1. Activity Sheet needs split pin.
2. Draw a story board or timeline of the events in Joseph's life.
3. With a partner, choose one of the following. Write a short story, or role play the scene to illustrate how you would show forgiveness: (i) your best friend has broken your favourite toy; (ii) your brother/sister has lost your pen; (iii) your mum/dad has thrown away your favourite reading book by mistake.
4. What might you need to be forgiven for, by: your mum/dad; your friends; your teacher?
5. What is famine? Show pictures and discuss the effects of little or no food/drink (available from various famine relief agencies).
6. "We Enjoy Plenty". Make a collage of food labels, parts of empty cereal boxes, cartons and other packaging, to show the ample supplies of food we have in this country.

Teacher's Notes

Summary: Ten of Joseph's brothers came to Egypt to buy corn. Joseph tested them to see if they had changed and were sorry for what they had done to him. Joseph realised that they had changed and had learned not to be selfish, but put others first. Eventually Joseph told them who he was. Joseph was also reunited with his father Jacob. Christians seek to obey the teaching of Jesus. They are willing to forgive those who have done bad things to them.

Point of Contact
Forgiveness
- Have you ever been deeply hurt by someone?
- What sort of words can hurt people?
- Have you ever found it hard to forgive someone who's hurt you, even when they have said sorry?

For the background to this lesson see "From Prison to Power".

A Change of Lifestyle
Could we find anyone who experienced a greater change of lifestyle than Joseph? One morning he was a prisoner chained up and later in the day he was ruler over the land of Egypt. In all this Joseph acknowledged that it was God who had given him his high position and change of life (Gen. 41:50-52).

His New Work
Joseph collected as much corn as he could during the seven years of plenty. He travelled throughout the land of Egypt making arrangements for storehouses to be built. Large harvests of many thousands of tonnes of corn had to be collected and stored. The Egyptians obeyed every order that Joseph gave them.

Famine!
After seven good years Joseph's word proved true. There was no rain and the crops would not grow. God had warned the Egyptians and because of Joseph's wise planning they were well prepared. The famine not only affected Egypt but many of the surrounding countries (show map), including Canaan where Joseph's family lived. People heard that Egypt had food. Many people travelled to Egypt to buy food.

The Brothers Arrive
One day Joseph's father, Jacob, sent his sons to Egypt to buy corn. He kept his eleventh and youngest son Benjamin with him and only sent the other ten. When they arrived in Egypt they approached Joseph to ask for corn. They bowed before him. Though twenty years had passed Joseph recognised them immediately, but they did not know who he really was. Joseph looked like an Egyptian and was wearing Egyptian clothing. It was then that Joseph remembered the dreams he had when he was still a teenager. His brothers were bowing down to him just as God had told him.

Joseph's Wisdom
Joseph could have felt angry towards his brothers. They had treated him in a very cruel way and even thought of killing him. Joseph was now in a position of authority and had an opportunity to take his revenge. He could have punished them or refused to sell them corn so they would die of starvation. However he decided not to tell them immediately who he was. He pretended he did not know them. He wanted to know if they had changed and if they were now sorry for what they had done to him.

Spies!
Joseph accused his brothers of coming as spies, in order to attack a weakened Egypt. They denied this, saying they were just poor farmers from Canaan, with a father and a youngest brother still at home. However Joseph put them in prison for three days. Here they had time to think and talk. They did not know Joseph could understand their language. He listened to their conversation and was amazed. The brothers said, "We are suffering like this because of the terrible way we treated Joseph. When we heard him crying out we would not have mercy on him." When Joseph heard this, he went away and wept.

Bring Benjamin
After 3 days, Joseph gave his brothers plenty of corn and told them to go home. But

there was a condition. They must bring back their youngest brother Benjamin. Joseph also kept one of the brothers as a prisoner. This was to make sure that they would return. The brothers did as Joseph told them, and although Jacob their father was distressed at Benjamin going to Egypt with them he soon relented.

Joseph Revealed!
When Joseph saw his brothers in Egypt again, he invited them all to a meal at his house. When Joseph had ordered all the servants to leave the room and he was alone with his brothers, he told them who he was. It must have been a very emotional moment for Joseph. His brothers were speechless.
Joseph said that he forgave them their bad treatment of him many years earlier. The brothers knew they did not deserve such kindness. They all embraced each other and returned home to tell their father Jacob the wonderful news.

Jacob's Joy
Jacob was now a very old man and wept with joy when he heard that his son Joseph was still alive. He travelled to Egypt to be reunited with Joseph.

Joseph's Provision
Joseph wanted to provide for his family, and so his father Jacob, his 11 brothers and their wives and families all settled in Egypt. Pharaoh was very pleased to meet Jacob and gave him and his family some of the best land in Egypt.

God's Word Fulfilled
Once again the brothers bowed down before Joseph. Joseph knew that the dreams he had been given when he was 17 had all come true. The brothers said, "Please forgive the sin of your brothers when we did evil to you." Joseph spoke kindly and said, "Do not be afraid. God has brought good out of it. I was sent here to save our family and many others from the famine."

Forgiveness
Jesus taught his disciples to forgive one another. He also said, "I say to you, love your enemies, bless those who curse you, do good to those who hate you, and pray for those who spitefully use you and persecute you" (Matthew 5:44). He also taught his disciples a prayer, "..forgive us our trespasses as we forgive those who trespass against us" (Matthew 6:12). Christians should be willing to forgive those who have treated them badly.

Illustration: Elisabeth Elliot - A Demonstration Of Forgiveness
Jim Elliot and his four friends went to the jungles of Ecuador where they sought to tell the Auca tribe about Jesus Christ. It appeared that the missionaries were building up a good relationship with the Aucas and had enjoyed happy times with them. They seemed to be responding to the words they were hearing and the kindness of the missionaries.

On Sunday, January 8, 1956, the men Jim Elliot had worked amongst and prayed for, for several years, suddenly attacked them, killing Jim and his four companions. It was a great tragedy for the missionaries' families and especially their young wives.

However, though so tragically bereaved, Elisabeth Elliot continued to pray for the Aucas and for the particular men who had killed her husband. She was not bitter towards them.

It was her joy to eventually hear of many of these Aucas becoming true Christians and finding forgiveness for the bad things they had done.

(*The story of Jim and Elisabeth Elliot can be found in an 'Omnibus Edition' of her books, by Elisabeth Elliot, published by OM Publishing, ISBN 1 85078 265 2)

Things to learn:
- Joseph forgave his brothers when he saw they were really sorry.
- Eventually Joseph was reunited to his brothers and father.
- The whole family moved to Egypt.
- The Bible teaches us that we should forgive those who are truly sorry.
- God forgives those who are truly sorry.

Discuss
- Should we be ready to forgive those who have been cruel or unkind to us?
- Should we want to see that they are sorry first?

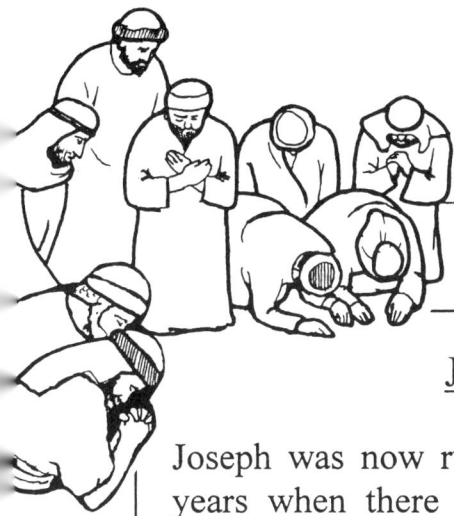

Joseph Forgives His Brothers

Joseph was now ruler of Egypt. He worked hard during the seven years when there was plenty of food. He travelled around Egypt telling the people how to build barns and store corn.

After seven years, famine came. The Egyptians were pleased that Joseph had told them to store their food. They now began to use the corn they had saved.

Joseph's father, Jacob, sent his sons to Egypt to buy corn. When they came to Joseph, they did not recognise him. Joseph knew his brothers straight away, but did not tell them who he was. As they bowed down to him he realised his dreams of many years ago had come true.

Joseph told his brothers that he thought they were spies. He put them in prison for three days. Here they had time to think and talk about how badly they had treated Joseph.

Joseph let his brothers go and told them to go home and come back with Benjamin, the youngest. Jacob did not want Benjamin to go to Egypt, but eventually he let him go. When all the brothers returned to Joseph he invited them all to a meal in his house. When he had told all his servants to leave the room, Joseph told his brothers who he was.

They were amazed! They couldn't believe that their brother Joseph was ruler of Egypt! Joseph told his brothers that he forgave them their unkindness to him.

When they went home to their father Jacob, they told him they had found Joseph. Jacob cried for joy. He travelled to Egypt to see Joseph for himself. How happy he was now!

Joseph wanted to help his father and his brothers. So they all came to live in Egypt.

Name.. Date.................................

JOSEPH FORGIVES HIS BROTHERS

Draw a line to the right endings for these sentences.

Joseph was now..............
The famine was..............
Jacob sent his sons.........
Joseph recognised..........
They bowed down............
Joseph pretended that ....
He said to them........
He wanted to see.............

.... "You are spies"
.... his brothers straight away
.................he did not know them
.... if they were truly sorry
.......very bad in many countries
.................a very important ruler
.... down to Egypt to buy food
...... to him just like in the dream.

Can you can fit these words into the grid

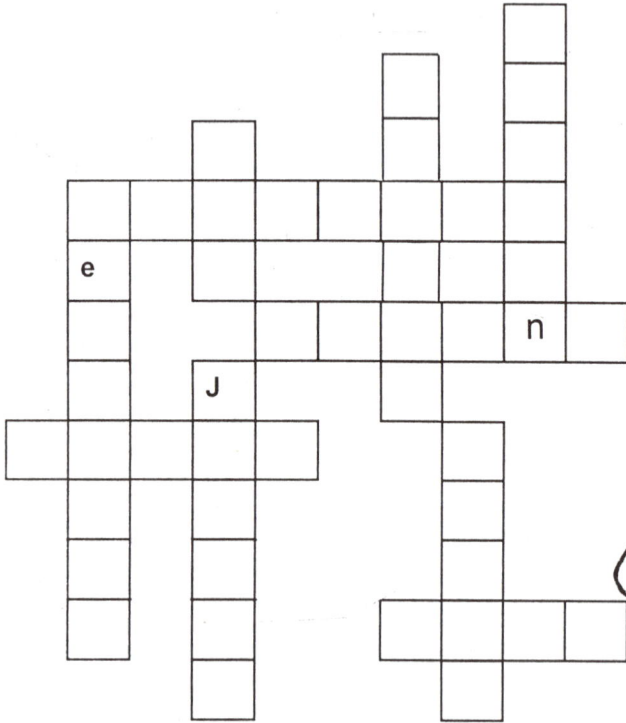

Jacob (5)   brothers (8)   famine (6)
spies (5)   bow (3)   Benjamin (8)
prison (6)   dreams (6)   Joseph (6)
test (4)

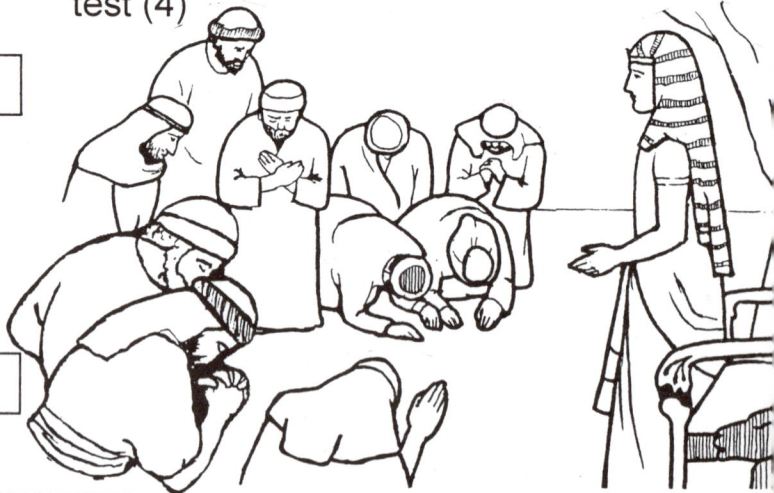

When Joseph left home he was..........   5 + 7 + 3 + 2 =   years
He lived in Egypt for...........................   9 + 1 + 2 + 1 =   years
He collected food in the good.............   3 + 1 + 2 + 1 =   years
                                                                                    _____ +
How old was Joseph when he saw his brothers again ?............... _____ years

How many years was it since Joseph had seen his brothers ?.... _____ years

Here is a picture of
Joseph meeting his
father. Join the dots
by following
the alphabet.

When Joseph's brothers bowed down before him, he remembered his dreams.

Gen.ch.42

make hole

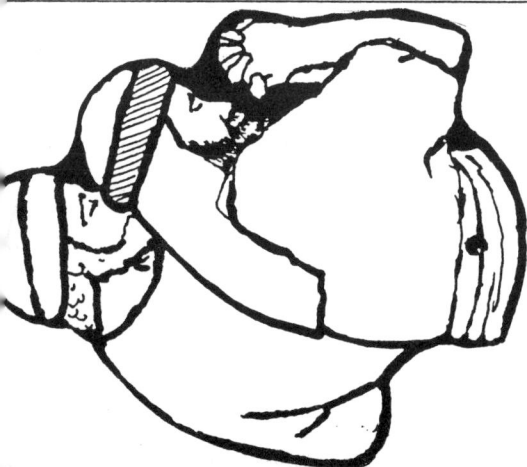

JOSEPH FORGIVES HIS BROTHERS – ACTIVITY SHEET

Cut out the two brothers. Make a hole for the split pin and fasten to the picture through the dot.

Moses' Birth and Call

Exodus 2, 3 & 4

Themes	God's Plan, Preparation

Aims	To teach the Biblical account of the birth and call of Moses. To consider preparation for future work and vocation. To teach that God will help and protect those who are willing to serve him and work for him.

Resources	Bibles, Children's Story Sheet, Puzzle Page, Activity Sheet, Map.

Other Ideas & Activities

1. Activity Sheet – follow instructions on Sheet.
2. Vocations and Careers: Ask the children to consider what they would like to be when they are older. They could then find out more about what that career involves with regard to the training, nature of the work and the qualities required of those who do the job.
3. Ask a parent to come in and speak to the class about their training and work.
4. Find out more about the Egyptians, e.g. what did they build and what were their kings called? Find out more about the Egyptian slaves and how they were treated.
4. Design and make a waterproof basket for a baby.
5. Ask your parents for any stories about what you did when you were a baby or very young. Were you ever in danger? What happened? Write about it and then report back to the class.
6. Think of all the good things God has given you and done for you, and ways that he has protected you. Make a list.

Teacher's Notes

Summary: Moses' parents had faith and trusted God to keep their son safe. It was in God's plan that the Egyptian princess should find the basket Moses was put in and adopt him as her own child. In the palace Moses had an excellent education. Moses chose to leave the riches of the Egyptian palace and go and live with his own suffering people, the Israelites. Moses became a shepherd. Here for forty years, God prepared him for the work he would call him to do. While in the desert God spoke to Moses from a burning bush. God called him to take the Israelites out of Egypt and back to Canaan. God often prepares people for special work.

Point of Contact

Training/Preparation

- What do you want to be when you grow up?
- What do you think you have to do to prepare yourself for this?
- How can you prepare further?

After Joseph

Joseph was taken to Egypt and here he became very powerful and influential. (See lessons on Joseph, from section "Beginnings".) His family went to live in Egypt with him. For about 400 years they stayed and grew in number, until there were about 2 million of Abraham's descendants living in Egypt, in an area called Goshen (show map.)

Another Pharaoh

A Pharaoh came to be King of Egypt, who didn't know about Joseph. He was afraid that the Israelites were becoming so numerous that they would soon be very powerful and take over the whole land of Egypt.

So he ordered the Israelites to work as slaves. They were very cruelly treated and were often whipped and beaten. The Israelites cried to God in prayer, asking him to help them. God answered them by sending Moses to rescue them and take them back to the land of Canaan (now called Israel). Abraham had been promised by God that one day his descendants would live in this land.

Moses' Birth

Pharaoh was still worried that the Israelites were becoming too powerful. He was a cruel and hard man. He ordered that, from now on, all the baby boys born into Israelite families must be thrown into the river and left to drown.

Moses' mother and father had two children already. Miriam was 13 and Aaron was 3. They were now expecting another baby. When Moses was born they decided that they wouldn't obey Pharaoh and allow their baby boy to be thrown into the river. So they trusted God to help them.

At first they hid Moses by keeping him in the house. After 3 months he grew bigger and his cry was louder. They could not keep his birth a secret any more. They had to think of another plan.

Baby In the Bulrushes

Moses' mother made a basket out of reeds from the river. She put Moses inside and covered the top with a lid. She hid the basket amongst the reeds. She told Miriam, Moses' sister, to sit at a distance and watch.

Pharaoh's Daughter

Pharaoh's daughter came down to the river to bathe in the cool, clean water. When she saw the basket she sent one of her maids to fetch it. When the princess lifted the lid baby Moses began to cry. She fell in love with him. She realised that some Israelite mother had left him there to save him from the cruel orders of her father Pharaoh. The princess decided to adopt baby Moses as her own child.

Miriam's Intervention

Miriam had seen what had happened. She ran up to the princess and said, "Shall I get someone to nurse the baby for you?" "Yes," replied the princess. Miriam told her mother and then brought her to see the princess. She ordered Moses' mother to take the baby and care for it. She promised to pay Moses' mother for doing this. How incredible! God had worked things out so that Moses" parents did not need to worry about hiding Moses any more. Not only that, but Moses' mother was now to be paid for looking after her own son!

The Palace
The years passed and soon the day came when Moses was old enough to go and live in the palace with the princess. Moses had a complete change of lifestyle. Instead of a poor home he now had all the riches and good living of a palace home. Now he was a fine prince wearing expensive clothes, eating delicious food and having servants to wait on him. Moses studied in the best schools and colleges of Egypt. He became a wise and intelligent man (Acts 7:22). Here he would have been trained how to lead people and rule over them.

A Choice
Although life at the palace was easy, Moses never forgot that he was an Israelite by birth. The Israelites served the Egyptians as slaves and life was extremely hard. Even though this was so, one day Moses chose to leave the palace and return to live with his own people. He was willing to leave all the riches and privileges he had and live in suffering with the Israelites (Heb11: 24-26). God had a plan for Moses.

Escape!
One day when Moses was defending an Israelite slave, he killed an Egyptian. When Pharaoh heard this he was furious and ready to kill Moses. Moses escaped to the desert. There God cared for him, giving him a home and a family.

A Burning Bush
Moses became a shepherd. For forty years he looked after sheep in the deserts near Egypt. One day Moses saw a strange sight. In the distance he saw a bush on fire. Moses went to have a closer look. He noticed a strange thing. Although the bush was on fire, it was not being burnt. As he came close to the bush he heard a voice calling, "Moses, Moses". He answered, "Here I am."

Then the voice said, "I am God." Moses was afraid and hid his face. He knew it was God speaking to him. Then God said, "I have seen the suffering of my people in Egypt. I have heard their prayers and am going to take them from Egypt back to their own land, the land of Canaan." The one who had learned to care for and look after sheep, was now going to care for and help God's people. It had taken forty years of patient preparation, but now Moses was ready to lead the Israelites back to the land of Canaan.

God Commands Moses
God said, "I will send you to Pharaoh to ask him to let my people leave Egypt." Moses didn't want to do the work and began to make excuses. He said, "I'm nobody. I am no good at speaking. They will not listen to me." God reassured him and told Moses that his older brother Aaron would help him. God showed Moses two miracles, which he could use when he saw Pharaoh to prove that God had sent him. Moses returned to Egypt to lead the Israelites back to Canaan.

Illustration: Long Preparation For A Life's Work
David Livingstone was born in Scotland in 1813. At the age of ten he took up factory work, but eventually he made up his mind to go abroad as a Christian missionary and doctor.

Although he was still employed in the local mill, he started to learn medicine by propping his books up on the spinning machine and, as he says "catching sentence after sentence" as he worked. After work Livingstone would read at home, often late into the night. He had a real hunger for knowledge and an ability to absorb it very quickly. He was also determined to learn all he could.

Soon he was earning enough to enable him to attend medical classes in Glasgow. Here he trained to be a doctor. In 1840, at the age of 27, and many years after he had first started his preparations, David Livingstone now felt ready to go abroad.

He went to Africa, where he stayed until his death in 1873. During this time he preached to many thousands about Jesus Christ. He was able to use his medical skills to heal people of their illnesses. He explored much of southern Africa. He travelled 29,000 miles in Africa and discovered six lakes and many rivers and mountains, including the highest waterfall in the world. All his preparation and study was of great use to him in the end. He is remembered for the missionary work that he did and also his great explorations of Africa.

(* "David Livingstone - Trail Maker" by Robert O Latham - Faith & Fame series, published by Lutterworth Press, ISBN 0 7188 2489 X - available from most Christian Bookshops.)

Things to learn:
- Moses' mother hid him from Pharaoh in a basket in the bulrushes.
- Moses chose poverty rather than the riches of Egypt.
- God had a special work for him to do and prepared him for it.
- God often prepares people to serve and work for him.

Discuss
- How did God protect Moses?
- How did God prepare Moses for his future work?
- What gifts has God given you?
- What do you want to do?
- How will you prepare for it?

Moses' Birth and Call

Pharaoh, the king of Egypt, was a cruel man. He made the Israelites work for him as slaves. They were often beaten and told to work harder. He did not want too many Israelites in Egypt. So one day, he ordered that all the baby boys born in Israelite families should be killed.

One day an Israelite mother had a baby boy called Moses. When he was three months old, it was difficult to hide him. So Moses' mother made a basket out of reeds. She put Moses inside and carefully hid the basket among the reeds on the river. She told Miriam, Moses' sister, to watch the basket.

Soon Pharaoh's daughter came down to the river to bathe. She saw the baby Moses and realised that this baby boy had been hidden to protect him from the cruelty of her father. She decided to adopt Moses as her own child.

Miriam saw what happened and ran to Pharaoh's daughter. Miriam told her that her mother would look after the baby. Pharaoh's daughter agreed. So Moses' mother was able to look after her son until he was old enough to go and live with Pharaoh's daughter at the palace. Moses had a comfortable life. But he never forgot that he was an Israelite.

Moses decided to leave the palace. He went into the desert and became a shepherd. Moses was a shepherd for forty years. One day Moses saw a bush on fire. As he went closer, he noticed that the bush was not being burned. Then he heard God calling his name, "Moses, Moses." Moses answered, "Here I am".

God told Moses that he wanted him to be the leader of the Israelites and help them to leave Egypt and return to their home country. Moses did not want to do this, and began to make excuses. God told Moses that he would help him, and that Moses' brother Aaron would work with him too.

So Moses went back to Egypt and became the leader of the Israelites.

MOSES' BIRTH AND CALL

Find the missing words and put them in the crossword.

1. Pharaoh ordered all the baby __ __ __ __ to be killed.
2. Moses' mother made a __ __ __ __ __ __ for Moses.
3. Pharaoh's daughter saw the basket in the __ __ __ __ __.
4. Miriam said that she would find a __ __ __ __ __ for Moses.
5. Moses grew up in Pharaoh's __ __ __ __ __ __ __.
6. The Israelites were treated badly by the Egyptians as __ __ __ __ __ __ __.
7. Moses went to the desert to be a __ __ __ __ __ __ __ __ __.

8. God spoke to Moses in a burning __ __ __ __.
9. God told Moses that he must lead the Israelites out of __ __ __ __ __ __.
10. Moses' brother __ __ __ __ __ __ would help him.

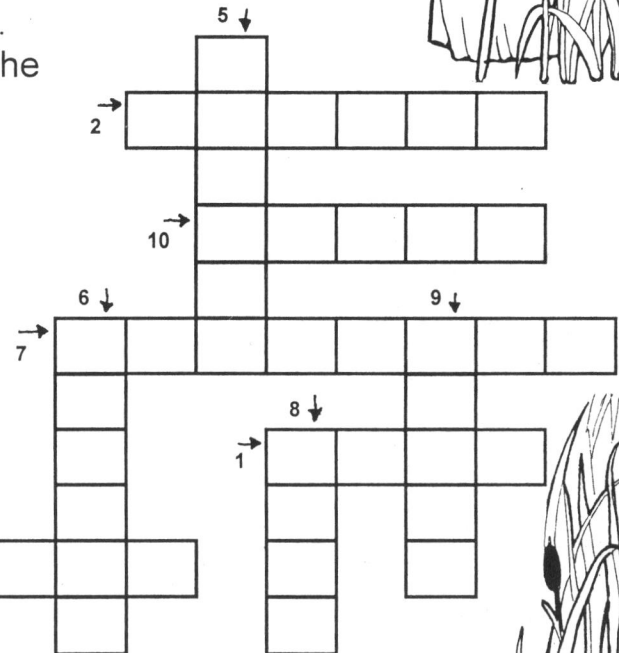

Find out what God said to Moses from the flames. Start at the arrow missing out the X's.

" __ __ __ __ __ __ __ __

__ __ __ __ __ __ __ __ __ __

__ __ __ __ __ __ __ __ __ "

from Exodus ch.3 v 17

Which choice did Moses make ?
Fill in the words, and colour in the right path.

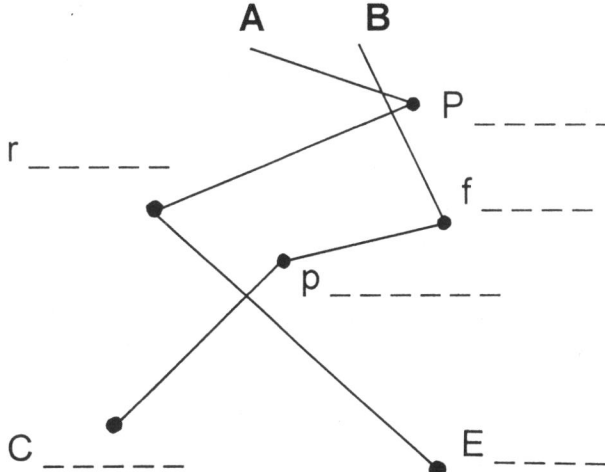

A   B

P _ _ _ _ _

r _ _ _ _ _ _ _

f _ _ _ _ _

p _ _ _ _ _ _

C _ _ _ _ _   E _ _ _ _ _

Prince, poverty, faith, Canaan, riches, Egypt.

Moses' mother hid him in the bulrushes and Pharaoh's daughter found him.

Exodus ch.2

Stick baby and basket here.

Fold up.

MOSES' BIRTH & CALL – ACTIVITY SHEET

First cut along wavy line. Then 'fringe' the reeds and fold upwards along dotted line. Next cut out basket and lid. Stick or staple where indicated. Stick or staple the flap on lid to fit over basket.

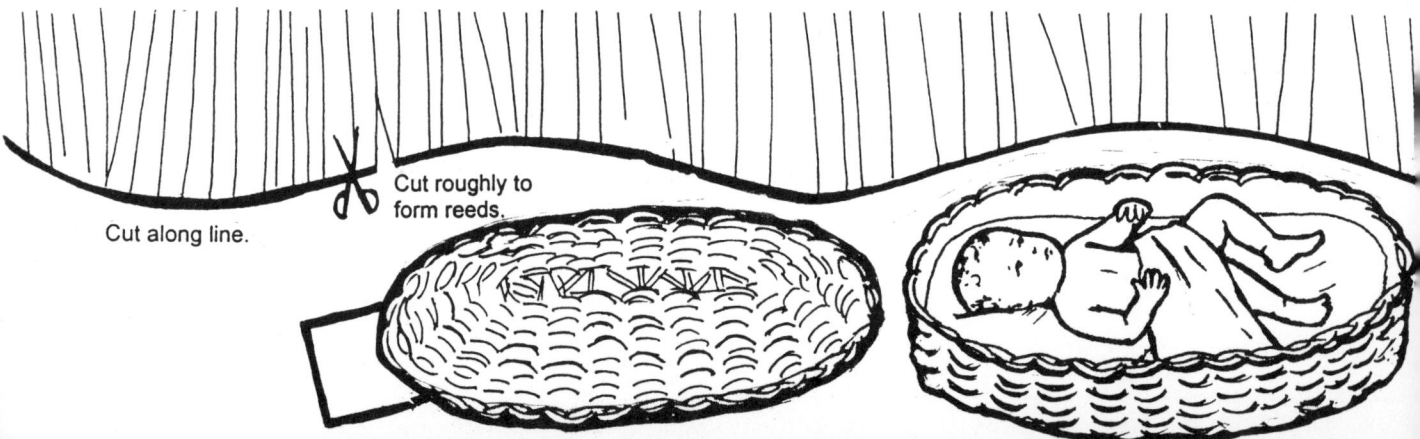

Cut along line.

Cut roughly to form reeds.

Pharaoh and The Plagues

Exodus 5 - 11

Themes	Stubbornness, God's Power

| Aims | To teach the Biblical account of Moses and the ten plagues.
To show God's power over all creation - the planets, animals, the weather, etc.
To consider stubbornness and its consequences. |
|---|---|

Resources	Bibles, Children's Story Sheet, Puzzle Page, Activity Sheet.

Other Ideas & Activities
1. Activity Sheet – best if background sheet is coloured; split pin needed.
2. Choose one of the first nine plagues. Draw a picture/write an account of what life was like for an Egyptian during the time of that plague. This could lead to a class display.
3. Write a list under the title "God is powerful". What things did God show he has power over, in the nine plagues.
4. Write a true story or make up one, in which you were stubborn. What happened? Did you learn not to be stubborn? Share and discuss.

Teacher's Notes

Summary: Pharaoh didn't want to let the Israelites leave Egypt. He wanted to keep them as slaves. God told Pharaoh, through Moses, to let his people go. Pharaoh refused, so God sent plagues on Egypt. There were ten plagues in all: waters turned to blood; frogs; lice; flies; sickness of animals; boils; hail; locusts; darkness and finally the most severe plague - the death of the firstborn. In all these plagues, Pharaoh showed great stubbornness. God showed his great power and that he alone is the true God, who has greater power than Pharaoh.

Point of Contact
Stubbornness
- Are you ever stubborn?
- Do you refuse to listen to your parents' or teachers' warnings?
- What happens?

For the background to this lesson see "Moses' Birth and Call".

Back To Egypt
After God had spoken to Moses from the burning bush he went back to Egypt. Here he met with his brother Aaron who was to be his helper. Together they went to see Pharaoh. Pharaoh was extremely powerful and still using the Israelites as slaves.

Moses Sees Pharaoh

When Moses and Aaron came before Pharaoh who was on his throne, they told him what God had said. "Let my people, the Israelites go, so they can go away into the desert and worship me." But Pharaoh still wanted the Israelites to work for him. He had no intention of letting them go. He said, "Who is God that I should obey him? I do not know God and will certainly not let the people go." Moses answered, "If you do not do what God says, then he will punish you." Pharaoh became very angry and sent Moses and Aaron away.

More Cruelty

Pharaoh now complained that the Israelite slaves had become lazy and needed to be made to work harder. They were making bricks for buildings. He ordered that if they did not produce the number of bricks he now wanted they would be whipped and beaten. The lives of the Israelites became unbearable, but Pharaoh was angry with them and their God and showed no pity.

Moses was discouraged that Pharaoh had ignored him, but God said to him, "I am the Lord and will rescue the Israelites from their slavery. Pharaoh will grow hard in heart but eventually he and all the Egyptians will know that I am the Lord." Moses knew that God would keep his word.

A Second Visit

Again Moses and Aaron went to the palace. Pharaoh said, "Show me a miracle to prove yourself." Aaron threw down the rod he had in his hand and it became a snake. Pharaoh asked his magicians to do the same, and their rods too became snakes. However Aaron's snake ate up all of the others. But even this made no impression on Pharaoh. He did not recognise God's superior power.

A River Of Blood (The First Plague)

Moses met Pharaoh by the River Nile. Again he said, "The Lord God says, 'Let my people go!' If you do not listen God will turn the water of this river to blood!" Pharaoh ignored the warning. He thought the God of the Israelites was not very powerful. Aaron held his rod out over the river and all the waters of Egypt turned to blood. For seven days no one could drink the water and there was the vile smell of dead fish.

Frogs Everywhere (The Second Plague)

Moses went to Pharaoh again. Moses said that if he did not let the people go God would fill the land with frogs. Pharaoh would not listen. Aaron lifted up his rod. Suddenly masses of frogs came up out of the river and started crawling all over the land. There were frogs in the houses, in beds, on tables and even in their food. Pharaoh cried out to Moses, "Pray to God to take these frogs away and I will let the people go!" When Moses did the plague of frogs died. But Pharaoh still did not let the people go.

More Plagues

Again and again Moses and Aaron went before Pharaoh to call upon him to let the people go. Again and again Pharaoh refused. So God brought further plagues upon Egypt.

Lice (3)　　　Lice descended on everyone and on all the animals, causing them to itch and scratch themselves.

Flies (4)   Swarms of flies covered the ground and filled the houses of the Egyptians, however the houses of the Israelites had no flies.

Sickness of Animals (5)   The Egyptians' cattle became sick and died, but the Israelites' cattle were untouched.

Boils (6)   Boils and sores broke out on all the Egyptians causing them great pain and discomfort.

Hail (7)   A great storm of hailstones fell on Egypt killing any men or animals that were in the fields and destroying plants and trees. However in Goshen, where the Israelites were, no hail fell.

Locusts (8)   Masses of locusts were blown over the land by an East wind. They covered the land of the Egyptians and ate every green leaf and plant that the hail had not destroyed.

When a plague came, often Pharaoh would agree to let the people go. But once the plague was gone he would change his mind.

Darkness (The Ninth Plague)

A darkness came on the land of Egypt. It was so black that no one could see to move about or get up for three days. Pharaoh could stand it no longer. He called Moses and told him and the Israelites to go, but leave their flocks and herds. But Moses said that the flocks and herds would have to go too. Pharaoh became angry and ordered Moses never to come to the palace again. Moses assured Pharaoh he would not see him again.

Pharaoh had been so stubborn. He had refused to obey God. This had caused much misery for the Egyptians. But God had decided that there would be one more plague. This tenth plague would force Pharaoh to let the Israelites go, and show the Egyptians how great God is.

Illustration: Jesus' Miracles Demonstrate God's Power

In performing his many miracles, Jesus again showed God's power over the forces of nature and the creation. He changed water into wine (John 2); calmed the storm (Matthew 8); cured leprosy (Mark 1:40); healed those who were paralysed (Matthew 9); gave sight to the blind ((John 9); cured disease (Luke 14); gave massive catches of fish (Luke 5) and raised the dead (Luke 7 & John 11).

Things to learn:

- Pharaoh was very proud and stubborn.
- He would not let the Israelites leave Egypt but treated them cruelly.
- God sent 10 plagues on the Egyptians.
- God was showing that he is the true and great God and has power over all creation.

Discuss

- Why didn't Pharaoh let the Israelites go?
- How do we know that these plagues came from God?
- Do you think God is pleased when we are stubborn and refuse to listen to our parents/teachers?

Pharaoh and the Plagues

Moses and Aaron went to Pharaoh, the king of Egypt and asked him to let the Israelites leave Egypt. But Pharaoh did not want the Israelites to leave as they were working as slaves for him. So he told Moses and Aaron to go away.

The first plague
Moses warned Pharaoh that God would punish him for not letting the Israelites leave Egypt. Pharaoh still would not listen. So God sent the first plague to Egypt. All the rivers in Egypt were turned to blood. For seven days no one could drink the water and all the fish died.

The second plague
Moses went to Pharaoh again and asked him to let the Israelites go. But Pharaoh would not listen. Aaron lifted up his rod. Suddenly the land was covered with frogs. Pharaoh begged Moses to take the frogs away. When Moses did this, Pharaoh still did not let the people go. So God sent more plagues to Egypt.

The third plague
Everything was covered in lice, including all the animals and people. The lice made them itch and scratch themselves.

The fourth and fifth plagues
Millions of flies covered the ground and filled the houses of the Egyptians. Then the Egyptians' cattle became sick and died.

The sixth and seventh plagues
The Egyptians were covered in painful boils and sores all over their bodies. Then a great hailstorm killed many Egyptians and their animals.

The eighth and ninth plague
The land was covered with locusts that ate all the green leaves and plants. Then Egypt became completely dark. It was so dark that no one could do anything for three days. Pharaoh called Moses to him and told him that the Israelites could leave Egypt. But again he changed his mind.

The tenth plague
So God decided that there would be one more plague – the death of the eldest child in the family.

PHARAOH AND THE PLAGUES

God sent 10 plagues. Draw in the missing pictures and fill in the missing words.

1.	2. Frogs.	3.	4. Flies.

5. Dead cattle.	6.	7. Hail, thunder and fire.	8.

9.	10. Death of eldest		

Take every second letter to find out what God's message to Pharaoh was.

Cross out the wrong words.

Moses asked <u>Pharaoh / Aaron</u>
but <u>Pharaoh / Aaron</u>
<u>would / would not</u> let the
<u>Israelites/Egyptians</u> go.
God sent <u>10 /12</u> plagues to the
<u>Israelites / Egyptians</u>

" _ _ _ _   _ _ _   _ _ _

_ _ _ _   _ _ _ _   _ _ _ _ _

_ _   _ _ _ _   _ _ _   _ _ _

_ _   _ _ _   _ _ _   _ _ _ _ "

Exodus ch. 9 v 14

PHARAOH & THE PLAGUES – ACTIVITY SHEET

Cut out plague circle and Pharaoh and fasten plague circle using a split pin to an A4 sheet of paper. Stick Pharaoh in bottom left corner.

The **10** plagues God sent

locusts
darkness
death of eldest
rivers into blood
frogs
lice
flies
cattle dead
boils
hail thunder fire

Pharaoh was angry.

The Passover

Exodus 11 - 14

Themes	Slavery and Freedom, Judgment & Deliverance

Aims	To describe the Bible's account of the first Passover.
	To teach the children that the Passover is still celebrated by Jews today.
	To highlight the New Testament's teaching regarding the Passover.

Resources	Bibles, Children's Story Sheet, Puzzle Page, Activity Sheet.

Other Ideas & Activities
1. Activity Sheet – photocopy on two contrasting colours; cut out and mix colours.
2. Describe and draw a Passover meal . The food could be drawn on a paper plate. This could be compared with what the Jews do today and the items they put on a Seder plate. Again, a Seder plate with its various items could be drawn on a paper plate.
3. Make some unleavened bread or by a box of 'Matsos' from a delicatessen or supermarket (freely available in most stores).
4. Draw the preparations for the Passover, using the instructions given under the heading "God's Orders" (see notes below).
5. Contrasts: What words would you use to describe (i) Pharaoh; (ii) an Israelite before the Passover; (iii) an Israelite after the Passover? What are the differences between them? How did God deal with them?
6. Children could be shown a remembrance day poppy or wreath and then discuss its meaning and significance (see 'Illustration' below).
7. Discuss events we remember which remind us of a great deliverance e.g. remembrance day, Christ's resurrection.

Teacher's Notes

Summary: God sent the tenth and final plague. Every firstborn Egyptian child died. However, God "passed over" the Israelite homes, where the Passover lamb had been killed and its blood put on the door posts. Pharaoh was now ready and willing to let the Israelites go. They hurriedly collected their belongings and began their journey. At long last they were on their way to Canaan. Every year Jews remember this special night called "Passover", when they were delivered from slavery in Egypt. The Bible says that the passover lamb and its death, is a picture of the death of Jesus (1Cor. 5:7).

Point of Contact
Anniversaries
- What is an anniversary?
- How often is an anniversary celebrated?
- Why do people remember anniversaries/important events?

For background to this lesson see "Pharaoh and the Plagues"

The Final Warning

After the plague of darkness, Moses and Aaron visited the palace for the last time. Pharaoh had not listened, even though God had warned him so many times, and there had already been nine plagues. Moses warned Pharaoh that there would be one last plague. The eldest child in every Egyptian family would die. Pharaoh's heart was hard as ever and he refused to let the Israelites leave Egypt. He became angry and said to Moses, "Get out and don't come back! If I see you again, I will kill you!" So Moses and Aaron left the palace for the last time.

God's Orders

God gave Moses these instructions for the Israelites.

(1) In the evening of the fourteenth day of the month, each family must take a lamb and kill it.

(2) Using the blood of the lamb, each family must use a bunch of herbs to paint blood on the doorposts of their house.

(3) The whole family must stay indoors and dress in their outdoor clothes ready to quickly leave Egypt.

(4) They must then roast the lamb and quickly eat it with bitter herbs and unleavened bread (bread made quickly without yeast).

Moses told the Israelites that during the night God would send his angel, who would go through the land of Egypt and kill the eldest child in every family. Moses explained that when God saw the blood on the doorposts of the Israelites' homes, he would "pass over" their house and not harm anyone there (Ex. 12:13).

So the Israelites obeyed God's instructions given to them through Moses. They must have had a very busy day, packing their things for the journey out of Egypt and making preparations for the meal. At last everything was ready. The Israelites waited.

The Midnight Cry

At midnight God's angel passed through the land of Egypt. In every Egyptian home the eldest child in the family died. From the prince in the palace to the prisoner in the prison, no one escaped the plague of death. A great noise was heard throughout the land, as the Egyptians cried out at the death of their firstborn.

Saved Because Of The Blood

When the angel of death went over the home of the Israelites and saw the blood on the doorposts he "passed over" and no one died. The sprinkling of the lamb's blood meant that all in the home were safe.

Pharaoh's Message

A distressed Pharaoh sent an urgent message to Moses - "Get out of Egypt before we are all dead. Take your flocks and herds and go!"

The Journey Begins

Quickly the Israelites gathered together their possessions and wrapped them up in bundles. The Israelite nation had been in Egypt for 400 years. Now they were on their way back to their homeland of Canaan.

"Do Not Forget"

When they left Egypt Moses had told the Israelites, "You must never forget the special night when you were delivered from slavery in Egypt. Every year on the same night you must celebrate and remember what God has done for you. Each year you must take a lamb and kill it, and put its blood on the doorposts of you homes. When the children ask, 'Why do you do this?', you must explain to them what happened in Egypt. Tell them how it was that God judged Pharaoh and the Egyptians, who would not let you go. But when God saw the blood on the doorposts of your homes, he "passed over" and did not kill."

This annual celebration is still kept today by Jewish people and is called the "Passover".

Another Passover

The Israelites believed what God had said. They trusted that when he saw the blood of the lamb on their doorposts he would not visit their homes with death. God kept his word and did not harm the Israelites.

In the New Testament Jesus is called the true Passover lamb (1Cor. 5:7). The Bible tells us that the Passover in the book of Exodus is something God gave to picture what Jesus would do many years later on the cross. The Israelites obeyed God and trusted that the Passover lamb would protect them. The Bible says that whoever trusts in Jesus and his death on the cross (where his blood was spilt) God will "passover" their sin and forgive them (John 3:16).

Illustration: Remembering Other Times of Deliverance

On the 11th day of the 11th month at the 11th hour, many people pause and remember how this nation has been delivered in two world wars. We are reminded that others gave their lives so that we can have our freedom.

Christians regularly remember Christ's death and resurrection. The Bible says that, because he gave his life, he has obtained the greatest deliverance for all who believe upon him (John 3:16).

Things to learn:

- The final plague on Egypt was the death of the firstborn.
- God's Angel "passed over" the Israelite homes where the blood had been put on the door posts.
- Passover is still celebrated every year by the Jews
- Christians believe that Jesus is the true Passover lamb.

Discuss

- What does the Passover story tell us about God?
- Why is the Passover so significant to Jews?
- What does it mean to Christians today?

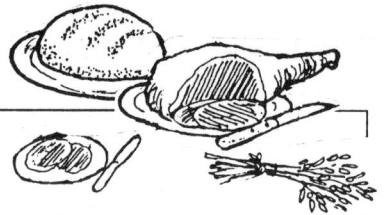

The Passover

God had sent nine plagues on Pharaoh and the Egyptians. Moses and Aaron went to Pharaoh for the last time. Moses warned Pharaoh that there would be one last plague - the eldest child in every Egyptian family would die at midnight. But Pharaoh still refused to let the Israelites go. He was angry with Moses and Aaron and told them to leave the palace at once.

God gave Moses some instructions for the Israelites to prepare for this last plague and to get ready to leave Egypt. He told each family to kill a lamb and paint the doorposts of their houses with its blood. The lamb should then be cooked and eaten by the family with herbs and unleavened bread. The people should be dressed in their outdoor clothes ready to leave Egypt quickly. The Israelites followed these instructions carefully and waited.

That night, at midnight God passed through Egypt and the eldest child in every family died. God passed over the Israelites' houses with blood painted on the doorposts and the people inside were safe.

All the Egyptian families cried aloud as their eldest child died. Pharaoh sent a message to Moses telling him to take the Israelites out of Egypt immediately. The people gathered their things together quickly and left their homes in Egypt. At last they were free to go back to their home country.

The Jews still remember this day and call it the Passover. The Bible tells us that Jesus was like a Passover lamb; he came to save his people.

THE PASSOVER

Cross out the wrong words.

God sent 20 / 10 plagues altogether. God told the Israelites to kill a lamb and put the blood / wool on the doorposts / roof of their house. At midnight God passed through the land killing everyone / the first- born of the Egyptians. Moses / God said that when he saw the blood then he would pass over, and not destroy. Now, Pharaoh told the people they must leave / stay in Egypt. The Egyptians gave the people gold, silver and clothes. How sad and angry / thankful and happy the Israelites felt as they left.

Put some red on the door posts.

aderb   baml

shreb

On the evening of the passover the Israelites ate a meal. Unscramble the words to find out what they ate.

—— —— —— —— , —— —— —— —— ——

and unleavened —— —— —— —— —— .

Unleavened bread is bread made without

aesty —— —— —— —— ——

That same night the Israelites left Egypt. Find out how their lives changed. Take the first letter from each picture and write it in the box it connects to.

Unscramble the 7 hidden letters to complete this sentence.
God told the Israelites to always r _ _ _ _ _ _ _ the passover night.

Draw in some more Israelites leaving Egypt.

THE PASSOVER – ACTIVITY SHEET

Cut out this window and glue over empty window on picture.

Cut out the door and staple or stick in position.
Children colour a patch of red on the door
posts and lintel (for blood).

Those who had blood on their d
posts when the angel
passed over were safe.

Ex. ch.11,1

Crossing the Red Sea

Exodus 12:37-51; 13:17-15:21 (Hebrews 11:29)

Themes	God's Power, Praise, Deliverance

Aims	To teach the Bible's account of how the Israelites crossed the Red Sea, but Pharaoh and his army were drowned.

Resources	Bibles, Children's Story Sheet, Puzzle Page, Activity Sheet, Map.

Other Ideas & Activities
1. Activity Sheet – photocopy on blue & green paper; cut out and mix colours.
2. Find ways of parting water/stopping water using dams, etc. What materals work best/worst and why?
3. Write a story/act out a short play or draw a series of pictures to describe an incident where you or a friend have been chased into a situation, from which it appears impossible to escape. What happens? Do you escape, and if so how?
4. Moses' Song of Praise – Exodus 15. Look at it and read it in groups. What does it tell you about God and Moses?

Teacher's Notes

Summary: Pharaoh gave orders to the Israelites to leave Egypt. They quickly gathered their belongings and left. Pharaoh changed his mind and chased after them, catching them up by the Red Sea. The people cried out to God for help. When Moses held up his rod, God parted the water, so that the people could walk through on dry land. When Pharaoh and his army followed, the water returned and they all drowned. The Israelites rejoiced that they were now free forever from slavery and thanked God for his goodness to them.

Point of Contact
Excitement
- Have you ever been excited because you are going away?
- As the day got nearer how did you feel?
- What happened when the day came?

For the background to this lesson see "The Passover".

Incredible News!
News spread quickly around the Israelites that Pharaoh had given orders for them to leave Egypt. Although they had been expecting to leave, now at last the day had finally arrived. They were very excited. They had spent all their lives as slaves suffering Pharaoh's cruelty and now they were going to be free.

Getting Ready

They quickly gathered their children, animals and belongings. The people were in such a hurry to leave that they didn't have time to finish baking their bread for the journey. They left the dough in bowls, wrapped it all up in a cloth and carried it over their shoulders. The bread, which they made from this dough, was called 'unleavened', because it had no yeast in it. At last they were going to Canaan, the country God had promised them. The Israelites gathered together out of the towns and villages in Goshen and formed orderly lines of people ready to begin walking.

The Journey Begins

It was well after midnight when their journey began. Later in the day they stopped and rested. As they sat by their campfires they finished baking their bread. This was the same bread which the Israelites had prepared in haste on the night of their departure from Egypt. It was without yeast ('leaven'). The Israelites still remember this time when they ate this bread which had no yeast. Each year they celebrate the Feast of Unleavened Bread.

Which Way To Go?

God had a special way of showing the Israelites the way to go. In the day a thick pillar of cloud went ahead of them. At night this cloud became a pillar of fire so that they had all the light they needed. Whenever the cloud moved, the Israelites packed up their belongings and followed it.

Pharaoh!

The cloud guided the Israelites right to the edge of the Red Sea (show map). Here they put up their tents and camped for the night. Suddenly the Israelites saw in the distance a great army coming towards them. Pharaoh had changed his mind and decided that he wanted his slaves back! He was coming to get them with six hundred chariots and thousands of horsemen and soldiers. It looked as if he would easily overtake them and capture them.

Trapped!

The Israelites were now trapped. In front of them was the Red Sea. Behind them was Pharaoh. How could they possibly escape? There were no bridges or boats and they could not fight the greatest army in the world. They were terrified.

Moses Encourages The People

In desperation the people cried out to God for help. The situation seemed impossible. Moses said, "Do not be afraid. Just stand still and watch what God will do for you today. The Egyptians you see today, you will soon see no more."

A Cloud Barrier

The pillar of cloud, which had been in front of the Israelites, moved behind them. It now stood as a barrier between them and the Egyptian army. When it was night-time, the pillar of cloud was shining brightly on the Israelite side, but on the other side of the cloud it was dark and the Egyptians could not see.

God's Great Power

Moses then stretched out his rod over the Red Sea. Immediately God made a powerful east wind to blow on the water. The water divided leaving a wide strip of dry land through the Sea. Now the Israelites were able to walk through on this dry path, past the water, which was standing high on either side. By the light of the pillar behind them they walked through the Red Sea during the night. When morning came they were all safely on the other side.

The Egyptians Follow

Then God removed the pillar of cloud and the Egyptians could once again see the Israelites. Pharaoh gave his army orders to continue chasing the Israelites through the Red Sea, along the dry sea bed. When they were in the middle of the Sea, God made their chariot wheels fall off, so that they had great difficulty in driving. The Egyptians began to realise that God was on the side of the Israelites and was helping them to escape.

Drowned!

From the other side, Moses once more stretched his rod out over the sea. Immediately the water came crashing down. Pharaoh, his chariots and his mighty army were all drowned.

Rejoicing

Watching from the other side, the Israelites saw all their enemies drown. Pharaoh and all the Egyptians, who had been so cruel to them, were gone forever. Now they were free and safe. They celebrated with music and singing. Miriam, Moses' sister, played the timbrel and all the women danced for joy. Moses taught his people a new song of praise to God.

Illustration: Dunkirk - Safe From Harm

During the war about $\frac{1}{3}$ million British troops faced either death or captivity across the English Channel, at a place called Dunkirk. Our king called for a national day of prayer. The deliverance was so amazing, many call it a 'miracle'. Hundreds of little boats left England and crossed the Channel on a calm sea and rescued the soldiers from the beaches of Dunkirk.

Once they had returned to the English coast they relaxed and felt safe. At last they had escaped from the enemy and were now home and free. Many thanked God for their deliverance from the enemy.

Things to learn:

- God delivered the Israelites from slavery.
- He showed his power by dividing the Red Sea.
- The people praised God for saving them.

Discuss

- What did God do to show to the Israelites that he was on their side?
- How do you think the Israelites felt about being free from slavery?
- What does this incident teach us we should do if we are ever afraid?

Crossing the Red Sea

After the tenth plague, Pharaoh told the Israelites to leave Egypt immediately. When the Israelites heard this they were very excited. At last they could return to their own country. So the Israelites met together and began walking. It was well after midnight when their journey began.

God showed the people the way to go. In the day, God put a thick pillar of cloud in front of them. The Israelites followed the pillar of cloud wherever it went. At night-time the cloud became a pillar of fire, giving the people light.

God used the pillar of cloud to lead the people to the Red Sea. They put up their tents and camped for the night. Suddenly they saw Pharaoh with his great army of chariots, horses and soldiers. They were coming towards them! The Israelites knew that they could not fight the Egyptians, and they could not run away. What were they going to do? The people asked God to help them.

God moved the pillar of cloud behind the Israelites so it was in front of the Egyptians. The Egyptians couldn't see where they were going.

Moses put out his rod over the Red Sea. Immediately God sent a wind to part the water in two. There was a dry path through the middle of the Red Sea. The Israelites walked on the path to the other side.

When all the Israelites were safely on the other side of the Red Sea, God took away the pillar of cloud in front of the Egyptians. At once the Egyptian army started to go through the Red Sea on the dry path. But God made their chariot wheels fall off which stopped them. On the other side of the Red Sea Moses put out his rod over the water again. The water came crashing down over the dry path. Pharaoh and his army were all drowned.

The Israelites watched this happen. How happy they were to know that they would never be slaves again! God had kept them all safe and shown them the way to go. They sang for joy and thanked God for his goodness to them.

Name............................ Date............................

CROSSING THE RED SEA
Draw a line to the right ending for these sentences

Pharaoh changed his
   mind about.....................
He got all the chariots
   of Egypt together..............
The Israelites saw them
   and were...........................
Moses lifted up his rod
   over the Red Sea..............
When the Egyptians
   tried to chase after them....
Moses stretched out
   his rod again.....................
When Israel saw how
   great God was...................

.....God made their chariot wheels
      fall off.
.....and the water came back
      and drowned all the Egyptians.
.....and God made a pathway
      through the water.
.....and chased after the
      Israelites.
.....very afraid and cried out
      to God.
.....they sang a song of praise
      to God.
.....letting the people go.

**Fit these words into
the crossword.**
Israelites (10)
Egyptians (9)
chariots (8)
drowned (7)
Red Sea (6)
Moses (5)
wind (4)
rod (3)

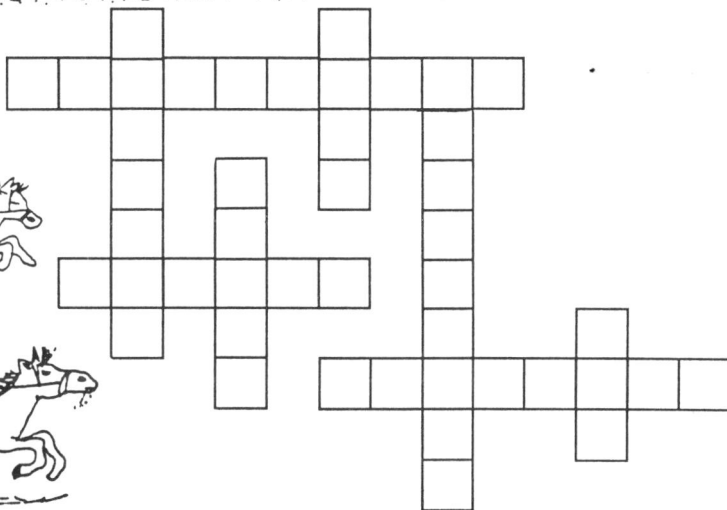

**Find out what Moses said to the people when they saw the Egyptians
coming after them. Match the jigsaw pieces and
write the words in the right order.**

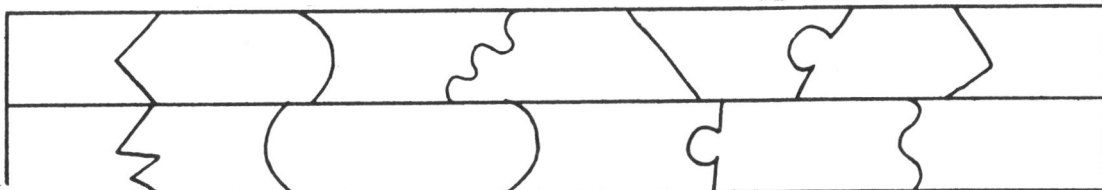

do   be   God   see   and   what

Do   will   afraid.   not   Stand   today.   still

The Israelites went through the Red Sea on dry land but...

... the Egyptians were all drowned.

Ex. ch.14

CROSSING THE RED SEA – ACTIVITY SHEET
Cut out Israelite and Egyptian strips, staple or glue one at each end of sea (⌒ shows you where).
Fold both line "A"s backwards and then fold to meet together at centre of seas (to dotted line).
The sea can be "opened" or "shut".

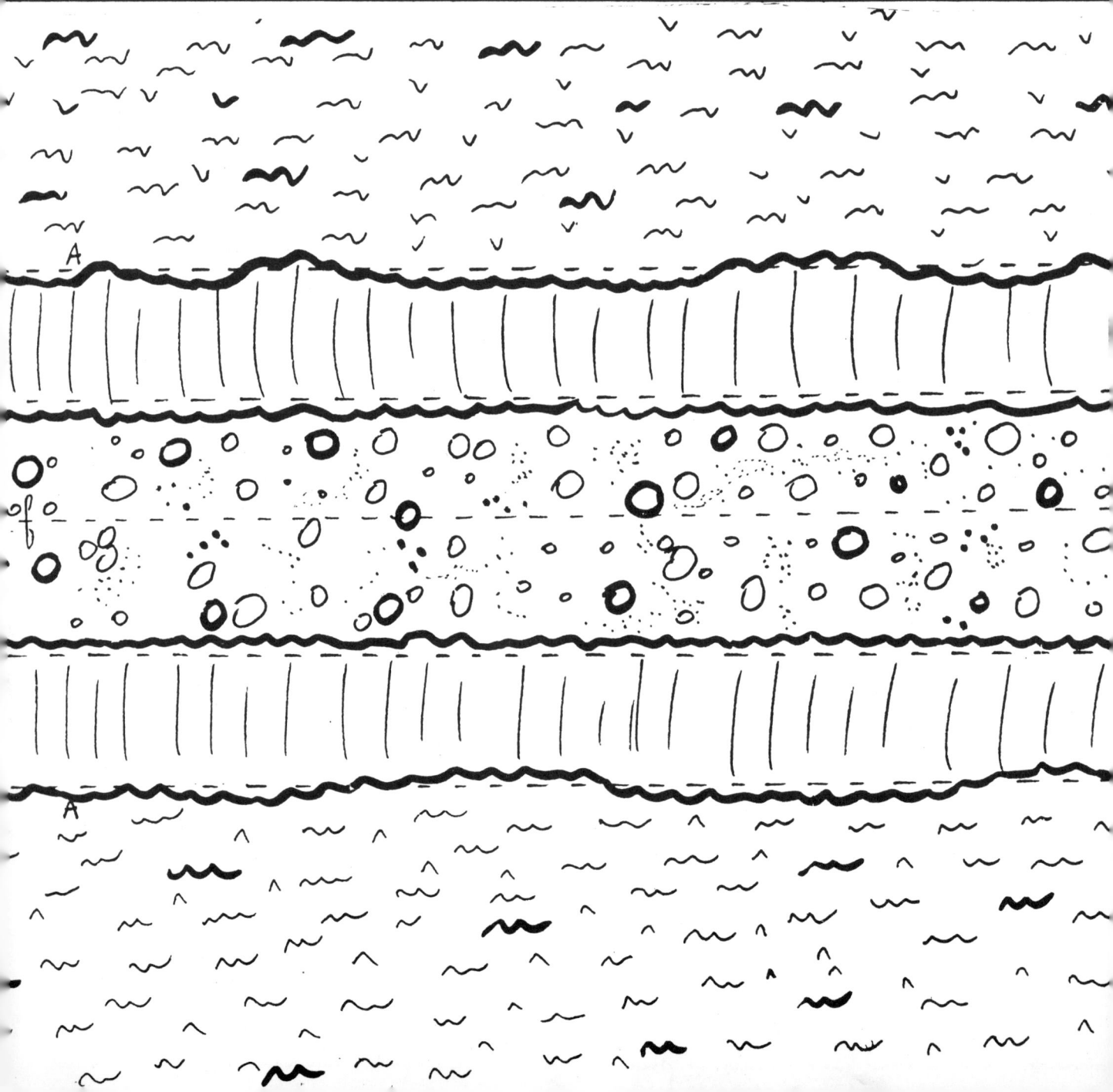

A

A

The Israelites in the Wilderness

Exodus 15:22-17:7, Numbers 11

Themes	God's Provision and Goodness, Complaining

Aims	To describe the Israelites' journey across the wilderness. To consider God's provision for people today. To encourage the children to be grateful/thankful for their daily food and not complain.

Resources	Bibles, Children's Story Sheet, Puzzle Page, Activity Sheets, Map.

Other Ideas & Activities

1. Activity Sheets – photcopy 'manna' sheet on yellow-creme paper; screw up white tissue paper tightly into small balls and glue on sheet. 'Water' sheet – needs blue tissue paper 12 x 4 cm, then follow instructions.
2. Using an atlas, draw a map of Egypt, the Sinai Peninsula and Canaan, and label the various parts referred to in the Bible such as Egypt, Goshen, The Red Sea, Sinai, the Wilderness of Paran, Edom, Moab, etc and the possible route of the exodus and entry to Canaan. Maps at the back of Bibles can supply all this information.
3. Show and discuss pictures of deserts. Find out more about deserts and people who live there.
4. Imagine you were going on a journey across a desert. Make a list of all the things you would need.
5. Saying grace – thanking God for food. Many Christians thank God before each meal. Why do they do this? (Not only does it show that a person is acknowledging God and his goodness but Jesus also gave Christians his own example to follow - see 1Cor. 11:23,24.) The children could learn a 'grace' they could use themselves to thank God.
6. Make a list of all that we can give thanks to God for on a daily basis.
7. Read the hymn, "Guide me, O Thou great Jehovah," by William Williams. How does the hymn use incidents taken from the time when the Israelites were in the wilderness? What does the writer use these incidents to illustrate?

Teacher's Notes

Summary: No food grew in the desert. God provided food for the Israelites by sending them manna everyday. When Moses struck the rock, water gushed out and supplied all they needed. After a year some complained and wanted meat. God sent them quails. God provided food, water, and clothes that never wore out for the forty years that they were travelling through the wilderness. However, the Israelites were still ungrateful and complained to God. Many Christians thank God for their food before each meal, because they believe that it is good to acknowledge that it is God who has provided for them.

Point of Contact
Hostile Environments
- Do you know where some of the hottest and coldest parts of the world are?
- Who lives there?
- How do they manage to survive?

For background to this lesson see "Crossing the Red Sea".

Safe At Last!
The Israelites were now safely on the other side of the Red Sea. Never again would they see Pharaoh and the Egyptians who had treated them so cruelly. It was now time for them to start the long journey to the land of Canaan, the country God had promised to give Abraham and his descendants (the Israelites) some 400 years earlier. The Israelites must have wondered how they were going to get to Canaan. There were between 1 and 2 million people, and it would be a long journey (show map). But God provided for his people during this time, in some amazing ways.

Which Way To Go?
The Bible says that God showed them which way they should go. He went ahead of them by day in a pillar of cloud. When they moved at night, he went ahead of them in a pillar of fire. Wherever these moved, the Israelites packed up their belongings and followed it. In this way God guided them.

What Could They Eat?
Soon all the food the Israelites had brought with them was eaten. They had now been in the wilderness for a month. It was obvious that they would not find food growing in this rocky soil and the sand of the desert. The people began to complain to Moses, because they were hungry. Moses prayed to God, who said, "I will rain bread from heaven and the people shall go out and gather food every day."

Manna
In the morning when the Israelites went out of their tents, they saw an amazing sight. God had sent bread down from heaven. The ground was covered with what looked like hailstones or small white beads. The people said, "Manna?", which translates as, "What is it?" The Israelites went out, collected the manna and found that it was tasty and nutritious, and that they could boil it, bake it or grind it up to make cakes from it. It tasted like wafer biscuits made with honey. When the sun came up it melted away.

God told the people, through Moses, that each day they should collect only enough for themselves and their families. On the sixth day they were to collect twice as much as a normal day, enough for the seventh day as well. On the seventh day, the Sabbath, God's special day, the manna did not appear.

Water
It is impossible to stay alive long without water. After three days in the wilderness the Israelites found some water which refreshed them and later they came to an oasis, where there were twelve springs and seventy palm trees. Here they enjoyed the water, but soon they had to move on again.

Thirst!

Now, after six weeks in the wilderness, their water bottles were empty and the people were extremely thirsty. Instead of praying to God, they grumbled to Moses and blamed him for their thirst. Again Moses cried to God in prayer. God told Moses to go to a large rock on the mountainside, where the people could see him. Here Moses hit this great rock and water poured out and flowed down like a river. Now the people and the animals could quench their thirst with the clear, cool water.

Complaints!

The Israelites had all they needed and should have been thankful to God. When they remembered all the good food they had enjoyed back in Egypt, like fish, meat, fruit and vegetables, they began to grumble. They said how they hated the manna and wanted to eat meat. How unthankful they were. When Moses saw them standing in the doorway of their tents, crying and complaining, he was cross. God was angry too.

God Provides

Moses prayed to God. God responded by telling Moses to say to the people, "Get ready, for tomorrow you shall eat meat. You will have sufficient meat to last the whole month." Even Moses found it hard to believe that this was possible. He said, "Even if we kill all the animals, that would not provide enough meat for so many people. " God said that they must wait and see his power.

Quails

God made a strong wind from the sea blow over the Israelites' camp. Flocks of small birds, called quails, were blown over the camp. The people went outside, caught the birds and killed them. Some were so eager to have meat that they worked hard catching birds for two days. After plucking their feathers they dried the birds in the sun. They could then cook them or keep them for later. Many died because they were greedy and ate too much.

Clothing

God also made sure that miraculously, the Israelites' clothes never wore out, for the forty years that they were travelling through the wilderness.

Sukkot

Today the Jews keep the 'Feast of Tabernacles' or Sukkot every year. They make huts out of leafy branches from trees and live in them for a week. Others take branches and put them around their rooms. They remind themselves of the time when the Israelites lived in tents in the desert and God provided all that they needed.

Still Ungrateful

Though God had provided so carefully for the Israelites and met their every need, they still complained. They were ungrateful for all the many things God had done for them.

Being Thankful

Christians believe that God is their heavenly Father and that he cares daily for them and provides for their needs. They remember to be thankful to God for all that he gives them.

Illustration: A Christian's Hymn Of Thanks

1. Lord of heaven, and earth, and sea,
To you all praise and glory be;
How shall we show our love to thee,
Who givest all?

2. The golden sunshine, spring time air,
Sweet flowers and fruits, your love declare,
When harvests ripen, you are there,
Who givest all.

3. For peaceful homes and health filled days,
For all the blessings earth displays,
We owe you thankfulness and praise,
Who givest all.

4. You did not spare your only Son
But gave him for a world undone,
And freely with that blessed One
You givest all.

5. For souls redeemed, for sins forgiven,
For means of grace and hopes of heaven,
Father, what can to you be given,
Who givest all?

6. To you, from whom we all derive,
Our life, our gifts, our power to give!
O may we ever with you live,
Who givest all!

Christopher Wordsworth, 1807-85

Things to learn:
- God provided bread and water for the Israelites while they were in the desert.
- God, in his kindness, gave them meat to eat.
- The Israelites complained about their food.
- Jesus taught us to pray for our daily food (Matt. 6:11).
- Christians often pray and say thank you to God for what he gives them.

Discuss
- What do you complain about?
- Who do you complain to?
- How do you feel when you complain?
- How do you think your parents feel when you complain about things?
- What things can you thank God for on a daily basis?

The Israelites in the Wilderness

The Israelites were safe on the other side of the Red Sea. They had a long journey ahead of them to their home country. They had to travel over deserts and over rocky ground. But God looked after them.

God showed them the way to go by putting a pillar of cloud in front of them during the day. At night-time the cloud turned into a pillar of fire, which gave the people light and warmth.

The Israelites soon ate up all the food they had brought with them from Egypt. They wondered what they would eat now. The people complained to Moses because they were hungry. Moses prayed to God for help.

The next morning the Israelites woke up and saw small pieces of bread all over the ground. They collected as much as they needed for the day. When the sun became hot, the bread melted away. They called this food, 'Manna'.

After they had been in the desert for six weeks their water bottles had become empty again and the people were very thirsty. They complained to Moses. Moses prayed to God. God told Moses to go to a large rock on the mountain side and hit the rock with his rod. When he did this, the people were amazed to see a great stream of cool clear water pour out of the rock. They all drank as much as they wanted.

Though God provided for the Israelites they always complained. One day they said how they would like to go back to Egypt. They hated the manna and wanted meat. Again Moses prayed to God. God made a wind blow small birds, called quail, to blow over the camp. The Israelites caught them and cooked them.

The Israelites were travelling through the desert for forty years. During all this time their clothes and shoes did not wear out. God gave them everything they needed. However, still the Israelites complained and were ungrateful.

THE ISRAELITES IN THE WILDERNESS

Name ....   Date ....

Fill in the missing words – they are all in the picture.

The Israelites complained to _ _ _ _ _ because they were very hungry. God heard them. He said that he would send bread from _ _ _ _ _ _. Every morning after the dew had lifted there was the _ _ _ _ _. It was small, round and _ _ _ _ _. It tasted lik wafers made with _ _ _ _ _. Moses told the people to _ _ _ _ _ _ _ what each family needed every day and not to have any _ _ _ _ _ _ _ _ _. On the sixth day they were to collect enough for two days so they could _ _ _ _ on the seventh day. The Israelites complained again because they were _ _ _ _ _ _ _ _. God told Moses to hit a large _ _ _ _ on the mountain with his rod. Immediately clean, cool _ _ _ _ _ poured out of the rock.

Moses   white   left over   thirsty   honey   collect   heaven   water   rock   manna   rest

The Israelites would have died without this......

1. The last letter of
2. The second letter of
3. The first letter of
4. The middle letter of
5. The last letter of

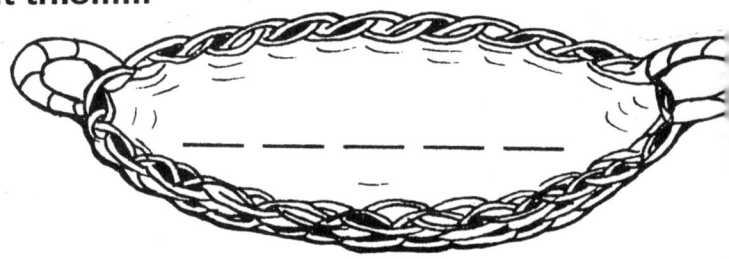

_ _ _ _ _ _

Work out the code to find this verse from the Bible.

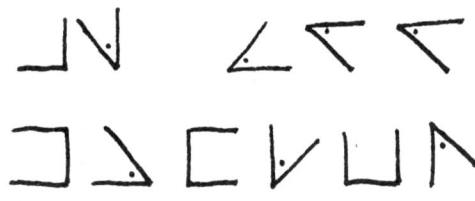

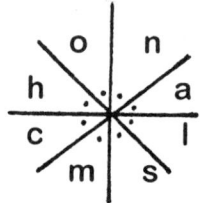

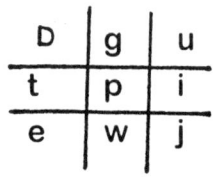

	o	n	
h			a
c			l
	m	s	

D	g	u
t	p	i
e	w	j

'   ,

_ _   _ _ _   _ _ _ _ _ _ _   _ _ _ _ _ _ _   _ _ _ _ _ _ _ _ _ _ _

Phil ch. 2 v14

God sent manna in the mornings for the Israelites to collect and eat.

Ex. ch.16

God sent manna in the mornings for the Israelites to collect and eat.

Ex. ch.16

God provided water from the rock.

Exodus ch. 17

Slit here

Push end of
tissue paper through
to form water. Stick
with sticky tape at
the back.

God provided water from the rock.

Exodus ch. 17

Slit here

Push end of
tissue paper through
to form water. Stick
with sticky tape at
the back.

The Ten Commandments

Exodus 19 -20:17

Themes	Law, Order, Right & Wrong

Aims	To teach the children about the Ten Commandments. To show that God has made the difference between right and wrong very clear. To show that the commandments are relevant to people's lives today.

Resources	Bibles, Children's Story Sheet, Puzzle Page, Activity Sheet, Map.

Other Ideas & Activities

1. Activity Sheet – photocopy on two contrasting colours; cut out and mix colours.
2. Draw two tablets of stone and list the commandments on them. (This could be done as a class activity on a larger scale.)
3. Talk about right and wrong, and the role of the conscience. (Pinocchio and his nose are a good picture. Just like Pinocchio's nose would inform him when he wasn't truthful, so our conscience does the same thing.)
4. Write a story where your conscience has told you what is right/wrong.
5. How could we break the sixth commandment? See what Jesus says – Matt. 5:21,22. What are the implications of this for the other Commandments (e.g. 5,6,8,9,10)?
6. Where do we have rules? Draw a table and list the place and the rules we find there (e.g. school, road, home, swimming baths).
7. Test the children's knowledge of the highway code. What would happen if there was no highway code or law on the roads? The children might like to draw their favourite sign(s) or make up a new one.

Teacher's Notes

Summary: The Israelites stood by Mount Sinai. When they saw the thunder and lightning, heard the sound of a trumpet and felt the earthquake, they knew that God was showing them that he was holy and powerful. Moses met God on the top of the mountain and received the Ten Commandments written on two stones. The Israelites were to obey them. They are the rules God has given, for us all to keep and live by.

Point of Contact
Rules
- What are rules?
- Why do we have them?
- Imagine there were no rules at school and everyone could do as they pleased - what would happen?

- What would happen if there were no rules on the road and people driving cars could do whatever they pleased?

For background to this lesson see "The Israelites in the Wilderness".

God's Goodness and Provision
It was now nearly three months since the Israelites had crossed the Red Sea. During the day God sent a cloud in front of them to guide them through the desert. At night time a pillar of fire guided them. God had been very kind to them. Not only had he released them from the Egyptians and the time of suffering they had there. God had also protected them and provided them with food and water. Eventually the cloud stopped in front of a very high rocky mountain called Mount Sinai (show map - the area is also known as Horeb). Here the people set up their camp.

God's Presence
On the morning of the third day a thick cloud covered the top of the mountain. Moses brought the people out of the camp to stand and watch. They were very afraid when they saw fire and smoke at the top of the mountain. Suddenly there was an earthquake and thunder and lightning. At the same time a trumpet sounded louder and louder. God wanted the people to realise that he was a great and holy God and had come down to say something important to them. God called Moses to go up the mountain to talk with him. He stayed there for forty days and forty nights.

The Ten Commandments
While he was on the mountain God gave Moses ten rules which he wanted the people to obey. These were written down on two tablets of stone, and given to Moses to take to the people. These commandments were very important and showed the people very clearly how they should live to please God. He wanted the people to know how he wanted them to behave towards himself and towards one another. If they did what was right they would be happy, but if they did what was wrong they would be unhappy. God still expects these commandments to be kept by everyone today.

The First Commandment
You must worship only God. God clearly says that we should love him more than anything or anybody else. God should be the most important person in our lives.

The Second Commandment
You must not make any idol to worship. God is not pleased when people bow down and worship idols made out of stone, wood or china. The Bible says that we cannot see the true God. Although he is invisible he still hears the prayers and praise of those who worship him (Isaiah 46:5 - 7; John 4:24).

The Third Commandment
You must not use God's name to swear. People do this a lot today, but the Bible says this makes God angry. It shows that those who use his name in this way do not respect him. God does not want us to use swear words when we are cross either.

The Fourth Commandment
Keep Sunday as God's special day. When God made the world he rested on the seventh day and he wants us to follow his example. Christians believe that because

Jesus rose from the dead on a Sunday, this is the day they should keep special. On a Sunday they go to church, learn about God, pray and sing hymns and also have a day where they rest from their usual weekly work.

The First Four Commandments
These first four commandments show how we should behave towards God. The next six show how we should behave towards each other.

The Fifth Commandment
Obey your parents & those who look after you. We should want to please them, by doing things willingly and cheerfully. All children are disobedient and break this commandment sometime. The Bible says that Jesus is the only child who never broke it.

The Sixth Commandment
Do not murder. These days we hear of many murders on the TV, radio and in the newspapers. It is very wicked to kill another person. We may think we would never murder but Jesus said we shouldn't even hate someone (Matt. 5:22).

The Seventh Commandment
Do not take anyone else's wife or husband. The Bible says that God wants a man to have one wife and live with her all her life (Genesis 2:24).

The Eighth Commandment
Do not steal. It's never right to take something that doesn't belong to us. We mustn't steal from shops, from school, from friends, from mum and dad or anyone. We might not think no one can see us do such things, but the Bible says that God sees all that we do (Psalm 139: 1-3).

The Ninth Commandment
Do not tell lies. It's always wrong to tell lies, even what are called "white lies". You should not lie to get yourself out of trouble. It is easy to tell lies. We must be prepared to tell the truth even when it's is hard.

The Tenth Commandment
Do not be jealous of others. We are not to keep wanting the things that belong to other people. We can think, if only we had our friend's dog, computer, bicycle, etc. This is jealousy. God wants us to be content with the things we have.

God's Wise Rules
These are God's wise rules for people to live by. Your parents or whoever looks after you may have wise rules at home and expect you to keep them. Maybe you have to be in bed by certain times, especially on school days. You must not eat too much between meals and you must brush your teeth before you go to bed. All these rules are meant for your good, so that you do well at school and keep fit and healthy. It is the same with the Ten Commandments. God gave them so that all people might live happily with each other and enjoy life.

Right And Wrong
Some people wonder at times whether something is a good thing or a bad thing. Is it right to take a watch which someone has left in a swimming pool changing room, or

should you hand it in to the reception? When mum discovers that all the biscuits have gone and it is because you've eaten them, should you blame someone else in the home? When your mum asks you to help lay the table, should you ignore her or do as she asks? The Ten Commandments show us what we should do. It is a standard God has given us, which shows us what is right and what is wrong.

Perfection

The Bible says that though God has given us his rules, there has never been anyone who has been able to keep them all (Romans 3:10), apart from one man. Jesus kept God's commandments and never broke any of them. Jesus was perfect and never said a bad thing nor thought a bad thought (John 8:46; Heb. 7:26). The Bible says that Jesus can forgive us all the wrong things we have done in breaking God's commandments (Eph. 1:7).

Illustration: The Ten Commandments And Their Effect

The story of "Mutiny on the Bounty" has been made famous by the film of the same name. However, the final part of the story is often left untold.

The fifteen men and twelve women mutineers from the ship the Bounty arrived on the deserted Pitcairn Island. Here they lived a life of immorality and lawlessness and broke nearly every one of God's commandments. Eventually, due to disease and murder, only two men were left, along with nine women and twenty children.

Then a change occurred. A man began to read the ship's Bible. He became a Christian. Eventually he was the only man left, as the other had died of asthma. He now took charge of the people and told them that they must rule their society according to the Bible and the Ten Commandments.

Many years later, when others arrived on the island, they were surprised to find a peace loving, kind and lawful Christian community. The Bible and the ten commandments had had a great influence upon what were once evil minded people, giving them a law abiding, happy and peaceful society.

Things to Learn:
- God gave Moses Ten Commandments, written on stone tablets.
- God expects everyone to obey them.
- Only Jesus ever kept them all.

Discuss
- How do we know what is right and wrong?
- Why has God given us the Ten Commandments?
- If we have done wrong, what should we do?

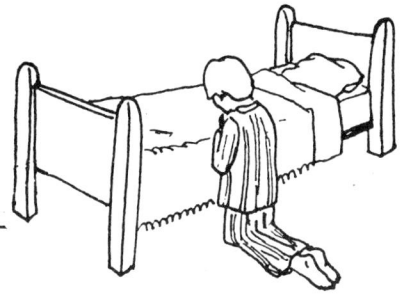

The Ten Commandments

The Israelites had left Egypt. God was guiding them through the desert by a pillar of cloud during the day and a pillar of fire at night. One day the pillar of cloud stopped in front of a very high rocky mountain - Mount Sinai. The Israelites set up their camp here and waited to see what God wanted them to do.

After three days, a thick cloud covered the mountain. Then the people saw fire and smoke at the top of the mountain. This was followed by an earthquake and thunder and lightning. The people were afraid. God called Moses to go up the mountain to talk with him.

God gave Moses ten rules (commandments) for the people to obey. God wrote these on two slabs of stone.

1. You must worship only God.

2. Do not make any idol to worship.

3. Do not use God's name to swear.

4. Keep Sunday as God's special day.

5. Obey and respect your parents.

6. Do not murder.

7. Do not take someone else's husband or wife.

8. Do not steal.

9. Do not tell lies.

10. Do not be jealous of other people and their belongings.

Moses was on Mount Sinai for forty days and forty nights. These commandments are important rules that show everyone how to live and how to please God.

THE TEN COMMANDMENTS

Fill in the missing words from the Ten Commandments, then fit the words into the grid.

1. Worship _ _ _ only.
2. Do not _ _ _ _ an idol.
3. Do not swear using God's _ _ _ _ .
4. _ _ _ _ _ _ _ _ _ God's day and keep it special.
5. Respect and obey your

   _ _ _ _ _ _ _.
6. Do not _ _ _ _ _ _.
7. Do not take anyone else's wife or

   _ _ _ _ _ _ _.
8. Do not _ _ _ _ _.
9. Do not tell _ _ _ _ _.
10. Do not _ _ _ _ what other people have.

Fill in the missing vowels. Jesus said....

"If y_u lov_ M_, k_ep My c_mm_ndm_nts."

John ch 14:15

I will take them when he is not looking.

Tick the pictures which show a commandment being *kept*. **Cross** the pictures which show a commandment being *broken*. Write underneath each picture the number of the commandment.

I will obey Mum and help with the washing up.

I'm not going to do what Mum says.

I hate him and want to hurt him.

I want to have her pram.

I will pay for my sweets at the till.

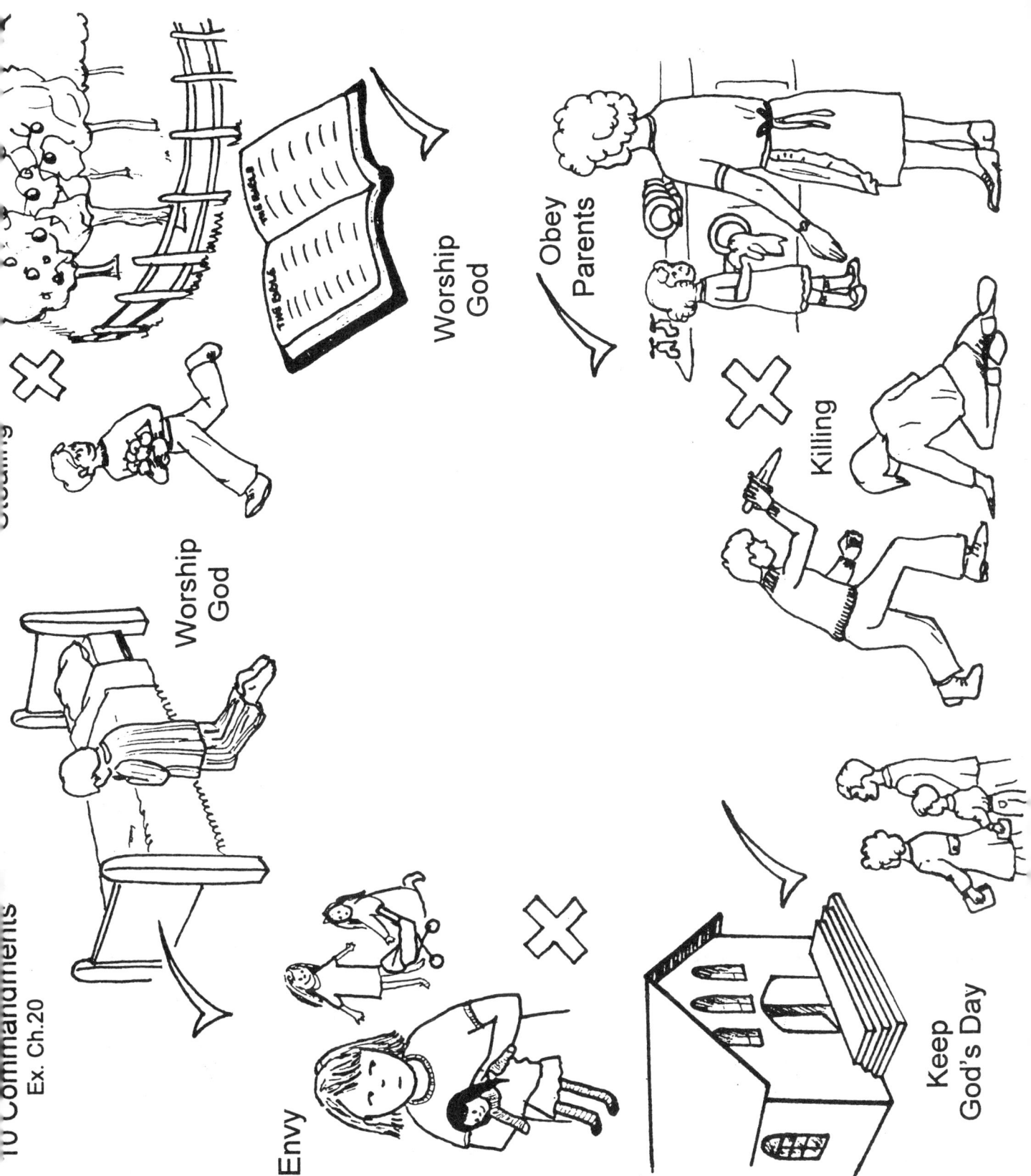

10 Commandments
Ex. Ch.20

Worship God

Worship God

Obey Parents

Killing

Envy

Keep God's Day

THE TEN COMMANDMENTS – ACTIVITY SHEET

...ut out the Commandments and stick to the
...ntre of the picture.

The Ten Commandments

1. Worship God only.
2. Do not make an idol.
3. Do not swear using God's name.
4. Remember to keep Sunday special.
5. Respect and obey your parents.

6. Do not murder.
7. Do not take anyone else's wife or husband.
8. Do not steal.
9. Do not tell lies.
10. Do not envy what other people have.

The Tabernacle and the Golden Calf

Exodus 25-32

Themes	Idols, Forgiveness, Worship

Aims	To teach the Bible's account of the Israelites and the golden calf.
	To describe the role and arrangement of the tabernacle.
	To consider what the Bible teaches regarding forgiveness.

Resources	Bibles, Children's Story Sheet, Puzzle Page, Activity Sheet.

Other Ideas & Activities

1. Activity Sheet – follow instructions on Sheet.
2. Do further research on the furniture in the tabernacle and draw the various pieces including the seven branched candlestick (which is still in use today).
3. Find the measurements of the tabernacle from the Bible and draw a plan of it to scale.
4. (Ambitious!) make a model of the tabernacle and its furniture.
5. The plans for the tabernacle were very accurate and detailed. Moses had to follow the instructions carefully. Discuss the importance of following instructions. This could lead to a piece of written work or role play.
6. Forgiveness - a major theme in the Bible. Using a concordance (if available) in pairs/small groups write a list of other stories which illustrate God's forgiveness (Old or New Testament).

Teacher's Notes

Summary: The Israelites rebelled against God and built and worshipped a golden calf. When Moses saw the golden calf he was angry and threw down the stones, on which were written the Ten Commandments, and smashed them. God showed Moses how to build the tabernacle. Here was a place where God could dwell amongst the Israelites, and where the Israelites could go to if they needed to be forgiven. The Bible says that the person and work of Jesus Christ is pictured in the tabernacle.

Point of Contact
Following Instructions
- When have you used instructions to make something or go somewhere?
- Did you follow the instructions carefully?
- What would have happened if you didn't follow the instructions and did your own thing?
- When is it very important to follow instructions?

For the background to this lesson see "The Ten Commandments".

Rebellion!

Moses had been up on Mount Sinai for forty days. Here God gave Moses the Ten Commandments written on two stones. The people had watched Moses disappear into a cloud on the mountain, as he went to meet with God. They became impatient when, after many days, Moses did not return. They came to Aaron, Moses' brother, and said, "You make us a god that we can worship." This was a wicked thing to do when God had done so much for them. They did not want to obey him but wanted to do their own thing.

The Golden Calf

Aaron should have refused to do what they asked, knowing that it was wrong to make idols. He told the people to take off their gold earrings and bring them to him. Aaron melted all the gold in a fire and formed it into the shape of a calf. This was similar to what the Egyptians worshipped at this time. The Israelites were copying them. When the people saw the calf they said, "This is the god who brought us out of Egypt."

The next day was a festival day. The Israelites spent the time eating, drinking, singing and dancing, and worshipping the golden calf. The Israelites were committing idolatry. They were worshipping something else and not the true God! They were breaking both the first and second commandments.

Broken Stones

After forty days, Moses came down from the mountain, carrying the stone slabs on which the commandments were written. He heard the noise of the people singing and dancing. Moses saw the golden calf and the people dancing round it in great excitement. Moses was furious and in his anger he threw down the stone slabs and they smashed in pieces at his feet.

Moses went straight up to the golden calf and threw it into the fire. Moses turned to Aaron and said, "Why have you allowed the people to sin against God like this?" Aaron responded by trying to blame the people.

Moses Prays

Moses told the people that they had sinned a great sin but he would go back to the mountain and pray to God asking him to forgive them. Although God was very angry, he promised Moses that he was willing to forgive and that he would still take the Israelites to the land of Canaan. Once more God wrote down his Ten Commandments on two slabs of stone.

The Tabernacle

While Moses was still up the mountain, God gave him instructions of how to build a special tent, where the people could worship him. Because they were travelling through the desert, this place of worship, called the tabernacle, had to be portable. It could be put up, then quickly taken down and folded away, and then later reassembled again.

Its Purpose

The purpose of the tabernacle was that it would allow God to dwell among the people in the middle of the camp. It would also be a place where the Israelites could come to worship and praise God. It was here that they could come and receive forgiveness for the wrong things they had done. Even those who had worshipped the golden calf and broken the 2nd commandment could come and receive forgiveness. The Bible tells us that the tabernacle pointed the Israelites to the person and work of Jesus Christ (see for example Hebrews 9:1 & 23, 24).

How To Build
God gave Moses the exact pattern of how to make the tabernacle. He told him the size of the building, the materials used and what furniture was to go inside. The people contributed gold, silver, bronze, precious stones, wood and animal skins to the making of the tabernacle. Craftsmen worked on all the materials and eventually it was completed.

Plain On The Outside, Beautiful Inside
The tent was about 14 metres long and 4 metres wide. This was divided into two rooms with a beautifully woven curtain, or veil, of red, blue and scarlet between them. In the larger room towards the front, called the holy place, were three pieces of furniture: a table, an altar and a candlestick.

In the small inner, back room, called the 'Holy of Holies' was the most important object in the whole tabernacle. This was a special box called the ark of God. The box was made of wood and covered with gold. Two golden angels stood with outstretched wings as if covering the ark. This ark was holy and a symbol of God's presence. Here God met with the High Priest when he entered the tabernacle. Here in the ark was placed the Ten Commandments.

Round the inner tent of the tabernacle, with its two rooms, was a courtyard surrounded by a high fence made of curtains, suspended on wooden polls.

Amongst The People
The tabernacle was put up in the centre of the Israelite camp. When the people looked towards it, they could see the shining cloud of God's presence over the tent, showing them that God was in the tabernacle. When the cloud moved on from the tabernacle the Israelites knew it was time to move camp. The Israelites would then pack up the tabernacle and their camp and follow the cloud.

The Way Of Forgiveness
The tabernacle showed the Israelites how they could approach God and also receive forgiveness for their sins. If an Israelite had done something wrong they would come to the tabernacle. Here they would give an offering to the priest who would take it to God. God would accept the offering and forgive them their sin. The Bible says that in this way God was teaching the people about Jesus Christ and what he would do at Calvary's cross (Hebrews 9:11-15). He would be the true offering who takes away the sin of the world (John 1:29).

Illustration: The Tabernacle - a Picture of Jesus
The Bible says that God was giving the Israelites a picture of what Jesus would accomplish when he came into the world. Once Jesus had come there was no need for the temple or the tabernacle.
- In the tabernacle there was the offering of a sacrifice to forgive sin. Jesus died on the cross so that sin could be forgiven (John 1:29).

- The High Priest went into God's presence in the tabernacle. Jesus is now in the presence of God in heaven (Hebrews 9:11, 12).
- There was just one way of entry into the tabernacle. Jesus is the only way to God (John 14:6).

Things to Learn
- The Israelites rebelled against God and his commandments.
- God gave Moses instructions for building the tabernacle.
- This was a place where the people could draw near to God and receive forgiveness for their sins.
- Christians believe that it is through Jesus' death on the cross that they are forgiven.

Discuss
- If you were an Israelite, how would you have felt when you saw the tabernacle in the middle of the camp? Would you have felt pleased or worried? Why?
- Why was Moses angry when he saw the golden calf?
- Why did God provide the tabernacle for the Israelites?
- Is there a way for God to forgive sin today?

The Tabernacle and the Golden Calf

Moses had been up on Mount Sinai for forty days. The people were waiting at the bottom of the mountain for him and wondered where he was. They began to get impatient. So they asked Aaron, Moses' brother, to make them a god to worship. They thought that God had forgotten all about them.

So Aaron collected gold jewellery from the people and melted it all in a fire. He then formed the gold into the shape of a calf. The people soon began to worship the calf as a god. They said, "This is the god who has brought us out of Egypt".

The next day the Israelites spent their time worshipping the golden calf, eating, drinking, singing and dancing. They forgot all about how good God had been to them.

God had finished talking to Moses, and Moses began to come down the mountain to join the people. He was carrying the two slabs of stone on which the Ten Commandments were written. When Moses saw what the people were doing he was very angry. He threw the two stone slabs on to the ground and they smashed into pieces at his feet. He then threw the golden calf into the fire.

Moses went back up the mountain to ask God to forgive the people. God agreed and wrote out the Ten Commandments again.

God also gave Moses instructions how to build the tabernacle. The people gave gold, silver, bronze, precious stones, wood and animal skins to make the tabernacle. Craftsmen used these materials and eventually it was completed.

The tabernacle was divided into two rooms by a beautifully woven curtain. In the larger room towards the front were three pieces of furniture: a table, an altar and a candlestick. In a smaller back room was the most important object in the whole tabernacle. This was a special box called the ark of God. The box was made of wood and covered with gold. Here God met with the High Priest when he entered the tabernacle. The Ten Commandments were kept in the ark.

The tabernacle was a special tent where the people could go to worship God and ask for his forgiveness.

THE TABERNACLE AND THE GOLDEN CALF

ue or false - put a tick in the right box.

	True	False
Moses was on Mount Sinai for a very short time.	❏	❏
The Israelites asked Aaron to make them a god to worship.	❏	❏
Aaron melted down their gold and made a golden calf.	❏	❏
The people did not worship the calf.	❏	❏
The people forgot about God.	❏	❏
After 40 days Moses came down the mountain.	❏	❏
When Moses saw the people worshipping the golden calf, he was very happy.	❏	❏
Moses threw down the tablets of stone which had the Ten Commandments written on them.	❏	❏
Moses asked God to forgive the people.	❏	❏

The tabernacle stood in the middle of the Israelite tents. The people came to worship God in the tabernacle.

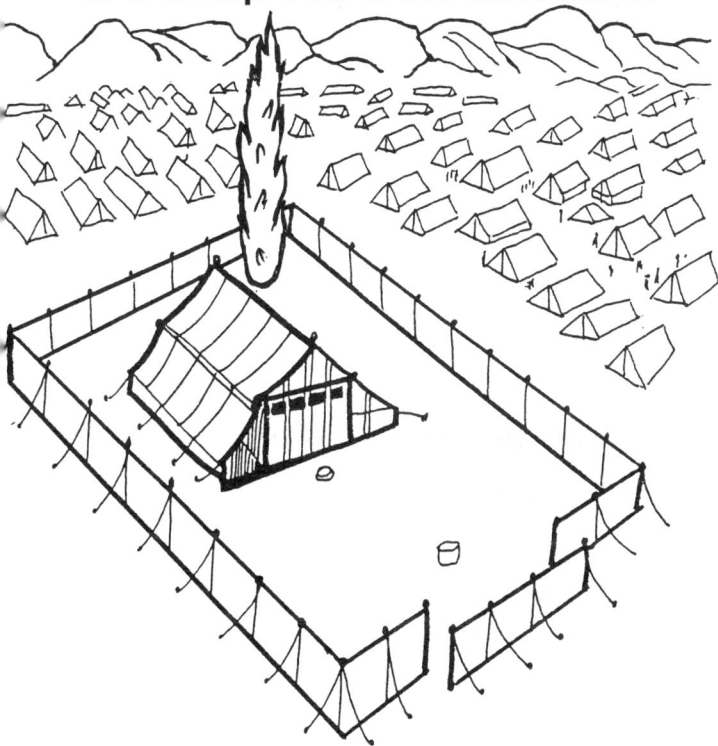

r	g	w	t	c	e	g	e
e	a	o	z	a	l	m	z
v	c	o	l	n	b	p	n
l	b	d	h	d	a	e	o
i	r	u	a	l	t	a	r
s	k	g	c	e	b	g	b
n	t	o	j	s	v	l	p
p	n	i	a	t	r	u	c
i	e	a	v	i	x	f	j
w	t	x	r	c	e	b	q
z	k	o	p	k	i	t	a

Find these words in the grid.

gold	curtain	silver
table	bronze	altar
wood	tent	ark
candlestick		

hat does the Bible tell us we should do when we have done something wrong?

e should ask God for...

Colour in the letters with a dot to find out the answer.

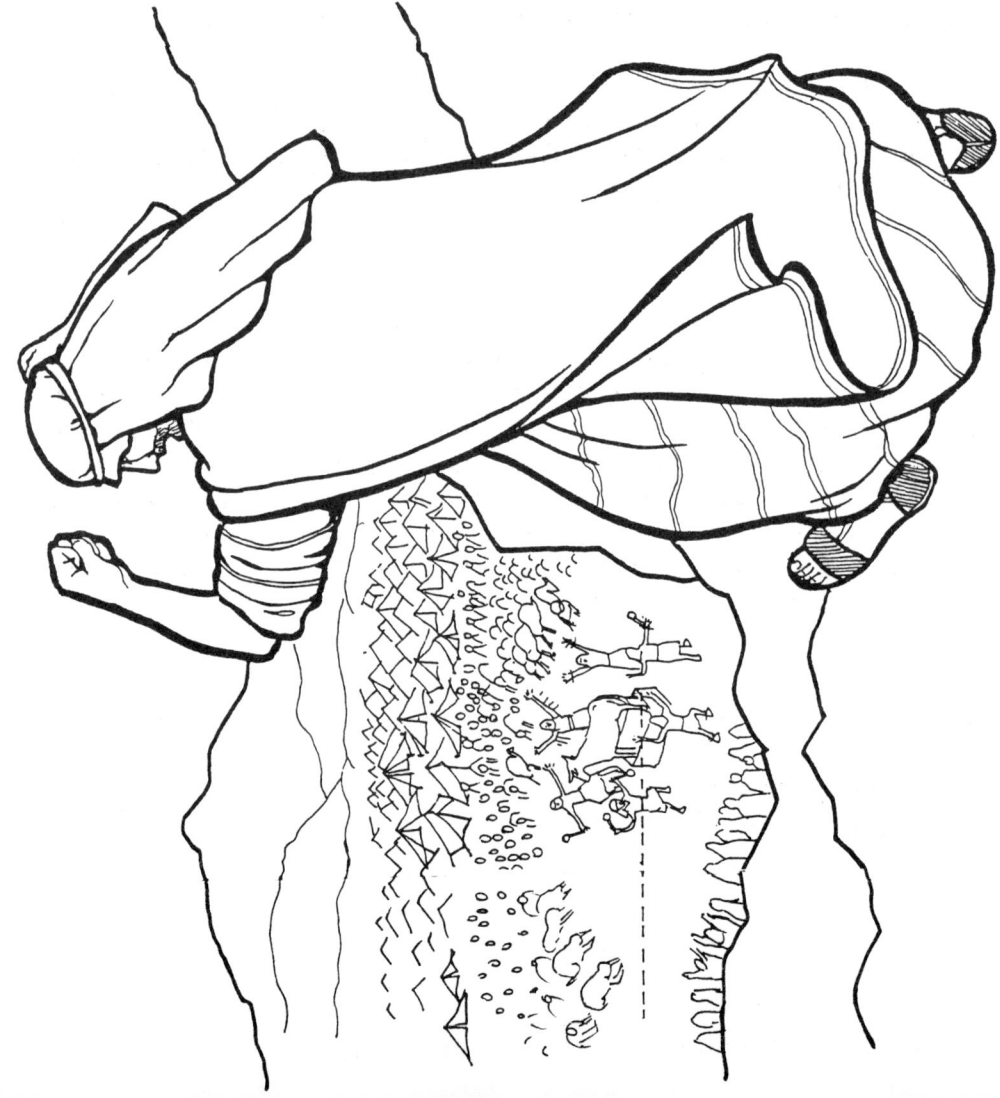

Moses was angry when he saw the golden calf and smashed the commandments. Ex. ch.32

Moses was angry when he saw the golden calf and smashed the commandments. Ex. ch.32

The Ten

1. Worship God only.
2. Do not make an idol.
3. Do not swear using God's name.
4. Remember to keep Sunday special.
5. Respect and obey your parents.

Commandments

6. Do not murder.
7. Do not take anyone else's wife or husband.
8. Do not steal.
9. Do not tell lies.
10. Do not envy what other people have.

The Ten

1. Worship God only.
2. Do not make an idol.
3. Do not swear using God's name.
4. Remember to keep Sunday special.
5. Respect and obey your parents.

Commandments

6. Do not murder.
7. Do not take anyone else's wife or husband.
8. Do not steal.
9. Do not tell lies.
10. Do not envy what other people have.

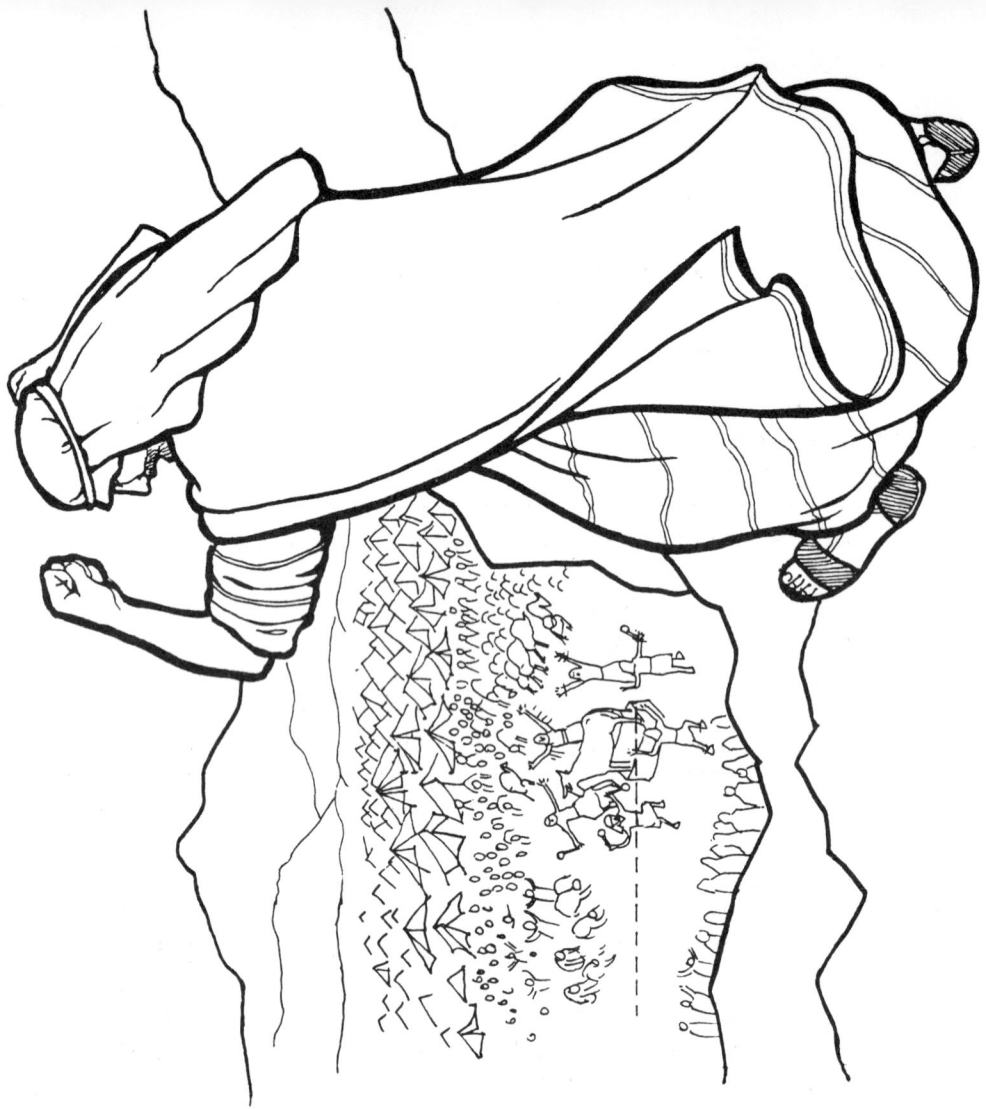

Cut out Commandments. Cut or tear into small pieces and stick at Moses' feet. Cut out calf (can be covered with gold foil) and stick on dotted line.

Joshua & The Walls of Jericho

Joshua 1 - 6

Themes	Faith, Obedience, Trust

Aims	To teach the Bible's account of Joshua's conquest of the city of Jericho. To consider why Joshua was such a courageous leader. To reflect on the faith and courage of Christians.

Resources	Bibles, Children's Story Sheet, Puzzle Page, Activity Sheets, Map.

Other Ideas & Activities

1. Activity Sheets – follow instructions on Sheets.
2. Draw a plan (bird's eye view) of the procession around Jericho. Draw/write the name of each part in boxes e.g. soldiers, priests blowing trumpets, priests carrying the ark, more soldiers, all the rest of the people. (See notes for details.) If possible divide the class into these sections and do your own procession!
3. Find out more about a ram's horn trumpet (a shofar). How do they work? Draw one and make a model one. How could you make it work? (Clue: how does a modern trumpet work?)
4. Walled cities. How were they designed to be secure? Make a plan of a walled city.
5. List other leaders mentioned in the Bible (see for example Hebrews 11: 23-32). List other well known leaders. What are their characteristics?
6. Compose a piece of music describing this event. Find trumpet sounds, procession sounds and crashing walls.

Teacher's Notes

Summary: God told Joshua not to be afraid. God promised to be with him and help fight his battles. Jericho was a great and strong city. The Israelites obeyed God and marched around the city once every day, and then seven times on the seventh day. At the sound of trumpets and the shout of the people, God made the walls of Jericho fall down. Only Rahab and her family were saved alive and the city was destroyed. Throughout history Christians have often shown great courage and boldness, even though they faced great difficulties or opposition. They were like this because they believed that God promised to be with them and help them.

Point of Contact
Great Responsibility
Imagine that the Queen came to your school, and you were asked to show her around.
- How would you feel?
- What would you have to remember?
- Would you like such a responsibility?

Note: Rahab's lie. Was it correct for Rahab to tell a lie in hiding the spies? The Bible says that we should always be truthful and not deceive one another in everyday situations (see Leviticus 19:11). However the Bible does concede that in certain war situations, where 'life and death' is involved, the use of deceit and cunning is permissible. (For example: in the attack on Ai., found in Joshua 8, Joshua is encouraged by God in his use of deceit, in order to take the city. In the Second World War, it was felt morally correct to use deceit, as much as possible, to confuse the enemy and so save lives.)

For the background to this lesson see the series on Moses.

A New Leader
Moses led the Israelites through the wilderness for forty years. Now the Israelites were ready to enter the land that God had promised to give them. When he died, God chose Joshua to take Moses' place. Joshua was well prepared for this position, being a brilliant soldier and having been Moses' assistant for several years. Even so, it was a big responsibility to take the people into Canaan and conquer the land. One day God came to Joshua and said, 'Be strong and do not be afraid, for the Lord your God is with you.' This reassured Joshua and gave him confidence to take Moses' place.

Crossing The Jordan
The first obstacle the Israelites met was the river Jordan (show map). They needed to cross this to enter the land of Canaan. Joshua obeyed God's instructions and (just like at the Red Sea some forty years before) the river Jordan opened up in front of them. The people walked over on dry land to Canaan. Joshua erected a monument of twelve stones, to remind the people in days to come, of God's great power and of his goodness to them.

Home At Last!
It was a happy day for the Israelites when they set up camp in their new country. This was the land that God had promised to give them and they were there at last. That same day, the manna stopped, as there was now plenty of good food. The Bible describes the land as one which "flowed with milk and honey".

Joshua's Is Encouraged
The next obstacle was the first great city that lay before them - Jericho. Its thick, high walls seemed impenetrable and the people wondered how they could possibly conquer such a city. Then God appeared to Joshua, dressed as a captain of an army and gave him specific instructions for conquering Jericho. Joshua knew that God would fight the battle with them.

The Spies
Joshua sent two men into Jericho. These brave men entered the city and stayed in the house of a woman called Rahab whose house was built into the city walls. The king of Jericho heard about the spies and sent soldiers to Rahab's house to capture them. Quickly Rahab hid the spies under some crops, which were drying on the flat roof of her home. She told the king's men that the spies had left the city before dark, and before the gates were shut. "Go quickly", she said, "and overtake them". *See Note on Rahab's lie.*

An Agreement
When the king's men had gone, Rahab went to the roof of her house and spoke to the spies. " I know that God has given this land to the Israelites. We have heard how he opened the Red Sea when you left Egypt and everyone is afraid. I believe that your God is the true God who is in heaven above and on the earth beneath. I have saved your lives. When you capture Jericho, please spare my life."

The spies agreed and promised to save Rahab and her family. As a sign she was to tie a piece of red cord in her window. When the Israelites came to capture the city they would know which was Rahab's house and keep her safe.

Escape!
As Rahab's house was built into the city wall, the spies were able to escape through a window. Rahab let down a rope and they disappeared into the darkness and returned to Joshua in the camp.

Instructions
Joshua obeyed the instructions God gave him as to how the city was to be taken. Every morning this grand procession marched around the city – first the soldiers, then the priests blowing trumpets, then the priests carrying the ark, followed by more soldiers. Finally, thousands and thousands of the Israelites followed behind. The people marched around the walls, like this, for six consecutive days.

Falling Walls
On the seventh day the people marched around the walls again seven times. The people circled the city for a final time. The priests blew their trumpets and, at a command from Joshua, all the people shouted as loud as they could. Suddenly the walls of Jericho came crashing down. It was not the noise of the trumpets or the shouting, but the power of God that brought the walls down.

Rahab Saved
The Israelite soldiers ran into the city and captured it. The two spies found the red cord in the window of Rahab's house and saved her and her family alive. Rahab's house was the only house on the walls still standing. Everything in the city was destroyed and burnt by fire. This was the first great victory for the Israelites in Canaan.

Courageous Christians
Throughout history Christians have often shown great courage and boldness, even though they faced great difficulties or opposition. They were like this because they believed that God had promised to be with them and help them.

Illustration: The Faith And Courage Of William Carey
William Carey had a great concern. He wanted to go to far away countries and tell the people there about Jesus. He wanted other Christians to be sent out as well.

He faced many obstacles. Not only did he have very little money to pay for such a journey, but also he faced the opposition of people in his home country of England. And even if he and the other missionaries were able to go abroad, they would face great difficulties, like, disease, different food and climate, hostility from people who did not want to hear what the Bible had to say.

However, William had great faith and believed that his God was able to help him achieve his goal. His motto was, "Expect great things from God; attempt great things for God."

Eventually William helped found the London Missionary Society, which sent Christians all over the world, telling people about Jesus. He too went to India, where he lived for 41 years until the day of his death. Here his work was greatly blessed by God. Unlike Joshua, William had not seen the walls of Jericho fall down. However, like Joshua, he had courage and faith in God, and was able to overcome many difficulties.
(* The story of William Carey can be found in 'William Carey' - by S Pearce Carey, published by the Wakeman Trust, ISBN 1 870855 14 0 - available from most Christian Bookshops.)

Things to learn:
- God encouraged Joshua to be strong and to have courage.
- Joshua obeyed all that God told him to do. This was the secret of his success.
- The walls of Jericho fell down, giving a great victory for the Israelites.
- Rahab was saved.
- Christians have often done great things for God, because they believed God would be with them and help them.

Discuss
- Why was it necessary for Joshua to have suitable qualifications for the task God gave him?
- How do you feel if you are given something which is extremely difficult to do?
- What was the secret of Joshua's success?
- How did God's promises help Joshua?
- What is the secret of a Christian's success?

Joshua and the Walls of Jericho

When Moses died, Joshua became the leader of the Israelites. Joshua was a good soldier and had been Moses' helper for many years. God spoke to Joshua, "Be strong and do not be afraid, for I will be with you wherever you go".

It was not long before the Israelites got to Canaan, the land that God had promised them. They had to cross the wide River Jordan to get into the land. Joshua asked God to help him. Joshua did as God had told him and the River Jordan opened up in front of all the people.

What a miracle! Now all the people could walk over on dry land to their new home. Joshua put up a pillar of stones in the middle of the river to remind the Israelites of what God had done.

The city of Jericho was nearby. The Israelites knew that they would have to conquer Jericho. But the city walls were so high and strong, it just seemed impossible. God spoke to Joshua and said that he would help them.

Joshua sent two men in to Jericho to find out more about the city and its people. The two men stayed in Rahab's house. Her house was built in the city walls. Rahab hid the two men on the roof of her house when some of the king' s men came to see her. The two men told her to tie a piece of red cord in her window, so the Israelites would know her house and not harm her.

At night-time, Rahab lowered the two men with a rope out of her window. The men returned to Joshua and told him all about Jericho.

Joshua asked God to help him conquer Jericho, and God gave him some instructions to follow. Every morning, for six days the Israelites marched round the city of Jericho. On the seventh day, as they marched around the city for the last time, the priests blew their trumpets and Joshua shouted his command. All the people shouted out loud and the strong, heavy stone walls of Jericho came crashing down!

The Israelite soldiers ran into the city and captured it. The men saw the red cord in Rahab's window and saved her and her family.

Name..

Date.................................

JOSHUA AND THE WALLS OF JERICHO

Fill in the missing vowels to find out God's promise to Joshua.

"Be str_ng _nd d_ no_
b_ afra_d, for th_ Lor_
yo_r God _s w_th y_u."

Fill in the missing words.

1. God chose Joshua to be the new l_ _ _ _ _ of the Israelites.
2. The Israelites had to cross the river J _ _ _ _ _ to get to their new land.
3. God parted the r _ _ _ _ so that the people could cross over.
4. Jericho was a city with strong, high w _ _ _ _.
5. Joshua sent two s _ _ _ _ in to Jericho.
6. Rahab h _ _ the spies.
7. The Israelites marched around Jericho, o_ _ _ a day for six days.
8. On the seventh day the people s_ _ _ _ _ _ _.
9. Jericho came crashing d _ _ _.
10. Rahab and her family were s _ _ _ _ _.

Now fit these words into the grid below. The words in the shaded squares spell out the secret of Joshua's success.

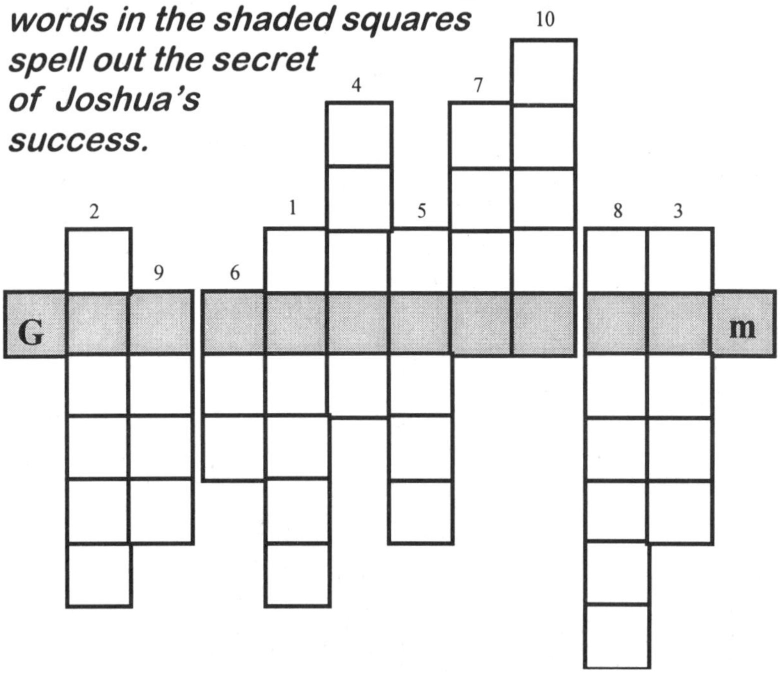

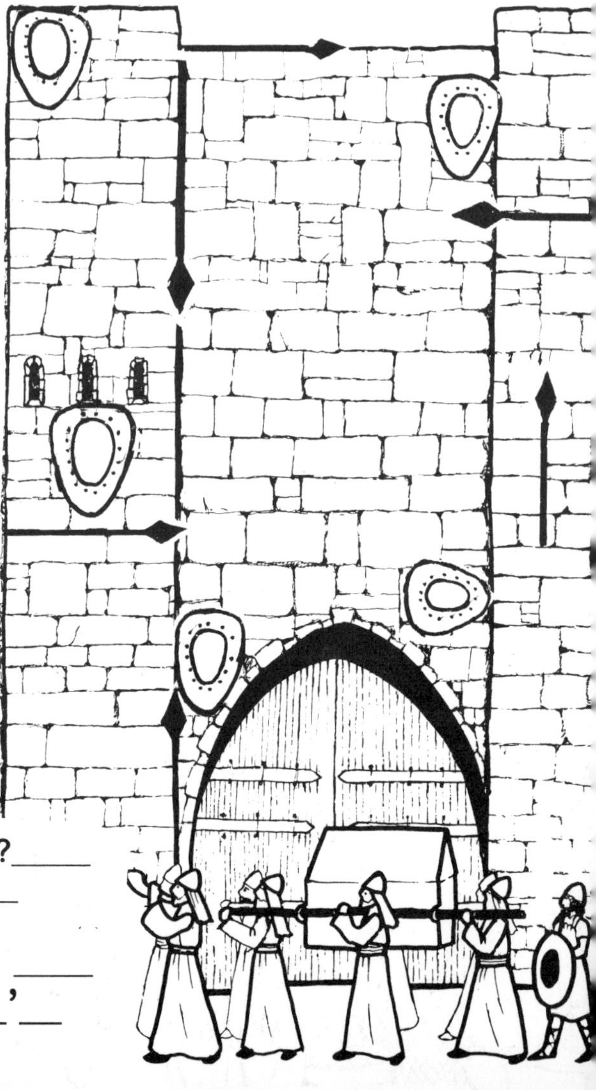

G m

How many spears can you find hidden in the wall ?_____
How many shields can you find ?   _____
Work out the difference between the two to find
out how many families in Jericho were saved.   _____
Whose family was it ?   R_ _ _ _'

The Israelites walked round Jericho seven times.....

JOSHUA & THE WALLS OF JERICHO – ACTIVITY SHEET (2)

Photocopy the two Joshua activity sheets back to back making sure one is upside down so that the solid black line is 'lined up' with Rahab's house. See diagram.

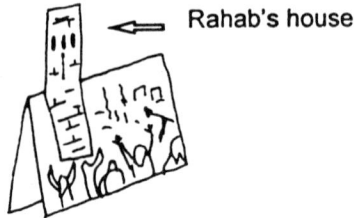

← Rahab's house

Fold forwards along this dotted line.

.... the trumpet sounded, the people shouted and the walls fell down flat.

Josh.ch.6

Cut along the solid black line. Stick red cord from the dot in Rahab's window.

Ruth - The Girl Who Put God First

Ruth 1 - 4

Themes	Choices, Unselfishness, Reward

Aims	To teach the Biblical account of Ruth. To show how unselfish Ruth was and how God rewarded her unselfishness. To consider the choices we make in life.

Resources	Bibles, Children's Story Sheet, Puzzle Page, Activity Sheet, Map.

Other Ideas & Activities

1. Activity Sheet – dried grass/straw could be used; follow instructions on Sheet.
2. Look at a stalk of wheat or barley. Show the process of getting enough grains to sell/grind into flour. It can be fun to grind some in a pestle and mortar to make flour.
3. Research farming methods in Biblical times - sowing, harvesting, winnowing, gleaning, etc.
4. Under a heading "Choices I have made" list the choices you have already made in your life. Under a heading "Choices I will make" list what important choices you will have to make. Now list what have been good and what have been bad choices.
5. The story of Ruth highlights the keeping of promises. Ruth made a promise to Naomi, putting Naomi's interests before her own. Boaz made a promise to Ruth, to look after her. Have you ever made a promise which has meant giving something up in order to keep it? Write a story about this.
6. The story of Ruth highlights some of the best ways in which people can care for each other. For example: - loyalty, thinking of others, working hard to provide for each other, sharing, welcoming strangers. These are Biblical attitudes valued by Christians. Ask the children to list ways in which they could demonstrate these in school, e.g. making newcomers feel welcome, helping others, etc.

Teacher's Notes

Summary: Naomi and her family went to live in Moab because there was famine in Bethlehem. While there her husband and both sons died, leaving widows. When Naomi decided to return home, Ruth her daughter in law decided to go with her. Ruth was willing to leave her home, family and friends, and all she had ever known, to go with Naomi and serve God. Ruth made the best choice. She worked hard in the fields to provide food for them both. The Lord rewarded Ruth by giving her a husband called Boaz and a baby. The Bible says that the best choice we can make is to live for and serve God.

Point of Contact
Famine
- What is a famine?
- Name some countries affected by famine.
- What caused the famine?
- What help did people try to give to those who were affected by the famine?

Famine!
Once there was a famine in the land of Israel. Elimelech, Naomi and their two sons lived in Bethlehem (show map). Elimelech decided to take his family away from the famine to live in the nearby country of Moab.

Moab
The people of Moab did not worship God. Instead they worshipped man made idols and other gods. Soon after they had settled, Elimelech died, leaving Naomi a widow. She had to look after her two sons on her own. When the boys grew up they married two Moabite girls, called Ruth and Orpah. After ten years both Naomi's sons died leaving Ruth and Orpah as widows!

Going Back
Naomi decided that it would be best to return to Bethlehem. She was very sad, having lost her husband and two sons. She wanted to be back home with her own people who loved and served God. Ruth and Orpah walked a little way with Naomi towards Bethlehem.

Naomi stopped and turned to the two girls. She said, "Now you two must go back to your own homes, back to your people, the Moabites." She wanted them to be happy and find husbands again. The girls loved Naomi and didn't want to leave her. They kissed her and cried at the thought of never seeing her again.

A Difficult Decision
After Orpah had kissed her mother in law, she set off to go back to her old home. Ruth hugged Naomi tightly and would not leave her. Naomi said, "Look, Orpah has gone back to her people. You go too, Ruth." But Ruth had made up her mind and said these beautiful words - "Don't ask me to leave you. Where you go I will go, and where you will live, I will live. Your people will be my people and your God shall be my God." Naomi gave way and together they continued along the road.

Back in Bethlehem
After a long journey Ruth and Naomi arrived in Bethlehem. Naomi's old friends were surprised and excited to see her. She had been away for ten years and now looked older and sad. Naomi told her friends how her husband and two sons had died and how she felt very upset. But now she rejoiced to be back home among her own people once again.

The Barley Harvest
Naomi and Ruth were poor and needed food and money. When the fields were harvested, the crops were cut with a scythe and put into bundles. Stray ears of barley would fall to the ground. People, who were called 'gleaners', then picked these up. Those who gleaned were allowed to keep what they collected. Ruth went into the fields

to glean, to get food for herself and Naomi. They could sell the barley and also make flour and bread for themselves.

Boaz the Boss

So Ruth went to glean in a field belonging to a man called Boaz. He was a very rich man. When he visited the field and saw Ruth, he asked the foreman, "Who is this young woman?" He could see she was from another country, by the colour of her skin, hair and the clothes she was wearing. The foreman replied, "She is Ruth. She came from Moab with Naomi."

Boaz talked with Ruth and was kind to her. He said, "I have heard about you. I know that you have been good and kind to Naomi. May God reward and bless you." It meant a lot to Ruth that Boaz did not despise her because she was a foreigner.

Boaz told the reapers to leave extra handfuls of grain for Ruth so that she would have plenty to pick up. All day Ruth was kept busy collecting the stalks of barley and beating out the grain.

The Day's End

After gleaning all day Ruth returned home to Naomi. She sold some barley and kept some to cook and eat. Ruth gladly worked hard to provide food and money for Naomi and herself to live on. How thankful they must have been to God for helping them at this difficult time. Soon the barley and wheat harvest was over and Ruth and Naomi wondered what they would do now.

Boaz Marries Ruth

God rewarded Ruth in a special way. By now Boaz had fallen in love with Ruth. They were married soon after. God rewarded Ruth for the unselfish choice she had made in coming to Bethlehem with Naomi, rather than returning to her own people with Orpah. She was now rich and Naomi also had all she needed. Boaz and Ruth had a baby boy. Everyone was delighted, especially Naomi, who now had a grandson. This baby boy was the grandfather of King David. From his family, Jesus was born.

The Best Choice

The best choice any one can make is to put God first in their lives. God helps Christians to make the right decisions and do what is right in their lives.

Illustration: Making The Right Choices

Jake and Tim were identical twins. Because no one could tell the difference they would often play tricks on people. Although they looked exactly the same they were opposites in their behaviour.

Jake was always disobedient and selfish. He always did his own thing and didn't care about anyone else. As he grew older he made bad choices and did many wrong things. He was lazy at school and played truant. He chose friends who encouraged him to lie and steal. When he was older Jake ended up going to prison.

His brother Tim was very different. At an early age he believed in God and was ready to learn all he could about Jesus. He chose to put God first in his life. As he grew older he made a lot of good choices. He chose to work hard at school so that one day he could be a pilot. He obeyed his parents, because he knew it was the right thing to do. He chose good friends who were a help to him. When he grew up he chose to be a teacher. He was able to encourage children to make the right choices.

There is no doubt that Jake made the wrong choices and ended with a lot of problems. Tim put God first in his life and God guided him in all the choices he had to make. Which of these do you think was happiest?

Things to Learn:
- Ruth was willing to leave her home, friends and all she had ever known, to go with Naomi and serve God.
- God rewarded her.
- The Bible says that the best choice we can make is to live for and serve God.

Discuss
- What difficult or important choices have you had to make?
- What difficult or important choices will you have to make?
- How will you decide?

Ruth - The Girl Who Put God First

Naomi lived in Moab. She had moved there with her husband and sons when there was a famine in their home country of Israel. But now Naomi's husband and two sons had died. She was left alone with her two daughters-in-law Ruth and Orpah.

Naomi decided to return to her home in Bethlehem in Israel. Ruth and Orpah walked with Naomi towards Bethlehem. Naomi stopped and told Ruth and Orpah to return to their homes and families in Moab. Orpah kissed Naomi and went back to Moab. But Ruth did not want to leave Naomi. She said, "Don't ask me to leave you. Where you go, I will go and where you live, I will live. Your people will be my people and your God will be my God". So Ruth went with Naomi back to Bethlehem.

Naomi was pleased to be back home again, and happy to have Ruth with her. Naomi and Ruth were very poor. When the fields were harvested, Ruth collected pieces of grain that had been dropped. This was called gleaning.

One day Ruth went to glean in a field belonging to a man called Boaz. He was a very rich man. He noticed Ruth gleaning and asked one of his workers about her. Boaz talked to Ruth and was kind to her. He told his workers to drop extra grain for Ruth to glean. Ruth had plenty of grain to take home that evening. Naomi and Ruth thanked God for giving them food to eat.

It was not long before Boaz fell in love with Ruth, and they soon married. Later they had a baby boy. Naomi was very happy for Ruth and Boaz and knew that God had been good to her.

RUTH - THE GIRL WHO PUT GOD FIRST

Join up the two halves of these sentences.

Naomi's family left Bethlehem.....	.....to go back to their own home
They went to live in Moab.....	.....to go with her to Bethlehem
When Naomi's husband and two sons died.....	.....and God rewarded he
She told her daughters'-in-law.....	.....and they had a baby boy
Ruth cared for Naomi and chose.....	.....gathering barley in the harvest fiel
Ruth worked hard.....	.....she decided to return to Bethlehem
Boaz married Ruth.....	.....because there was a famin
Ruth put God first in her life.....	.....where their two sons marrie

```
a  b  d  o  G  d  e  v  o  l  l
d  o  u  g  b  c  h  k  o  h  u
l  o  b  v  a  k  p  v  a  o  f
a  g  o  r  m  n  i  z  q  e  p
y  v  i  g  m  n  x  n  d  r  l
o  n  b  c  g  m  p  e  d  b  e
g  h  s  i  f  l  e  s  u  n  h
```

loving

unselfish

loved God

helpful

kind

caring

good

**Ruth was a very special person.
Find the words that describe her
in the wordsearch.**

**Follow the footprints from the arrow
to find out what Ruth said to Naomi.
Then write the words in the spaces.**

"
_ _ _ _ _   _ _ _ _ _   _ _ _

_ _ _ _ _   _ _ _   _ _ _ _ _

_ _ _ _ _ _ _   _ _ _   _ _ _

_ _ _ _ _   _ _ _ _
_ _   _ _ _   _
"

Ruth ch.1 v 16

God.

God

my

Your

people

shall

be

people

and

Ruth gathered barley to sell.

d up along dotted line. Cut
ng solid line then fringe the
er to form 'barley'. Cut out
ch of barley. Cut slits either
e of Ruth's arm and slot
ley in.

RUTH – THE GIRL WHO PUT
GOD FIRST –
ACTIVITY SHEET

Samuel Listens to God

1 Samuel 1 - 3

Themes	Prayer, Obedience

Aims	To teach the Biblical account of the birth and call of the prophet Samuel. To consider prayer and its role in the life of a Christian. To show how Christians obey God today.

Resources	Bibles, Children's Story Sheet, Puzzle Page, Activity Sheet.

Other Ideas & Activities

1. Activity Sheet – stick on black/dark paper/card; also needs yellow/orange tissue.
2. Research the furniture and arrangement of the tabernacle. Make a display showing the tabernacle and its various parts, incorporating drawings, models and writing.
3. The hymn "Hushed was the evening hymn", by James Drummond Burns, summarises the incident where God calls to Samuel in the tabernacle. Read, sing and discuss the words.
4. Discuss prayers - e.g. the Lord's prayer. Why do Christians pray? Write your own prayer for the next class/school assembly.

Teacher's Notes

Summary: Hannah longed for children of her own. She prayed for a baby boy and God gave her Samuel. She gave Samuel back to God to work with Eli in the tabernacle. Samuel was a wonderful child. He put God first in his life. While Samuel was still young God spoke to him and told him things that would happen in the future. Samuel was ready to obey God and do whatever the Lord told him to. Christians pray to God and read the Bible and want to do what he says.

Point of Contact
Being Made Fun Of

- Have you ever been laughed at or made fun of about something you cannot change?
- How did you feel?
- What did you do?
- Have you ever laughed at someone in this way?
- Did you say sorry afterwards?

No Children!

Hannah and her husband Elkanah, lived in Ramah. They were very happy together, except for one thing - they had no children. Hannah was very upset about this and must have wondered why God did not give her children. Another lady was unkind and made fun of Hannah because she had no children. This made Hannah cry. But Elkanah, her husband, comforted her, and told her that he still loved her.

Visiting The Tabernacle
Once every year, Hannah and Elkanah would travel to Shiloh to worship God. Shiloh was where the Israelites had put the tabernacle, that had travelled with them during the forty years that they were in the wilderness. People from all over the country would travel here to pray for God's forgiveness and thank him for his kindness. It was usually a happy family time.

Hannah's Distress And Prayer
One year, during their visit to Shiloh, Hannah felt very unhappy. She cried and cried because she was so upset that she had no children. When Elkanah saw her not eating her food and being so unhappy, he tried to comfort her but it did not help.

Hannah slipped away to find a quiet place in the tabernacle where she could be on her own and pray to God. She knew that God would understand how she felt, so Hannah told God everything. She asked him to help her in this difficult situation and to give her a baby boy. She promised that she would give the child back to God to work for him for the rest of his life.

Eli
Eli, the high priest, was watching Hannah in the tabernacle. He saw Hannah's lips move but did not hear any words. He thought she must be drunk, and was just mumbling to herself. He told her off, telling her to go and no longer touch the wine which she had been drinking. But Hannah explained to Eli how she had been telling God all about her troubles in prayer. Eli said, "Go in peace and may God give you what you have asked." Hannah returned home feeling happy and peaceful, believing that God had heard her prayer and would give her what was best.

Samuel Is Born
A few months later Hannah had a baby boy. How happy she was now! She called him Samuel (which means 'heard by God'). She sang a wonderful song of praise to God. God had been so kind in answering Hannah's prayer and she wanted to thank him. Later on Hannah had many more children.

Hannah Keeps Her Promise
When Samuel was old enough to look after himself Hannah took him back to the tabernacle in Shiloh. She kept her promise to give Samuel to God, to work for him. Hannah said to Eli the high priest, "For this child I prayed and the Lord has granted me what I asked him for."

Although Samuel was still young, he was a great help to Eli doing small jobs in the tabernacle. He was happy serving God in this way. Every year Hannah visited Samuel and took him a new little coat that she had made especially for him.

God Calls Samuel
One night when Eli and Samuel had gone to bed in the tabernacle a wonderful thing happened. It was dark, apart from the low flickering of the lamps in the tabernacle. God

came to Samuel and called out his name. The boy woke up and ran quickly to Eli thinking that he had called him. Samuel said, "Here I am, you called for me." Samuel was an obedient and willing child who wanted to do whatever Eli wanted. Eli said, "I didn't call for you. Go and lie down again."

A second time God called Samuel's name and again he got up and went to Eli. Once more Eli told him to go back to bed.

God then called Samuel for the third time, "Samuel, Samuel", and again he went to Eli and said, "Here I am, for you did call me". Then Eli realised that it was God who was calling Samuel. So he said, "Go and lie down again and when God calls you this time say, 'Speak Lord, for your servant is listening' ".

God Calls Again
So Samuel went back to bed and waited to hear his name again. Again God called Samuel's name. Samuel said, "Speak Lord, your servant is listening." Samuel was ready to listen carefully to every word that God said to him.

It was bad news that God told Samuel. He said that, because Eli's sons had done many bad things when working for their father at the tabernacle, he was now going to punish them.

The Next Day
Samuel was too afraid to go and tell Eli the bad news, so he lay quietly in bed until the morning. When it was light Samuel got up and opened the doors of the tabernacle, as usual. Eli then wanted to know what message God had given Samuel. Samuel told Eli that God had said he would punish his sons for all the wicked things they had been doing. Eli knew that his sons deserved to die and said, "Let God do what seems good to him."

Soon after this God's word to Samuel came true and Eli's sons died in battle.

Samuel As A Man
Samuel grew up and became a great leader of the Israelites. The Bible tells us that God was with Samuel and spoke through him to the people - he was a prophet.

Christians Today
Like Hannah, Christians pray to God and tell him about their troubles and needs and ask him for his help. They also give thanks to him for all that he gives them and does for them, just like Hannah did, when she was given Samuel. Christians also believe that God speaks to them and shows them how they should live in the Bible. Like Samuel they want to obey God.

Illustration: A Young Christian King
King Edward VI was the son of Henry VIII. His father insisted that the young Edward should be taught by Christian teachers who loved the Bible. As a result , by the time he became King at the age of nine he was a convinced Christian.

As a young boy Edward, like Samuel, wanted to   obey God. He only ruled England for six years, dying at the age of fifteen. However the boy king did all he could to help

Christians in his own country and encouraged the reading of the Bible. He established several schools and hospitals for the poor.

Things To Learn:
- When she was upset Hannah told God everything in prayer.
- God answered her prayer and gave her Samuel.
- When God spoke to Samuel he was ready to listen and obey.
- Christians pray to God and obey what God tells them in the Bible.

Discuss
- Is it important to listen to parents/teachers/friends? Why?
- How does God tell us what he wants us to do?
- Can we pray at any time and anywhere?
- Can we pray to God about our troubles?

Samuel Listens to God

Elkanah and his wife Hannah had no children. This made Hannah very unhappy.

Every year Elkanah and Hannah went to Shiloh to worship God in the temple. One year, when they were in Shiloh, Hannah was very unhappy. She cried and cried and would not eat any food. She went quietly to the temple to pray to God. She knew God would understand, so she told him everything. Hannah asked God for a baby boy and promised that he would work for God in the temple.

Eli, the priest in the temple, watched Hannah praying. He asked her what she was doing, and Hannah told him that she was praying to God. Hannah went home feeling much happier.

A few months later, Hannah had a baby boy. She called him Samuel. She rejoiced and thanked God for hearing her prayers.

When Samuel was older, Hannah kept her promise to God and took him to the temple. Samuel worked with Eli the priest doing jobs in the temple. Every year Hannah visited Samuel and brought him a new coat that she had made.

One night when Samuel and Eli were in bed, Samuel heard someone calling his name. He thought it must be Eli calling him, so he went to Eli and asked him what he wanted. Eli said that he had not called him. Samuel went back to bed. Again he heard a voice calling his name, "Samuel, Samuel". Samuel went to Eli again. Eli said that he hadn't called him and told him to go back to bed.

When Samuel heard the voice a third time, he went to Eli again. Eli realised then that it was God speaking to Samuel in a special way. He told Samuel, "Go and lie down again and when God calls you this time say, 'Speak Lord, for your servant is listening'". Samuel did as Eli had told him. When he heard God's voice, Samuel said, "Speak Lord, for your servant is listening". Samuel listened carefully to what God told him. The next morning Samuel told Eli what God had said. It was sad news for Eli. His two bad sons would soon be dead.

Samuel grew up to be a great leader of the Israelites. He was a prophet which means that he was God's messenger.

SAMUEL LISTENS TO GOD

Go through the maze to find out what
Hannah told Eli the priest.

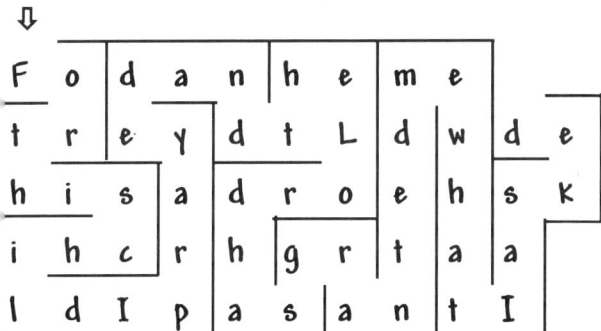

⇩

F	o	d	a	n	h	e	m	e	
t	r	e	y	d	t	L	d	w	d	e
h	i	s	a	d	r	o	e	h	s	k
i	h	c	r	h	g	r	t	a	a
l	d	I	p	a	s	a	n	t	I

Fit these words in to the crossword.

Eli	night	Lord	Samuel
old	voice	name	wicked
bed	speak	morning	asleep
die	hears	listen	servant

_ _ _   _ _ _ _   _ _ _ _ _   _ _   _ _ _ _ _
_ _ _   _ _ _   _ _ _ _   _ _ _   _ _ _ _ _ _
_ _   _ _ _ _   _   _ _ _ _ _ .

Sam.ch.1v27

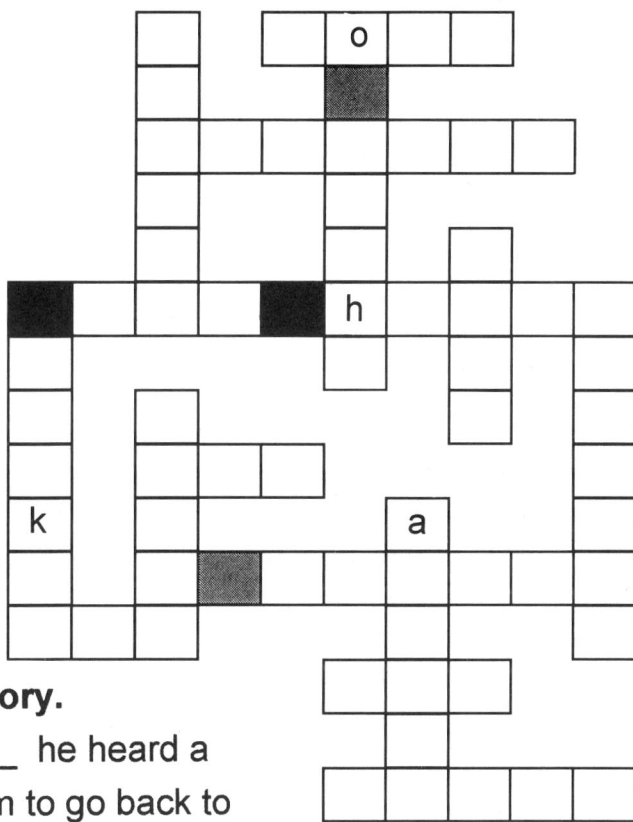

Now use the words to help you with the story.

One_____ when _____ was _____ he heard a
_____ calling his _____. _____ told him to go back to
_____ and _____, then to say, "_____ _____ for your _____ _____ .
In the _____ Samuel told Eli the message that God had given him.

CcGxconxdcnccnnxsx
npecxaxcknnscc xntno
ccux xsn ncfrxconm
ctxnhnecc Bxxinbnlen.

How does God speak to us today ?
Cross out all the letters 'c', 'x' and 'n'
to find the answer. Write it below.

....

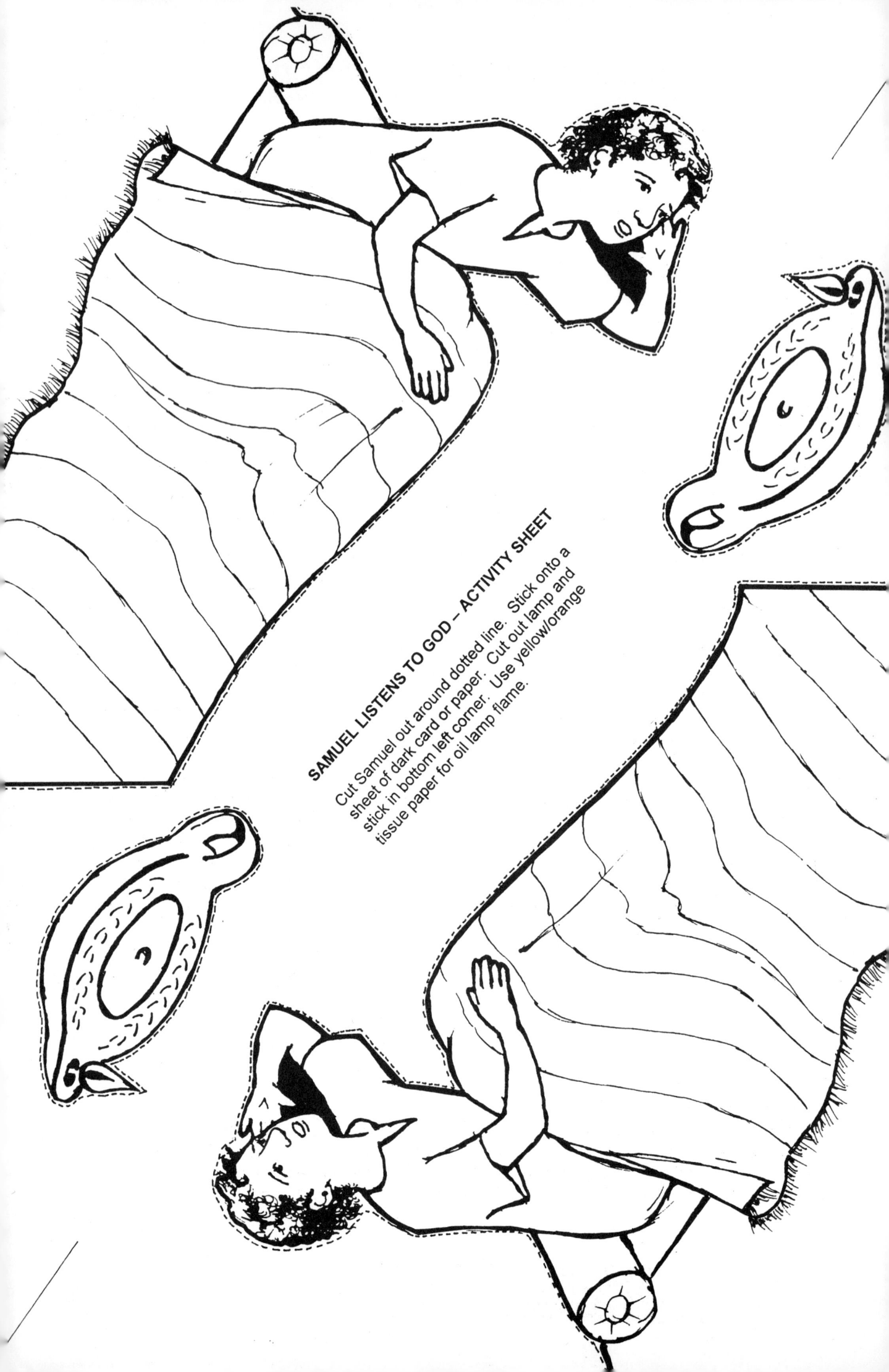

SAMUEL LISTENS TO GOD – ACTIVITY SHEET

Cut Samuel out around dotted line. Stick onto a sheet of dark card or paper. Cut out lamp and stick in bottom left corner. Use yellow/orange tissue paper for oil lamp flame.

David & Goliath

1 Samuel 16 & 17

Themes	Danger, Trust, Bravery

Aims	To teach the story of David and Goliath. To show how God helps those who trust Him.

Resources	Bibles, Children's Story Sheet, Puzzle Page, Activity Sheet.

Other Ideas & Activities
1. Activity Sheet – make sling with 20 cm string; glue to hand; draw in 5 stones.
2. Read Psalm 23. What did David say about who God was and what he did for him? Learn the psalm or a few of its verses. As a class sing the psalm (The metrical and other equivalent versions are found in nearly all hymn books)
3. Find out more about shepherds in Biblical times and today.
4. Look at the psalms in the Bible. Choose a short one, or part of one, and read it to the whole class.
5. Look at and discuss pictures of military armour through the centuries.
6. In groups compare David and Goliath; their size, their clothing and their attitude to their fight. Share and discuss your ideas.

Teacher's Notes

Summary: David was a shepherd boy who learned to trust God in the face of danger from wild animals. David trusted God to help him in the battle with Goliath. David had been chosen by God to be the future King of Israel. God does not change his plans or his mind so David knew that he would not die at the hand of Goliath. David was anointed king secretly, but it was a long time before he came to the throne. He had many dangers and troubles to face but through it all his trust in God never failed. Christians trust in God and believe he can help them when in trouble.

Point of Contact
Facing Danger
- What you would do if you found yourself suddenly in danger?
- Imagine that you saw a wild animal that had escaped from a zoo prowling round your garden. What would you do?

David the Shepherd
David was the youngest of eight brothers. His father's name was Jesse and the family lived in Bethlehem. David's job was to look after his father's flocks of sheep. He was a good shepherd and took great care of the sheep. He would find them fresh grass and water and watch out for any danger there might be around. Lions and bears roamed in

the countryside where David lived. More than once David had rescued lambs from the mouths of these animals. He trusted in God to help him and was able to attack the lion or bear and pull the lamb from its jaws. If the wild beast turned on David he killed it with a blow from his shepherd's staff.

The Music Maker
David was not only a shepherd; he was a musician and a poet as well. He played the harp and wrote many psalms which people still sing today. The most well known is probably the twenty third psalm in which David speaks of God as being his shepherd.

The Future King
One day Samuel, a prophet (God's Messenger), visited Jesse's home in Bethlehem. He had come to choose one of Jesse's sons to be king. The present king, Saul, had disobeyed God on several occasions and made God angry. He was no longer fit to be king.

Jesse's eldest son was tall and good looking and Samuel thought that he looked like a king. But God said, "No". He said, "People look on the outward appearance, but God looks on the heart." Jesse showed Samuel each of his sons, but each time God told Samuel that this was not the next king of Israel. Finally David, the youngest of Jesse's eight sons, was brought to Samuel and chosen and appointed to be the next king. Although David was good looking, with rosy cheeks and bright eyes, the Lord did not choose him for his looks, but because he had a good heart. David loved and trusted God.

Goliath's Challenge
David's three eldest brothers had joined King Saul's army and were away from home fighting the Philistines. Jesse gave David some food to take to his brothers and asked him to find out how they were getting on. So David left the sheep with a keeper and went off to the army camp. When David arrived the Israelites and the Philistines were facing each other across a valley, preparing for battle.

David found his brothers and as they were talking an enormous Philistine giant called Goliath, came towards the Israelites. He was wearing heavy armour from head to foot and carried a sword and shield. Goliath shouted across the valley, "Choose a man from your side to come and fight me. I challenge the God of your army. If you kill me, we will be your servants and if I kill him you will be my servants."

For forty days, Goliath had appeared every morning and evening and had made the same challenge. When the Israelites heard the roar of his voice they were terrified. No one was brave enough to fight him.

David Decides
David was angry that Goliath was not only challenging the Israelite army, but was also challenging God. David spoke to some of the Israelite soldiers. He said that he was prepared to trust God and go and fight the Goliath.

When King Saul heard of David's offer, he ordered that David should be brought to him. David told him, "I will go and fight this Philistine." The king told David that he was too young, but David explained how he had fought with lions and bears, when they took his sheep, and how God had helped him to kill them. He said, "If the Lord kept me safe from the lion and the bear, he will keep me safe against Goliath the Philistine."

Out To Meet Goliath

The king told David that he could wear his armour, but David refused, as it was much too heavy for him and he was not used to wearing it. Instead, David took his staff in his hand and went to the stream in the bottom of the valley. here he chose five smooth stones which he put into his shepherd's bag. With his sling ready in his hand he went to meet the giant Philistine.

Goliath challenged David and said, "Come to me and I will give your body to be eaten by the birds of the air and the beasts of the field." He was so sure of his own strength he was convinced that he was going to kill David.

David replied. " I come to you in the name of God. The God of the armies of Israel, whom you have challenged. This day the Lord will deliver you into my hand .... that all the earth may know that there is a God in Israel."

Victory!

David took one of the five stones from the bag and put it in his sling. He swung the sling round and round. The stone flew out and with an extremely accurate shot, hit Goliath in the forehead and he fell to the ground. Quickly David ran up to Goliath, took his sword and cut off his head. When the Philistine army saw that their champion was dead they all fled in fear. What a tremendous victory for the Israelite army. They had won the battle and David the shepherd boy, was the hero.

David had been chosen as king by Samuel. It was a long time before he came to the throne. He had many dangers and troubles to face but through it all he trusted in God, and God never failed him.

Illustration: God's Protection

Early in the last century a man, named James Fraser, went to China to be a missionary. Life was not easy for him there and he was often in danger. He was captured by bandits and robbed, he was threatened by thieves and burglars at night. He was shot at and once nearly drowned in quicksand.

In all this God preserved James' life. One day he went to preach to some people. These men and women lived by hunting. They did not want to hear about Jesus! They were angered by the message James brought them.

One of the men, sword in hand, chased after James, wanting to kill him. James ran as fast as he could and as he ran, he prayed. At last he reached a friendly village and he slowed down and looked back. The angry tribesman had stopped his pursuit and was going back to his tribe. Once again God had preserved the missionary's life. Like David, James trusted in God and God helped him.

Things to Learn:

- David killed the Philistine giant Goliath by using a stone from his sling.
- He was able to do this because he trusted in God.
- David wrote psalms about trusting in God.
- The Bible says that we can pray to God and ask him to help us.

- Christians read psalms and find them a help in times of trouble.

Discuss
- Why did Goliath feel brave?
- Why did David feel brave?
- Can we ask God to help us when we face something which is difficult?
- If we read the psalms in the Bible, can they help us?

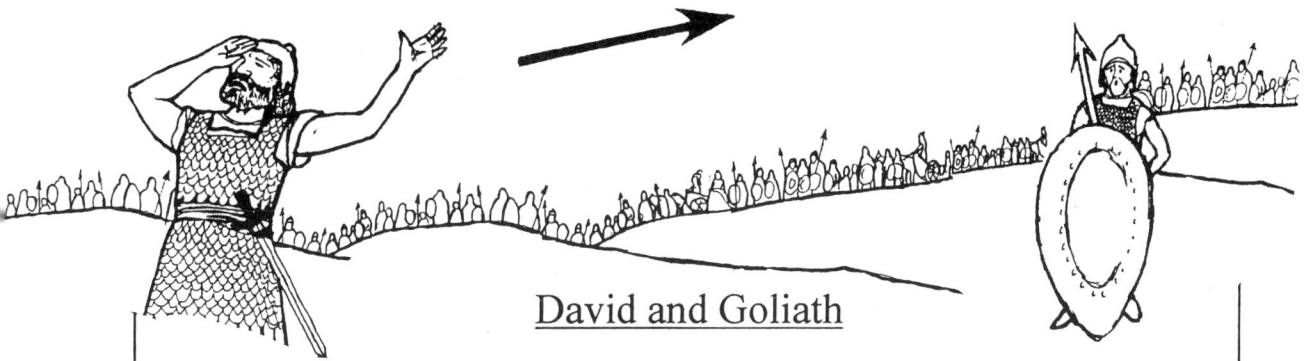

David and Goliath

David was the youngest of eight brothers. He looked after his father's sheep. Sometimes a lion or a bear would try to take one of the lambs from the flock. God helped David to rescue the lambs and to kill the lion and the bear.

David's three oldest brothers were in the army. One day, Jesse, his father told David to take some food to his brothers and to find out how they were getting on. David found someone to look after the sheep for him and went to the army camp.

The Israelite soldiers were ready for battle against their enemies, the Philistines. David found his brothers and was talking to them when a Philistine giant, named Goliath, shouted across to the Israelites. "Choose someone to come and fight me," he said, "If he wins, we will be your servants, but if I win, you will be our servants." The Israelites were afraid.

David was angry with Goliath for saying this. The king heard about David and sent for him. "I will fight this giant," said David.

The king thought that David was too young but David told him how God had helped him to kill both lions and bears. The king then agreed to let David fight the giant.

Goliath was wearing heavy armour and a helmet; he had a spear, a sword and a shield. David had his shepherd's crook and his sling. He chose five smooth stones from the nearby stream, and went to meet Goliath.

Goliath shouted his challenge to David. David said, "I come to you in the name of God." Then he put one of the stones in his sling and spun it round and round. The stone flew out and hit Goliath in the middle of his forehead and he fell on his face to the ground. When the Philistines saw that their champion soldier was dead they ran away.

Name .... Date ....

DAVID AND GOLIATH

Join the word bubbles to the correct person.

Take some food for your brothers.

You are too young to fight.

God helped me to kill a lion and a bear.

I will fight this giant.

Saul

David

Goliath

Jesse

Choose someone to come and fight me.

I come to you in the name of God.

I am a shepherd

I am a king

I am a father

I am a Philistine

Take the letter in the alphabet that comes *before* each letter and write out verse.

u s v t u j o u i f M p s e

_ _ _ _ _   _ _   _ _ _

_ _ _ _   _ _ _ _   _ _ _

_ _ _ _   _ _ _ _ _ .

Proverbs 3:5

x
j

u i b m m z p v s i f z q s

Goliath trusted his

_ _ _ _ _ _ _ _ .

David trusted in

_ _ _ .

God helped
David to kill
Goliath.
1 Sam. ch.17

David – The Man Who Loved His Enemy

1 Samuel 18 - 20, 24, 31 & 2 Samuel 2

Themes	Jealousy, Loving Your Enemies

Aims	To relate the Bible's account of how David was persecuted by Saul before he became king. To teach that we should have a loving attitude toward those who hate us.

Resources	Bibles, Children's Story Sheet, Puzzle Page, Activity Sheet.

Other Ideas & Activities

1. Activity Sheet needs plain material 9 x 4 cm.
2. Taking the text Matthew 5 verse 44, "Love your enemies...." write a story about a situation where someone showed a loving attitude to a person who was unkind to them.
3. Look at Psalm 18. When was it written? (The clue is in the psalm heading.) What did David trust in? What was he going to do?
4. Jonathan was David's best friend. Write down what makes someone a best friend.
5. Make a text card. Write out "Do good to those who hate you" on a card in 'open' letters and colour in.
6. Listen to some harp music - how does it make you feel?
7. In groups, compose a short piece of soothing music. Perform to the rest of the class and discuss.

Teacher's Notes

Summary: David won many victories over Israel's enemies and became very popular. King Saul hated him for this and wanted to kill him. For many years he hunted David, but never caught him. During this time David trusted in God, and also showed his enemy, Saul, great kindness. After Saul's death he became the greatest king Israel has ever had. The Bible says we should love our enemies. Jesus is the greatest example of someone being kind to those who treat us badly. He prayed for those who crucified him and asked God to forgive them.

Point of Contact
Popularity
- What things make a person popular?
- What things can make a person unpopular?
- Do you like to be popular?

For the background to this lesson see "David & Goliath"

David The Hero
David was a very popular man. The people thought that it was wonderful that he had killed Goliath, the champion of the Philistine army. The people praised David for giving

them the victory over their enemy.

David Honoured
David was made a captain in King Saul's army. David fought another battle, and again he was victorious. As he returned home the Israelite women went out to meet David and his soldiers. They were singing, dancing and playing musical instruments. They sang a song which said that King Saul was a good soldier, but David was ten times better than Saul!

Saul's Hatred
When King Saul heard the women praising David he became very jealous. He knew that David was good and wise and that the people thought highly of him. Saul couldn't stand to see him so popular. He was afraid that the people would prefer David to be their king instead of him! Now Saul's one aim was to kill David.

Attempted Murder
Saul had times where he was very bad tempered and moody. David could play the harp, so he was asked to play when King Saul was depressed. The music helped to soothe Saul and made him feel better. One day when Saul was in a particularly angry mood, David was asked to play for him. Suddenly in a fit of temper, King Saul threw a spear straight at David, intending to kill him. David dodged the spear and quickly escaped from Saul's presence and from the palace.

Escape!
David was married to Michal, King Saul's daughter. When David returned home, and told her what Saul had done, she was worried. "You must run away, before my father kills you," she said. That night she let David down from an upstairs window, by a rope and David escaped. To give David more time, Michal put a pretend body in the bed and told Saul's men that David was ill. Saul was very angry when he discovered David had escaped.

A Friend's Encouragement
Even though Jonathan was Saul's son, he became David's best friend. He was kind to David. David and Jonathan met in secret when David was hiding from Saul. Jonathan encouraged David to trust in God to help him and look after him.

On The Run
Saul was determined to be rid of David. So it wasn't long before he sent his soldiers to search for him. David hid in the woods and mountains. He was always changing his hiding place so as not to be caught and killed.

One day, when David and his men were hiding in a large cave, they saw Saul walk through the entrance. They hid in the darkness and watched as Saul stood in the cool of the cave and then lay down and went to sleep. David's men tried to persuade him to kill Saul. They said that surely here was a golden opportunity to get rid of the man who wanted to kill him. But David refused. He said it would be wrong to kill the man who God had made king. David knew that God would not want him to take revenge in this way.

David's Kindness
David quietly crept up as Saul slept, and cut off the corner of his robe. A little later Saul

got up and left the cave, David followed him at a distance. He then called out to Saul, "Saul, this day I have spared your life. Look I have the corner of your robe in my hand. I could have killed you but I did not. Can't you see, Saul, that you have nothing to fear from me? Why do you try to kill me?"

Saul replied, "Yes David, you are right. You have shown kindness to me, whereas I have shown you nothing but evil. May God reward you for the kindness you have shown to me this day."

After this David and Saul went their separate ways. However, though Saul appeared sorry, it wasn't long before he was once again hunting David in order to kill him. Also on a second occasion David let Saul go free, when he could have killed him (see 1 Sam. 26). However, David knew that Saul could not be trusted, and that he would always want to kill him.

David had to spend many years on the run, in order to escape from Saul.

David's Faith
Throughout this difficult time, David did not become bitter or resentful. He trusted God and so he remained kind and patient. David would often pour out his troubles to God in prayer. David knew a deep sense of peace, because he knew that if he trusted in God, God would keep him safe and not let him down. David's prayers often ended up with him praising and thanking God for his kindness in looking after him.

David wrote down and kept many of these prayers, and we can read them today in the Bible, in the Old Testament book called the Psalms. These Psalms of David tells us how David felt during these times. (For one example see Psalm 18.)

The King Is Dead!
During another battle with the Philistines, David's best friend Jonathan was killed. King Saul was also wounded and later died. Despite Saul's unkind treatment of David, he was deeply upset and grieved to hear that the King was dead.

David Is King
There was great rejoicing that now at last David could take his rightful place as king. David showed Saul's family great kindness. When he discovered that Saul had a disabled son, he invited him to live in his palace as one of his family.

David was the best king Israel ever had. He loved God and cared for all the people in his kingdom. He ruled over the land for 40 years.

A Great Example
During all the time when Saul treated David so badly, David did not retaliate or kill Saul when he could have done. He was patient and kind, even with his enemy. The Bible says that we should love our enemies (Matthew 5:43,44). Christians ask God to help them to show kindness and love to those who treat them badly. The greatest example of someone loving their enemies, and being kind to those who hated them, is the Lord Jesus Christ. He prayed for those who crucified him (Luke 23:34) and asked God to forgive them.

Illustration: Overcoming Evil With Good - A True Story

Aeneas Sage became the first minister of the highland village of Locharron in Scotland in the spring of 1726. The villagers did not like the thought of a man coming to tell them about what the Bible said, and about Jesus Christ. The only accommodation they were offered was a barn whose walls were made of wickerwork. The wind could pass through very easily and make their home very cold. However, the family made the best of it and settled down to sleep.

That night a man left his home in the village and went to the barn, carrying a lighted flame. He stepped very carefully towards the wall of the barn, making no sound. He then held the torch to the side of the barn. In no time the barn wall was alight. Quickly he moved along and held the flame to another part of the barn, and then another. Soon the whole building was alight!

Inside the barn Aeneas and his family were now awake. He leapt to the door just in time to glimpse someone throwing away the flaming torch and running off into the dark. Aeneas gave chase . The villager ran for home, but before he could a mighty hand took hold of him from behind. Aeneas was a very strong man, with a powerful grip!

Mr Sage put his captive down in the centre of the barn floor and asked:
'Did you set the barn on fire?'
'Yes.'
'Why did you do it?'
'To get rid of you, the new minister. But now I am in your hands, and you can take revenge.'
'We'll take revenge all right,' said Mr Sage. 'But you watch how we do it.'

Food and drink were put before the frightened man and Aeneas prayed thanking God for it and asking that God would bless it to the man. The man had expected a beating, but instead he got a good meal. He was very hungry, so he ate the meal up gladly. Soon word went round the whole village. In time Aeneas Sage had a great effect upon the people of the area, who came to love and respect their minister. They realised that here was a Christian, who though he was stronger than them all, preferred to show good in return for evil.

(* The story of Aeneas Sage is found in "They Shall Be Mine" by John Tallach, published by The Banner of Truth Trust, ISBN 0 85151 320 4 - available from most Christian Bookshops.)

Things to Learn:
- David had a loving attitude towards King Saul, even though Saul was trying to murder him.
- The Bible says that we should love our enemies.
- Jesus is the best example. Though he had done no wrong, he was crucified. Even then he prayed for those who treated him so cruelly.
- Christians ask God to help them to be kind to those who treat them badly.

Discuss
- Do you think David was right to have a kind attitude towards Saul?
- What do you do when someone is unkind to you? How do you feel?
- Is it easy to be kind to someone who has treated you badly?
- Should we ever tell on those who are cruel to us?

David – The Man Who Loved His Enemy

King Saul was jealous of David. The people began to say that David was a better soldier than the king. Saul did not like this and he began to think of a way to kill David.

King Saul often became bad-tempered. At these times he would ask David to play his harp which made him feel better. One day, when Saul was feeling very angry, he asked David to play for him. As David was playing his harp, Saul suddenly picked up a spear and threw it straight at David. David dodged the spear and quickly escaped from the palace.

David went home and told his wife what had happened. She told him that he must run away immediately before the king killed him. So that night she let David down from an upstairs window with a rope and David ran from the city. She put a pretend body into David's bed and told Saul's men that David was ill. When Saul and his men discovered that David had actually escaped, he was very angry.

Saul was now even more determined to kill David. He sent his men to search for him. David hid from the soldiers in the woods and mountains.

One day, when David and his men were hiding in a large, dark cave, they saw Saul come into the front of the cave and lie down to rest. As they watched, David's men tried to persuade him to kill Saul. But David said that he would not kill Saul. He knew that God wanted him to love his enemies.

Instead, David quietly crept up to Saul and cut off a corner of his robe. When Saul woke up and left the cave, David followed him at a distance and called out to him, "Look, I have the corner of your robe in my hand. I could have killed you today, but I did not. Why are you trying to kill me?". Saul called back to David and said that David had shown kindness to him, even though Saul had been trying to kill him.

However, Saul continued to hunt David to kill him. During this time David was patient and trusted God. When Saul died, David was deeply upset, even though Saul had treated him so badly. Soon after this David became king of Israel. He was a good king and cared for his people.

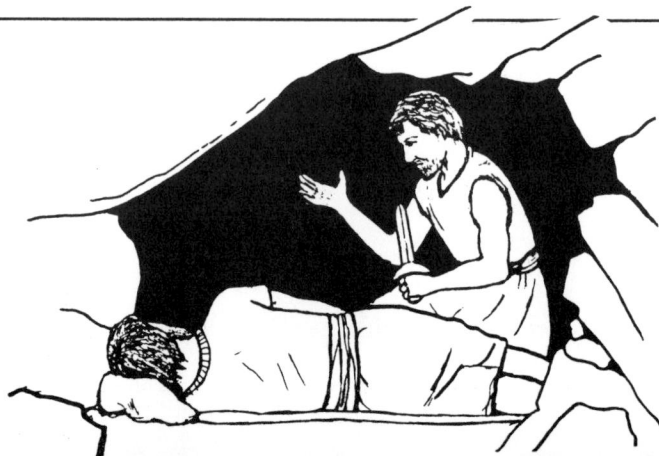

Name .... Date ....

DAVID - THE MAN WHO LOVED HIS ENEMY

Fill in the missing words.

Saul was j __ __ __ __ __ __ and wanted to kill David. David's wife helped him to e __ __ __ __ __ __. She pretended D __ __ __ __ was in the b __ __. Saul was a __ __ __ __ when he found David was not there. David hid from Saul in c __ __ __ __, forests and mountains. Once when David was in a cave Saul came in and went to s __ __ __ __. David crept up and c __ __ off a piece of Saul's r __ __ __.

Now find the words in the grid.　　　　　　**Colour the shapes with a dot in.**

```
p c u t z h j
e p a c s e d
e k x v a i a
l b v l e n v
s k o m g s i
w u q r q b d
s d y g b e d
```

What does this tell us about David?..

Write down the first letter of each object. ## Jesus said.....

— — __ — — — __ — — — — — — — —

— — — — — — — — — — __. Matthew ch.5 v 44

Give an example of how you can be kind to someone who is unkind to you.

....

....

....

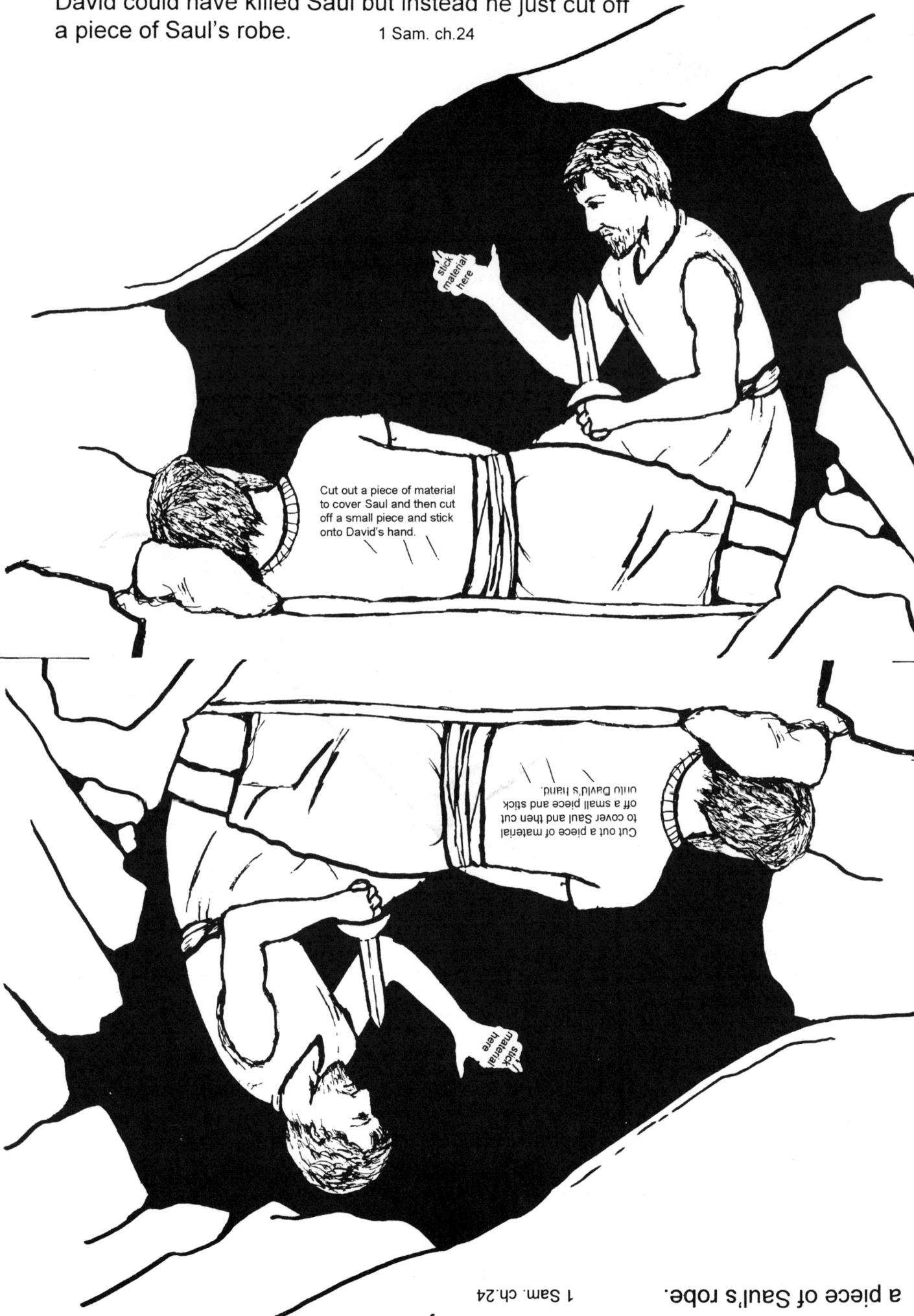

David could have killed Saul but instead he just cut off
a piece of Saul's robe.   1 Sam. ch.24

Cut out a piece of material
to cover Saul and then cut
off a small piece and stick
onto David's hand.

Solomon - The Wise King

1Kings 1 - 10, Proverbs, Ecclesiastes, Song of Solomon

Themes	Riches, Wisdom, Putting God First

Aims	To describe the wealth and wisdom of King Solomon. To reflect on the importance of wisdom. To show where wisdom can be found.

Resources	Bibles, Children's Story Sheet, Puzzle Page, Activity Sheets.

Other Ideas & Activities

1. Activity Sheets – photocopy babies on light pink/buff paper; needs tin foil 2 x 5 cm.
2. Research the furniture and arrangement of the temple. A display could be done, showing the temple and its various parts, incorporating drawings and writing. (A helpful resource here is 'The Student Bible Guide', published by Candle Books, pages 12 & 13, ISBN 0 948902 56 6 available from most Christian Bookshops.)
3. Proverbs: Wisdom to live by. Look at some of the proverbs in the book of Proverbs. In pairs choose a proverb (or teacher select some to do e.g. 1:5; 3:27,28; 6:6-11; 12:11; 12:18; 15:1; 16:18; 22:2; 22:24,25). Write a story to try and illustrate its wisdom. Share/discuss. *(A helpful resource here is 'Signposts from Proverbs' by Rhiannon Weber, published by The Banner of Truth Trust, ISBN 0 85151 517 7 available from most Christian Bookshops.)
4. Find proverbs to put under these headings: Money, laziness, work, pride, honesty, how to treat others, patience. See * above.
5. Ecclesiastes. Read chapter 3:1-8 - and discuss.
6. Look at how Solomon starts the book of Ecclesiastes in chapter 1 verses 2 -11. What conclusion does he come to at the end of the book - chapter 12 verses 13 & 14?
7. Listen to Zadok the Priest by Handel. (Zadok was one of Solomon's chief advisors and priests.) What does the music tell us about Solomon?

Teacher's Notes

Summary: When God asked Solomon what he would like he chose wisdom. God gave him wisdom and also great wealth. Solomon showed how great his wisdom was in dealing with two women who both claimed a baby as their own. Solomon built the temple and wrote several books of the Bible. His wisdom, power and wealth became known all over the world. The Bible says that Jesus is a greater king than Solomon.

Point of Contact
Choices
- If you could choose to have anything, what would it be?
- Why?
- Would it make you happy? Would it last?

Solomon's Choice

When King David died Solomon his son became King of Israel. One night God spoke to Solomon in a dream and said, "Ask what you like and I will give it to you". Solomon answered, "You have made me king instead of my father David, but I am still young and feel like a child. Please give me understanding so that I shall be wise and know how to give advice to others, as to what is good and what is bad, when they come and ask me to make decisions for them. Then I will be a good king, and do what is best for the people."

God was pleased with Solomon's request for wisdom rather than for riches, or long life or things for himself. He granted Solomon's request and gave him wisdom. He told Solomon that he would become the wisest man who ever lived.

But God said something else. "Not only have I given you what you asked for, I have also given you something you did not ask for. I have given you riches. You will also be the richest king that ever lived."

When Solomon woke up he knew that God had spoken to him and granted him his request. He thanked God and worshipped him.

Wisdom Tested

One day two women came to Solomon with a problem. They explained how they both lived in the same house. Both of them had recently given birth to a baby boy. One night one baby died, so his mother quietly swapped her dead baby for the living baby. When the other mother awoke in the morning she found a dead baby lying beside her. As she looked closely at the baby, she realised it was not hers, but belonged to the other woman.

Both women claimed that the living baby was theirs. It seemed like an impossible situation . How could Solomon possibly know which woman was lying and which woman was the true mother?

Wisdom Demonstrated

King Solomon listened to the two women and then said, "Bring me a sword". He continued, "Cut the living baby in two and give half to each mother." Of course, Solomon did not truly intend to kill the baby. He was testing the women to see who was the true mother.

When the real mother heard this she cried out, "No! Don't cut the baby in two, but give it to the other woman." As she was the real mother, she had a deep love for her baby and couldn't bear the thought of it being killed. She would prefer to see it given away, so long as it was not harmed. But the other woman didn't care and was quite happy for the baby to be cut in two.

Solomon could see from the women's responses who the true mother was. He declared, "Give the baby to the first woman. She is the mother."

News of what had happened with these two women, and the great wisdom Solomon had shown, soon spread around the country. The people could see that God had given Solomon great wisdom.

The Temple
Solomon wanted to build a temple where the people could worship God. For some 500 years, since the time that the Israelites were in the wilderness, the ark of God had been kept in a tent, called the tabernacle (see "The Tabernacle and Golden Calf"). Solomon knew that it was now time for God's ark to be put in a permanent building.

The temple was built on a hill in Jerusalem. It took thousands of men seven years to complete. Solomon was now a very wealthy king, so he did not have to worry about the enormous cost of building the temple. It was a magnificent building being beautifully decorated. Even the walls were covered with pure gold.

When it was complete, great crowds gathered for a special service of dedication. Solomon knelt down and prayed before the people asking God to bless the temple. As they were singing a wonderful light from heaven filled the building. God was showing his presence with them in the temple.

Books of the Bible
Solomon was a very knowledgeable man, who took great interest in all the plants and animals which lived around him in the land of Israel and beyond. He used his skills in writing about these and many other things. He wrote over 1,000 songs and 3,000 proverbs, or wise sayings. God used Solomon in another way. He helped him to write three books which have become part of the Bible. These are the books of Proverbs, Ecclesiastes and the Song of Solomon. The proverbs in the Bible are full of wisdom and instruction. People still use them today in everyday speech.

Solomon's Fame
Though he had not asked for riches, God blessed Solomon with them. He was now the richest man in the world. We know that Solomon built many exotic houses and gardens. He kept 40,000 horses, 12,000 horsemen and thousands of servants. He had an abundance of gold, silver, precious stones and valuable articles. He was so powerful that during his reign none of his enemies dared attack him. The land of Israel and the countries around about enjoyed a great time of peace.

The news of Solomon's wisdom and wealth, and the wonder of the temple which he had built, spread all over the world. A very wealthy lady, the Queen of Ethiopia, heard about Solomon and decided to come all the way to Jerusalem to visit him. She travelled several hundred miles. When she arrived she gave him gifts of gold, jewels and other precious things. She asked Solomon some difficult questions. With his wisdom, Solomon was able to answer them all. The Queen was amazed to see all Solomon's wealth and achievements and to learn of his remarkable understanding.

One Greater Than Solomon
When Jesus was on the earth he talked to some Jewish people about Solomon (Matthew 12:42). He spoke of his great wisdom and how Solomon was known throughout the whole world, and how the Queen of Ethiopia came to visit him. Yet he said a strange thing! He said that, "one greater than Solomon is here!" He was making it clear to these Jewish people, that though Solomon was a great man, one greater than Solomon was there with them now. The Bible says that Jesus is the greatest king who ever lived (Phil. 2:9-11; Rev. 19:16).

The Most Important Thing

Solomon teaches us that it is much more important to be a wise person, who takes the right decisions in life, than to be someone who enjoys lots of wealth and good things. That is why he chose wisdom before riches. Solomon tells us in one of his wise sayings that, "the fear of the Lord is the beginning of wisdom" (Proverbs 9:10). What Solomon is saying is that, if we have a respect for God and obey him, do what he tells us in the Bible and aim to please him, *then* we will be wise. God will show us what is best for us.

Illustration: Riches or Wisdom

Fred Charrington's father owned an enormous brewery in the East End of London, and many pubs throughout the country. His father was a multi-millionaire. Fred was expected to follow on in the family business. He too would inherit the vast wealth which had been built up.

Through the influence of a close friend, at the age of twenty, Fred became a Christian. He also became aware of the misery alcohol was causing in the slums and depressed areas of many cities in the country. Walking past one of his family's own pubs one night, he saw a starving woman outside with two poorly clothed children. She called in to her husband to give her some money to feed them. The husband came out and beat her and the children and then went back inside to carry on drinking.

Fred decided that he wanted nothing more to do with the brewing business. This caused great problems at home. His father was furious. He warned Fred that he would lose his income of £1,000 per week (perhaps close to £100,000 in today's money) and also his inheritance. Fred refused to be influenced by money.

Instead Fred involved himself in helping the poor and needy. He sought to tell others about Jesus. He started meetings in the Mile End district of London. Here he would preach from the Bible to all who came. Out of his own pocket, and through the contributions of others, he provided work for the unemployed, clothing and food for the destitute, and helped many others in distress. He continued this work for the rest of his life and had a marked effect on London's poorest districts.

Fred had turned his back on a life of wealth, ease and riches. Instead he put God first and served him. Do you think he was wise?

(* The story of 'Fred Charrington' can be found in "Men of Purpose" by P. Masters, published by the Wakeman Trust, ISBN 1 870855 04 3 - available from most Christian Bookshops)

Things to Learn:

- God was pleased that Solomon chose wisdom.
- He became a great king because God gave riches as well as wisdom.
- Solomon wrote Proverbs, Ecclesiasties and the Song of Solomon.
- Solomon tells us that, "the fear of the Lord is the beginning of wisdom."

Discuss

- What does it mean to be wise?
- Why did Solomon ask for wisdom and not riches or something for himself?
- How did Solomon use his wisdom?

Solomon – The Wise King

One day God said to King Solomon, "Ask what you like and I will give it to you". Solomon asked God to give him wisdom so that he would know how to help others and make wise decisions. God gave Solomon great riches as well as wisdom. Solomon thanked God for his wonderful gifts.

One day two women came to King Solomon. Both women had a baby boy and lived in the same house. That night, one of the babies had died. His mother quietly exchanged her dead baby for the living baby. Both women said that the living baby belonged to her.

Solomon listened to the two women and then said, "Bring me a sword. Cut the living baby in two and give half to each mother". When the real mother of the baby heard this, she cried out, "No! Don't cut the baby in two. Give it to the other woman". She did not want her baby to be killed, and preferred it to be given away. The other woman did not care about the baby and told Solomon to cut the baby in two. Solomon, of course, was just testing the two women and when he heard what they said, he ordered the baby to be given to the first woman, his real mother.

King Solomon built a temple in Jerusalem, where the people could worship God. It took seven years to build and was a beautiful building. The walls were covered in gold.

Solomon also loved the wildlife God had created, and spent a lot of time finding out more about plants and animals that lived in Israel. He wrote many books about the things he discovered. He wrote three books of the Bible - Proverbs, Ecclesiastes and the Song of Solomon. King Solomon also had many grand houses and gardens, horses, servants, gold and other valuable things.

News of King Solomon spread to other countries. One day the Queen of Ethiopia travelled many miles to visit Solomon in Jerusalem. When she arrived she gave him gifts and asked him many questions.

The Bible tells us that, although Solomon was a rich and wise man, Jesus was even greater than Solomon.

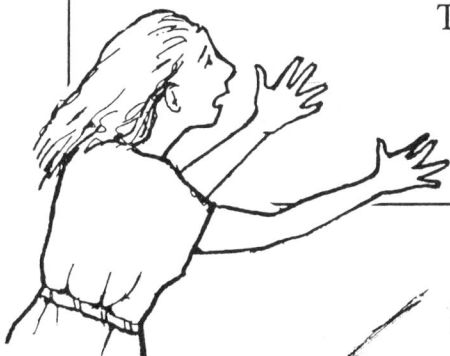

SOLOMON - THE WISE KING

Circle the correct answer.

1. Over which country was Solomon king? (a) Israel (b) Egypt (c) Spain
2. What did Solomon ask God for? (a) money (b) wisdom (c) children
3. What else did God give Solomon? (a) slaves (b) nothing (c) riches
4. Which queen came to visit him? Queen of.. (a) Syria (b) Ethiopia (c) Egypt
5. What did she ask Solomon? (a) for food (b) questions (c) for mone
6. How did she feel after the visit? (a) amazed (b) upset (c) disappoint

Answer these questions.

What were the two mothers arguing about?

....

....

Which mother said 'Don't kill the baby

....

What did this show everyone about Solomon?

....

....

If *a = 1 and Z = 26,*
crack the code to find out who is happy.   Proverbs ch.3 v 13

8 1 16 16 25   9 19   20 8 5   16 5 18 19 15 14

__ __ __ __ __   __ __   __ __ __   __ __ __ __ __ __

23 8 15   6 9 14 4 19   23 9 19 4 15 13.

__ __ __   __ __ __ __ __   __ __ __ __ __ __

What did Solomon build for God ?

p   m   e   T   e   l

Find the letters in the building and write them in the right order. __ __ __ __ __ __

King Solomon was very wise, he solved
a difficult problem. 1 Kings ch.3

Stick baby here.

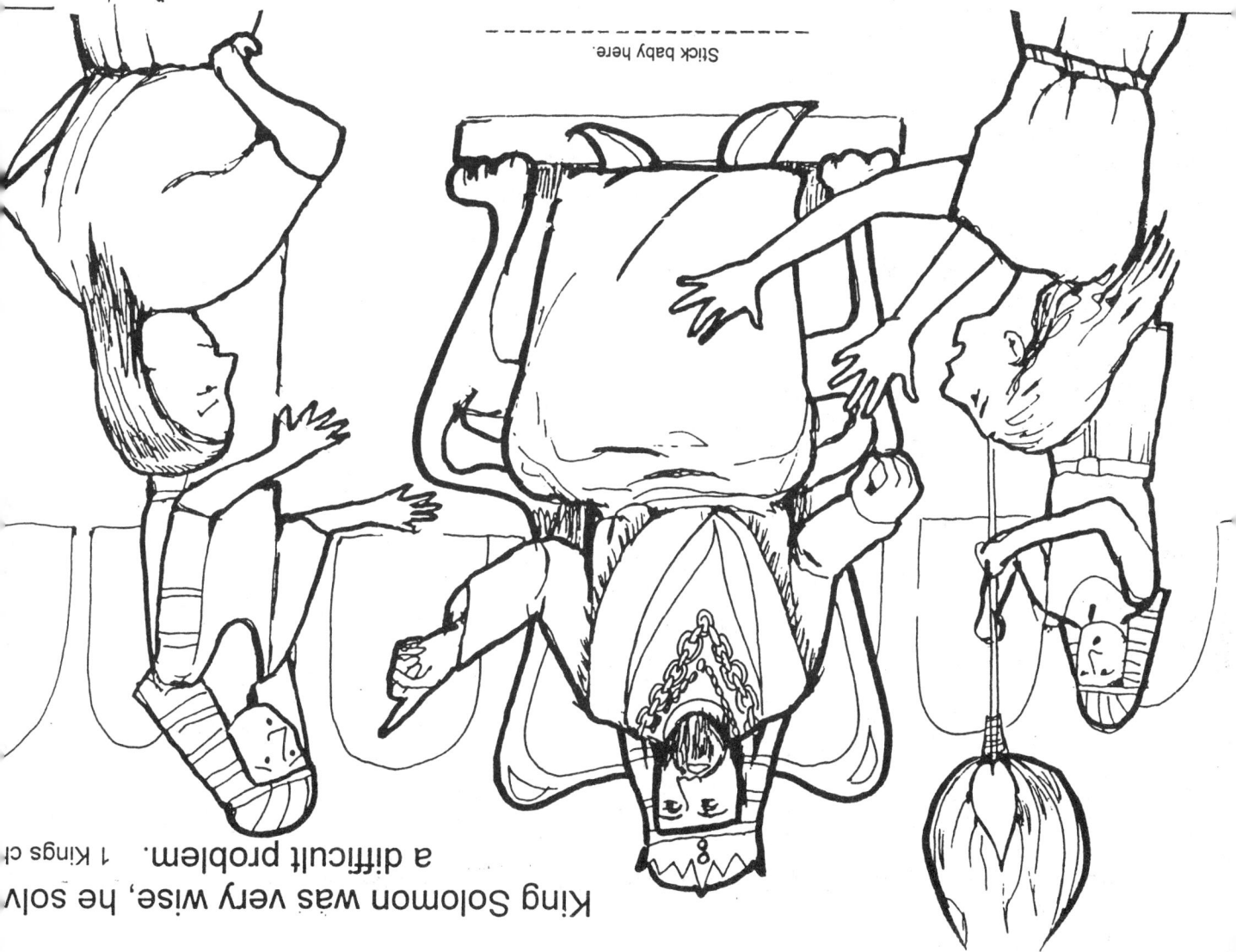

- -

- -

Stick baby here.

a difficult problem. 1 Kings ch
King Solomon was very wise, he solv

Cut out baby and stick where indicated on main picture. Using tin foil (2 x 5cm approx)
roll up to form a sword then glue or sellotape to servant's hands.

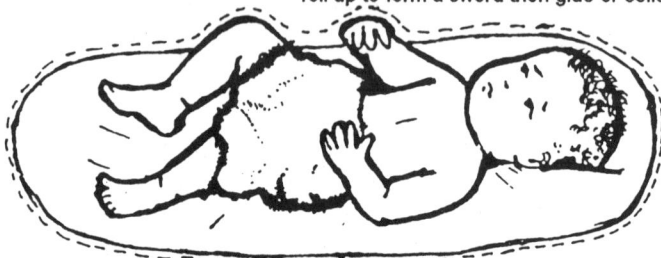

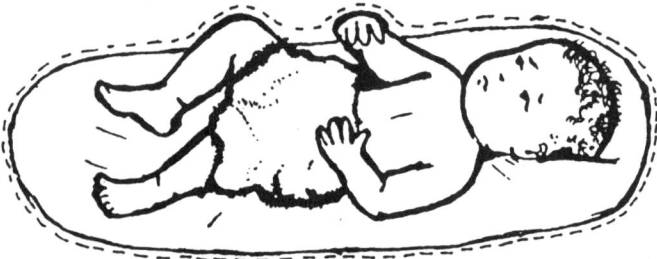

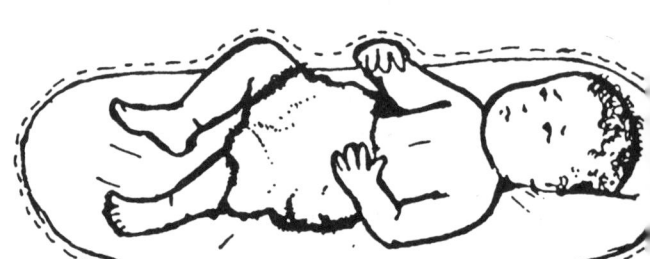

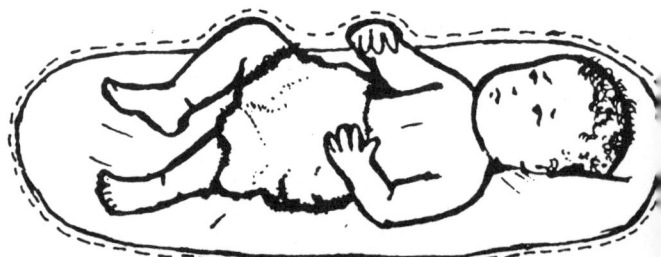

Jonah - Preacher On The Run

Jonah 1 - 4

Themes	God's Presence, God's Forgiveness

Aims	To teach the Biblical account of Jonah and the fish.
	To show that the Bible teaches that God is everywhere.
	To illustrate God's kindness and willingness to forgive.

Resources	Bibles, Children's Story Sheet, Puzzle Page, Activity Sheets, Map.

Other Ideas & Activities

1. Activity Sheets – preferably photocopy sea on blue/green paper.
2. Using a Bible Atlas, on a map of the Mediterranean, mark the places in the story - Joppa, Tarshish (Spain), Nineveh and Israel. Mark some other well known places and features such as Egypt, Greece, the Mediterranean Sea and the Nile. Draw arrows from Joppa to Tarshish and from Joppa to Nineveh and label one "the way Jonah went" and the other "the way he should have gone".
3. Under two headings, make a list of 'What Jonah Did' and 'What Jonah Should Have Done'.
4. Read Jonah chapter 1 and write out the story in your own words. Or: pretend you were a sailor on board Jonah's boat. Write what you saw and heard.
5. Read through Psalm 139 and list all the things it tells you about God.
6. Find out more about whales/large fish. Compile a table of data on average weight and length. Present this using a bar chart, if possible using the computer.
7. Write a story about someone who tried to hide or forget about something, but eventually, after many years, the truth was revealed!

Teacher's Notes

Summary: Jonah disobeyed God and refused to take God's message to the people of Nineveh. He boarded a ship going in the other direction to Tarshish (Spain). But Jonah couldn't run away from God, because God is everywhere. After a great storm Jonah ended up in the sea where a great fish swallowed him and took him back to dry land. Jonah went to Nineveh and preached to the people. When they heard that God was going to punish them for the bad things they had done they were sorry and asked for his forgiveness. The Bible says that God is a God who delights to show mercy and forgive those who are truly sorry (Numbers 14:18a).

Point of Contact
Hoping It Will Go Away
- If mum or dad asked you to do something you didn't want to do, what would you do?
- Have you ever gone into your bedroom and hoped mum/dad would forget?
- What happened?

Unwilling
Jonah was a prophet of God, who lived in the land of Israel. One day God said to him, "Go to the city of Nineveh and tell them that I have seen all the bad things they are doing and I will punish them."

Nineveh was the capital of Assyria. It was a very strong, powerful and rich city. The Assyrians were the Israelites' enemies and they were terrified of them. Jonah did not want to go to Nineveh and take God's message to the Assyrians.

The Wrong Way
So Jonah decided to run away from the work God was calling him to do. He went to Joppa, a port on the coast of Israel and boarded a ship for Tarshish (Spain), which was right across the other side of the Mediterranean Sea (show map). Instead of travelling 500 miles East to Nineveh he went in the opposite direction, intending to sail over 2000 miles West to Spain. Jonah thought he could run away from God, but he couldn't, because God is everywhere (Psalm 139: 7-12).

A Great Storm
After paying his fare Jonah went below deck and fell asleep, as the boat started its journey across the sea. It was not long before God sent a violent storm. The wind blew and the waves crashed over the ship. The sailors were afraid and thought that the ship was about to break up. So they threw cargo overboard to lighten the ship.

They began to cry out to their gods to save them. The sailors were superstitious and believed that the storm was sent to punish someone on board the ship. So they drew lots (like throwing a dice) to discover the trouble maker. The lot fell on Jonah. The captain woke Jonah up, and the sailors fired questions at him. "Tell us why this trouble has come? Who are you? Where are you from and what is it that you do?"

It's My Fault
Jonah replied, "I am an Israelite and I worship the God of heaven who made the sea and the dry land. This is my fault, because I am trying to run away from God."

They said, "What shall we do to you so that the sea will become calm again?"

"Take me and throw me overboard," Jonah said.

The sailors were very reluctant to do this, so they rowed hard to try and bring the ship safely to land, but the storm just grew worse. So asking for forgiveness from God they picked Jonah up and threw him overboard. Immediately the sea became perfectly calm, the wind died down and the waves became peaceful. The sailors were amazed and now believed that Jonah's God was the true God.

A Great Fish!
Jonah sank down into the sea. However, he did not drown because God had prepared a great fish (the Bible does not say a whale) to swallow him. For three days and three nights Jonah lived inside the fish. Here Jonah prayed to God for help and forgiveness. After three days God made the fish spit Jonah out onto dry land.

Go To Nineveh!
Again God spoke to Jonah telling him to go to the city of Nineveh and preach to the people. Jonah had another opportunity and this time he was ready to obey God. He travelled the long, hot and difficult journey to Nineveh. When he arrived he walked through the city preaching to the people, "Because of your wickedness, in forty days, Nineveh will be destroyed." The Ninevites were well known for their cruel and vicious deeds.

A Great Response
When the people heard this message they believed what God had said. The people showed they were sorry for the bad things they had been doing. They dressed themselves in sackcloth and cried out, asking God to have mercy on them, and not punish them as they deserved. Even the king took off his royal clothes, dressed in sackcloth, got down from his throne and sat in the dust. The king made a decree saying how all the people should stop doing the violent and bad things they had been doing and cry to God to have mercy on them.

God Forgives
When God saw how sorry the people were and how they had turned from their bad ways and wanted God's forgiveness, he said he would not punish them. Because of Jonah's message, the people's lives were changed and they began to serve the true God.

Jonah's Response
Jonah was upset. "This is just what I thought would happen," he told God. "I knew that you were a loving and kind God ready to show mercy and forgive." He still found it hard to see Israel's enemies being forgiven and blessed by God.

God Speaks
God showed Jonah how kind he was to him. He provided a lovely vine to shade Jonah as he sat in the sun. Eventually the lovely vine died. Jonah was angry that this lovely plant had withered.

God spoke to Jonah. "You are concerned about that little vine! Yet when I am concerned for the people of Nineveh, a great city with many people in it and many animals, you get upset. Should you really be angry Jonah?" God showed Jonah how selfish he was to be so concerned for a vine, and yet to show no concern for the people of Nineveh.

God Is A Merciful God
The Bible says that what God taught Jonah is one of the most important messages in the Bible. God is a God who delights to forgive people for the wrong things that they have done. If they are truly sorry, ask God to be merciful to them and believe on the Lord Jesus Christ, the Bible says that God is willing to forgive them (Psalm 130:4; Daniel 9:9; John 3:16).

Illustration: An Example of God's Willingness to Forgive
God gave David Brainerd a concern to go to the native Americans in New York State, America, and tell them about Jesus Christ. (This was 250 years ago when the area was very wild.)

These native Americans were very fierce and violent towards one another and other

155

neighbouring tribes. It was a terrifying experience to see them dressed for war. David watched them as they danced with their painted faces and feathered head dresses. They shrieked and yelled as they acted out what they would do to their enemies with their long spears. David feared for his life. The witch doctors held a powerful influence over the people. They made up magic potions for those who were ill, which often killed instead of curing the patient.

David spent many years in very harsh conditions, but he continued to tell the native Americans to turn to God and put their trust in Jesus. Eventually, however, he grew weak and then became very ill. However, he still persevered. He continued his work though the native Americans showed no interest in what he was telling them.

Then quite unexpectedly things began to change. The people began to listen to what David had to say. Within a very short space of time hundreds of people turned to God and became Christians. They had been extremely violent, but now they were peace loving and kind. One Sunday thousands of men, women and children came from the surrounding villages to hear David preach about Jesus.

The only way David could account for the dramatic change in their beliefs, behaviour and life was the power of God. These native Americans had come to see that they were doing many things which did not please God. They were sorry and asked to be forgiven. God did not refuse them.

Just as the people of Nineveh had turned from their evil ways, to believe Jonah's message, so these native Americans turned from their violent and warlike ways and became Christians. They too came to know that God is a merciful God who delights to forgive.

(* The story of David Brainerd is found in "God Made Them Great" by John Tallach, published by The Banner of Truth Trust, ISBN 0 85151 190 2 - available from most Christian Bookshops.)

Things to Learn
- Jonah was disobedient and ran away from God.
- But he couldn't do this because God is everywhere.
- He spent three days and nights in a large fish.
- Eventually he preached to the people of Nineveh, who responded to his message.
- God delights to forgive those who are truly sorry.

Discuss
- Why was Jonah reluctant to go to Nineveh?
- What does learning the hard way mean? How does this apply to Jonah?
- What lessons did Jonah learn about God?
- What does the story of Jonah tell us about God?

Jonah - Preacher On the Run

Jonah was God's prophet. One day God told him to go to the city of Nineveh. Nineveh was a rich and powerful city, but the people did not obey God.

Jonah did not want to go to Nineveh, so he decided to run away. He went to Joppa and got on a ship that was going to Tarshish. This was in completely the opposite direction to Nineveh! Jonah was trying to run away from God. He had forgotten that God is everywhere.

Jonah went to his cabin and fell asleep. The ship began its long journey. But it was not long before there was a great storm. The wind blew and the waves crashed over the side of the ship. The sailors were afraid and thought the ship was going to break. So they threw some heavy cargo overboard. They began to ask their gods to help them. The sailors thought that the storm must be sent to punish someone on the ship. So they drew lots and Jonah was chosen.

The sailors woke Jonah up and asked him questions. "Who are you? Where are you from? What do you do?" Jonah replied, "I am from Israel and I worship God who made heaven and earth. This storm is my fault because I am trying to run away from God."

Jonah told the sailors that if they threw him overboard, the sea would be calm again. The sailors did not really want to do this to Jonah, but the storm began to get worse. So they picked up Jonah and threw him into the sea. Immediately the wind stopped and the waves became calm. Jonah did not drown because God sent a large fish (like a whale) to swallow him. For three days and nights Jonah was inside this fish. Then the fish spat Jonah out on to dry land.

God spoke to Jonah again and told him to go to Nineveh. This time Jonah went and told the people about God. The people of Nineveh were sorry for all the bad things they had done and asked God to forgive them. When God saw how the people of Nineveh had changed, he forgave them.

Jonah was not pleased about this and complained to God. God explained that he did not want to punish the people of Nineveh. God loves to forgive those who are truly sorry.

JONAH AND THE FISH

Find out what happened on Jonah's two journeys.

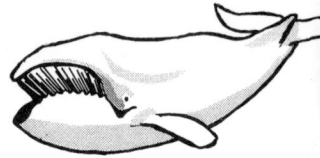

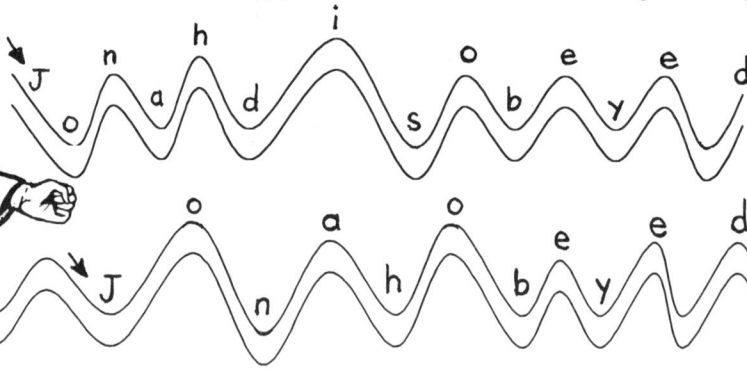

J o n a h d i s o b e y e d

God

J o n a h o b e y e d

Ninev

God

Fill in the verbs using the words in the fish below.

When Jonah was on the ship God __ __ __ __ a great storm. The sailors believed that Jonah was to __ __ __ __ __ __ and __ __ __ __ __ __ him overboard. God sent an enormous fish which __ __ __ __ __ __ __ __ __ __ __ Jonah up. He was inside the fish three days and nights and he began to __ __ __ __. The fish __ __ __ __ __ him out onto dry land. Jonah then went to Nineveh and __ __ __ __ the people that God would __ __ __ __ __ __ __ them. The people were sorry for their sins and __ __ __ __ __ __ __ God to __ __ __ __ __ __ __ them.

blame

threw

spat

told

sent

pray

asked

forgive

punish

swallowed

Draw Jonah in the fish.

God answered the prayers of the people of Nineveh.
Write out the verse below to find out why.

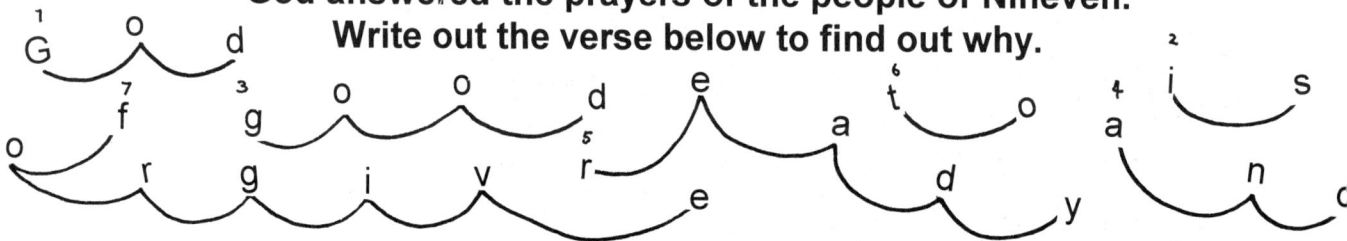

God is forgiving and ready to

__ __ __ __ __ __ __ __ __ __ __ __ __
1   2   3   4   5   6

__ __ __ __ __ __ __ __ __.
7

Psalm ch.86 v 5

Jonah got himself into
trouble by disobeying God.

Jonah ch.1

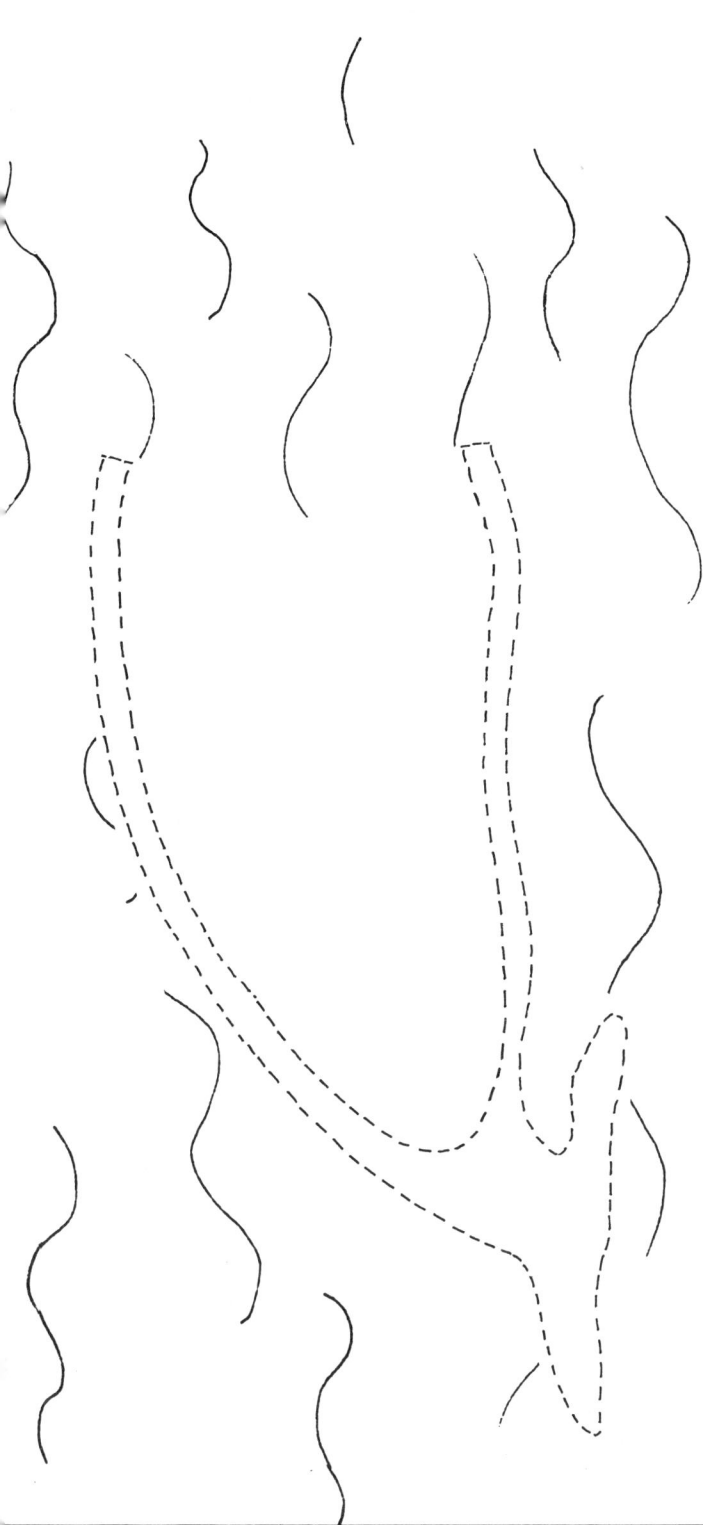

JONAH & THE FISH – ACTIVITY SHEET (1)

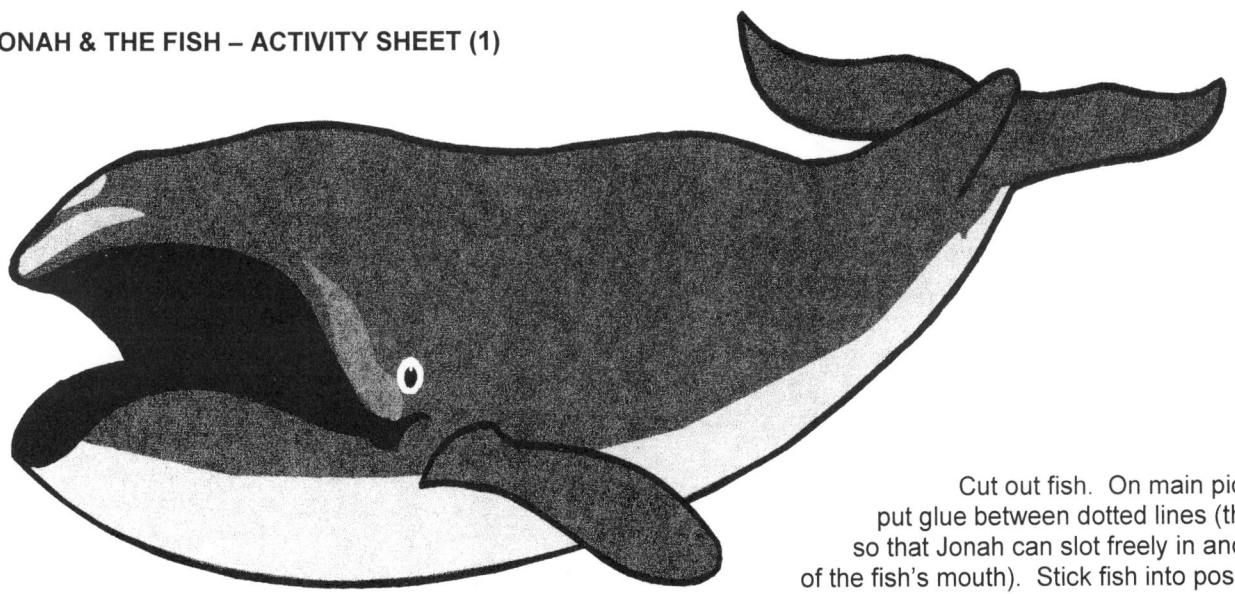

Cut out fish. On main picture
put glue between dotted lines (this is
so that Jonah can slot freely in and out
of the fish's mouth). Stick fish into position.

JONAH & THE FISH – ACTIVITY SHEET (2)

Cut out Jonah and slot him in and out of the fish.

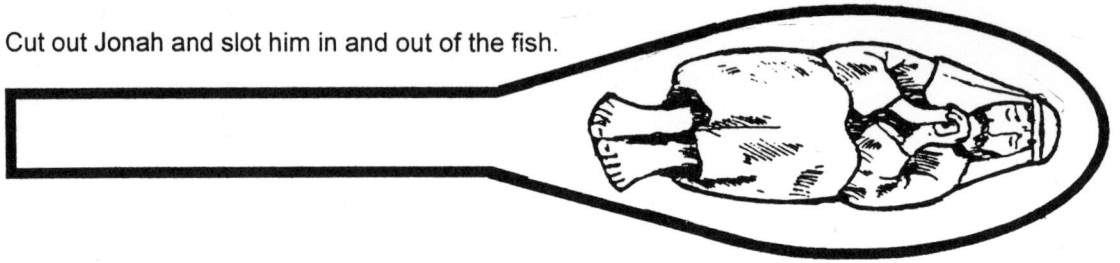

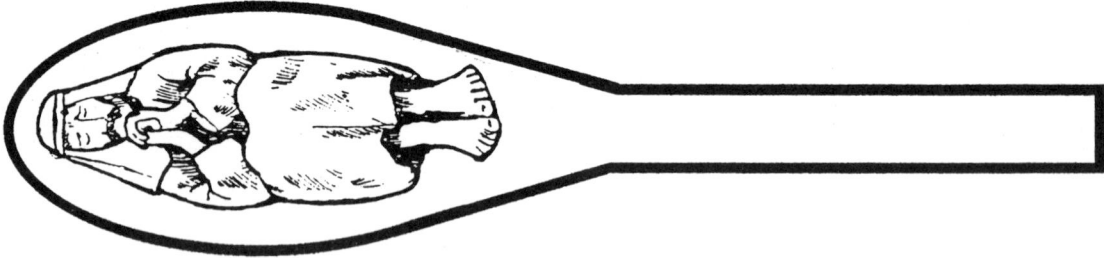

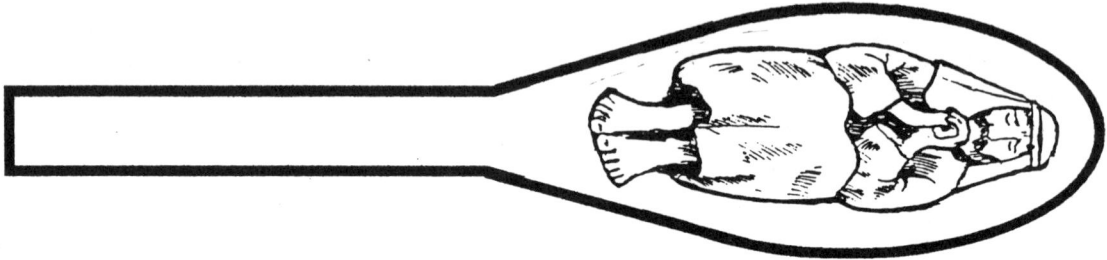

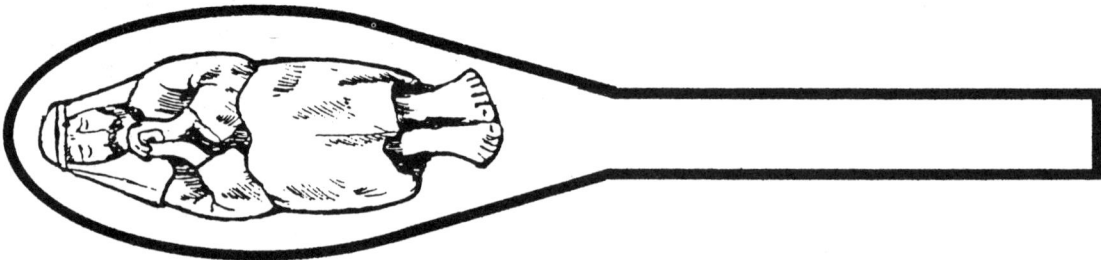

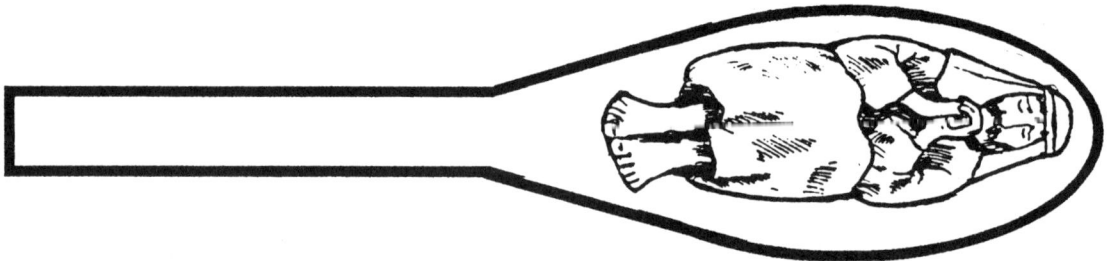

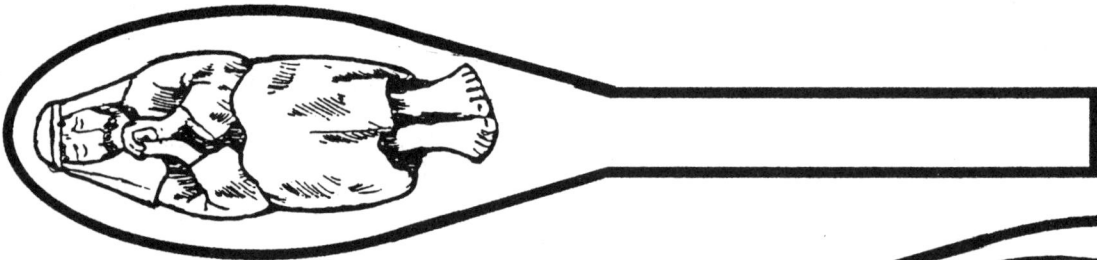

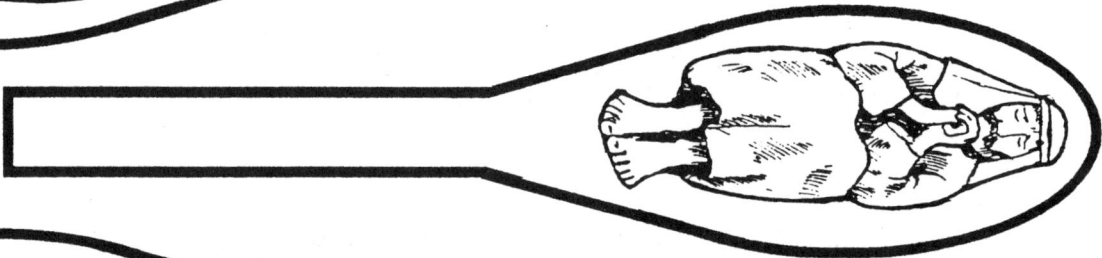

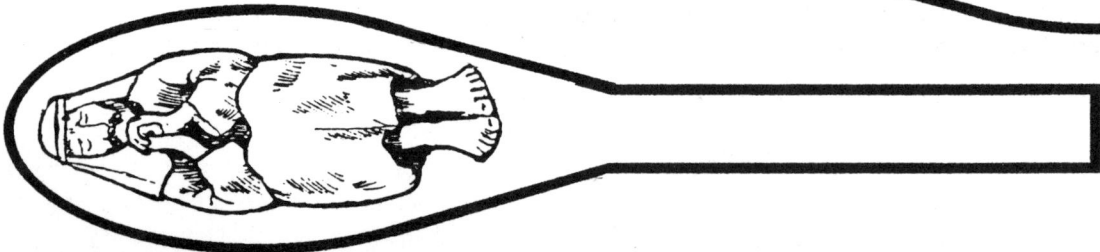

Elijah on Mount Carmel

1 Kings 17 & 18

Themes	God's Character, God's Power, Prayer

Aims	To recount the story of Elijah on Mount Carmel.
	To teach that the Bible shows there is only one God who is living and powerful.
	To show that the Bible teaches that God answers prayer.

Resources	Bibles, Children's Story Sheet, Puzzle Page, Activity Sheet.

Other Ideas & Activities
1. Activity Sheet – follow instructions on Sheet.
2. Elijah - a prophet - gave a message that it would not rain and it didn't. Can the children find or think of other examples where prophets or preachers brought a message from God concerning the future, which eventually came true? (E.g. Noah and the flood, Joseph's dreams, Moses & the plagues, Daniel and Nebuchadnezzar - see Dan. 4, Jesus - predicting his death & resurrection.)
3. Elijah wanted to prove that the fire which consumed his offering was miraculous and came down from God. What conditions are needed for a fire to burn? What conditions make it difficult to light a fire?
4. Compare/contrast God and Baal. How were they different? Write on a piece of card an adjective which describes God. Use these to make a class display about the character of God.

Teacher's Notes

Summary: King Ahab had encouraged the people of Israel to stop worshipping God. Instead he encouraged them to worship the false god Baal. Elijah challenged Ahab and 450 priests of Baal to a contest. The God who sent fire to burn up the offering was the true God. When Elijah prayed, fire fell from heaven and burnt up his offering. God showed the people that the God of the Israelites is the only true God. The Bible teaches that God hears and answers the prayers of Christians.

Point of Contact
Good/Bad Rulers or Kings
- What do you think a good king or queen should be like?
- Do you think that a good king or queen helps their people to be good?
- Is the opposite true?

A Bad King
David and Solomon were good kings of Israel because they loved God and kept his commandments. Later there were many other kings who refused to obey God. Ahab

was one of the worst of these kings. He did many evil things. He worshipped a false god called Baal. He encouraged the Israelites to ignore God and worship Baal and he had 450 men selected to be the priests of Baal.

Elijah's Message
At this time Elijah was God's prophet (God's messenger) in Israel. God sent Elijah to tell King Ahab that, as a punishment for his wicked ways and the bad ways of the people, God would not send rain for several years. Elijah was very brave to take this message to the palace. King Ahab was exceedingly angry with Elijah and wanted to kill him. Elijah had to escape quickly.

The Great Contest
Elijah had been hiding for three and a half years. One day God told him to go to King Ahab and say, "All this trouble has come to us because you have turned away from the true God to worship the idol Baal. Send now and gather the priests of Baal and the people and meet me on Mount Carmel."

On the chosen day, the King, the priests and a great crowd gathered on the mountain top. Elijah said, "I am the only prophet of God and you have 450 priests of Baal. Let us both build an altar of stone. Let us put wood on the altar, as fuel for a fire, and then let us both put a dead bull on this wood as an offering. Then let us both pray. You call to Baal and I will call to the God of Israel. The one who answers by sending down fire to burn up the offering, he is God." Everyone agreed to this challenge.

No Reply From Baal
Elijah watched as the worshippers of Baal built their altar. They then began to call out to Baal to send fire down to burn their offering. Baal was their 'fire god', so they were confident he would answer them. For hours and hours the people shouted out, "O Baal hear us, O Baal hear us," but nothing happened. Elijah began to make fun of them. "Shout out louder," he said, "maybe your god is asleep, or busy or on a journey." The priests of Baal leaped and danced frantically around their altar all day, but still no fire came.

Elijah's Turn
In the evening it was Elijah's turn. He said to the people, "Come and watch". Elijah repaired a broken down altar that had once been used to worship God. He built it up with wood and stone and dug a ditch (or moat) around it. He put wood on the altar and laid the bull on top, as an offering to God. Then Elijah commanded his helpers to fill water pots and fill the ditch around the altar. He then told them to pour water over the offering. He told them to do this, not *once* but *three* times, until the wood was soaking wet and the moat was filled with water! How could a fire possibly be lit now, when everything was so wet?

The Moment of Truth
The eyes of the king, the priests of Baal and the people were all now fixed on Elijah. Would his God hear his prayer and have the power to send fire and burn up the offering?

Elijah prayed a short prayer. "Hear me O Lord, hear me," he said, "That these people may know that you are the true God." Immediately God sent fire from heaven and burnt

162

up the offering. The fire was so powerful that it also burnt up the soaking wet wood, the stones and the dust and even dried up all the water that was in the ditch. It was an amazing miracle which only God could do.

A Great Victory

The people watching were afraid and fell down with their faces to the ground saying, "The Lord, he is God, the Lord he is God." All the people saw that God is the true and living God and that Baal was just a dead idol. Many stopped worshipping Baal and turned back to worship and serve the God of Israel.

The New Testament tells us that Elijah is an example of someone who believed that God would hear and answer his prayers (James 5:17-18).

Illustration: The True God

John Paton was on an island in the Pacific. Here was there to teach the people who lived on the island about Jesus and the God of the Bible. Many of those he spoke to would kill the other natives they didn't like and then eat the victim's body.

The island he was on had no fresh water, apart from a water hole which was kept by two bad men. This hole filled with water when it rained, but the two men pretended they filled it and would then get the poor people of the island to pay them large sums for the water.

John decided to dig his own deep well so as to get free fresh water for everyone to drink. The people of the island thought he was mad. They said that rain comes only from above. How could he possibly get rain from down below? John knew it was likely that there was a fresh water supply somewhere down below, if only he could find it.

As he prepared to dig, he realised that the people were watching. He had told them that he believed in the God of the Bible. He then realised that if he didn't find water, the people might not think much of him or his God! They might feel that his God was not able to help John. He was no better than the other god's the people worshipped.

John prayed that God would guide him to find water. He took a pick, a spade and a bucket and asked God for help. He chose his spot and began to dig. It took many days of hard work. He went lower and lower, twenty feet, thirty feet. Still the ground was dry. Then one day a little trickle ran into the bottom of the hole.

The people wondered what was going on? As they looked down the hole they could see John on his knees praying and giving thanks to God. Then he was shouting excitedly. He came up the ladder out of the hole. What was he carrying? A jug! An empty jug he had taken down was now full. But full with what? The chief on the island tasted it. It was fresh water! John had found fresh water. Soon the hole was full, and the people could obtain all the water they wanted.

Later the island people dug seven other wells at different sites. In every case the people could not complete the well because they hit solid rock, or if they did, they only found salt water. Truly God had heard John's prayers and guided him to dig his well in just the right place. The people could see that John's God was the true God who hears and answers prayer! From that time onwards they listened to all he taught them about God.
(* The story of John Paton and "Rain From Below" is found in "They Shall Be Mine" by John Tallach, published by The Banner of Truth Trust, ISBN 0 8551 320 4 - available from most Christian Bookshops.)

Things To Learn:
- Elijah God's prophet in Israel, challenged the priests of Baal on Mount Carmel.
- God powerfully demonstrated that he is the only true God who hears and answers prayer.
- The Bible teaches that God hears and answers prayer when Christians pray.

Discuss
- Why did Elijah soak his altar and offering in water?
- How did God show he was the only true God?
- What did Baal do?
- How does the story show that God hears and answers prayer?

Elijah on Mount Carmel

Elijah was God's prophet in Israel. King Ahab did not love God, but worshipped a god called Baal. King Ahab did not like the messages that God was telling Elijah to tell him, so he ordered that Elijah should be killed. Elijah escaped from King Ahab by hiding in the country. God provided food for him even though there had not been rain in Israel for a long time.

After three-and-a-half years God told Elijah to go to King Ahab and say, "All this trouble has come because you have turned away from God to worship Baal. Gather the people and meet me on Mount Carmel".

So, on the chosen day, the king, the priests of Baal, Elijah and a great crowd gathered on Mount Carmel. Elijah said, "I am the only prophet of God. You have 450 priests of Baal. Let us both build a stone altar, put wood on it and a bull on top as an offering. Then you call to Baal, and I will call to God. The one who sends down fire to burn up the offering is the true and living God". Everyone agreed to this.

Elijah watched as the priests of Baal built their altar and began calling out to Baal. Baal was their fire god so they were sure he would answer them. For hours and hours the people shouted out, "Baal, hear us!". But nothing happened.

In the evening it was Elijah's turn. He built the altar and dug a ditch around it. When the wood and the offering were in place, he told his helpers to pour water over the offering. Elijah told them to do this three times. Now the offering and the altar were so wet, how could it possibly be lit by a fire?

All eyes were fixed on Elijah as he prayed to God. Immediately, God sent fire from heaven which burnt up the offering. The fire was so powerful, it even burnt up the wet wood and dried up all the water in the ditch!

The people watching were afraid and fell down to the ground. From that day many people began to worship God. Nothing had happened when they had asked Baal to help them. They knew now that God was the only living and powerful God who hears and answers prayer.

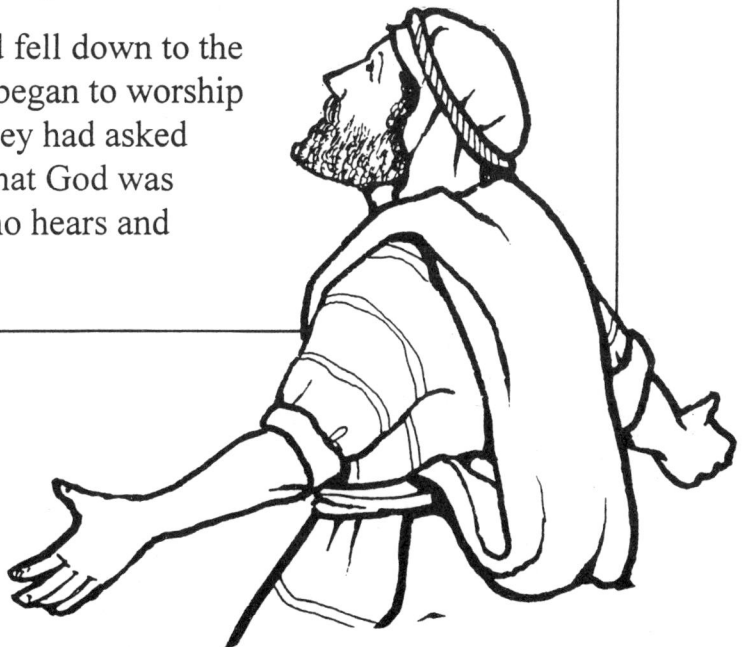

ELIJAH ON MOUNT CARMEL

Cross out the wrong words.

Ahab the *queen/king* and the people *did/did not* worship God. God punished them by not sending *rain/wind.* Elijah the prophet met the priests of Baal on *Mount Carmel/Ararat.* The God who answered prayer by sending *lightning/fire* to burn the altar was the true *king/God.* The priests of Baal built an *altar/house* and called to Baal for *hours/a few minutes.* Nothing happened. Elijah built an altar and poured *water/oil* all over it. He prayed to God. God *did/did not* hear Elijah's prayer. God sent *fire/stones* from heaven which burnt up *everything/nothing* on the altar. The people said, "*Baal/the Lord*, he is God."

Colour all the words about God in red and all the words about Baal in black

DOES NOT HEAR PRAYER

hears prayer

invisible

Baal

God

powerful

man-made

not alive

alive

no power

The people had to decide who was the true God. Match the stones in the altar and write in the Bible verse.

this

you

will

whom

you

day

choose

serve

Joshua 24:15

Only the true God could send me down from heaven and burn up

Elijah's sacrifice. 1 Kings ch.18

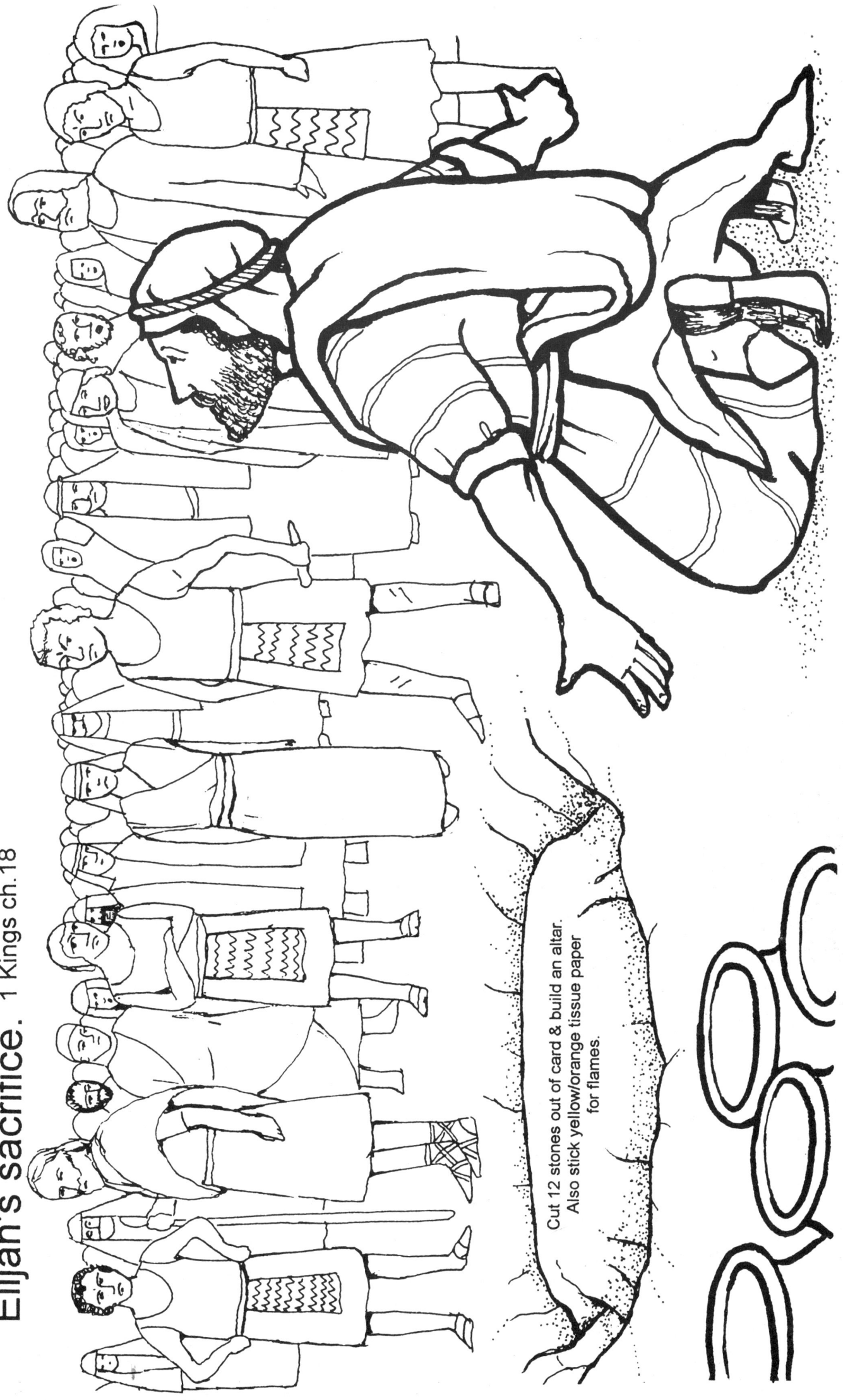

Cut 12 stones out of card & build an altar.
Also stick yellow/orange tissue paper
for flames.

Daniel In The Lions' Den

Daniel 1, 2, 3 & 6

Themes	Good Behaviour, Doing What Is Right, Standing Firm

Aims	To tell the Biblical account of Daniel in the lions' den. To highlight the importance of good behaviour. To show that we should not be afraid to stand firm for what we know is right.

Resources	Bibles, Children's Story Sheet, Puzzle Page, Activity Sheets, Map.

Other Ideas & Activities
1. Activity Sheets – photocopy lions on yellow; glue orange/brown wool for lions' manes.
2. Research the Babylonians. List their famous kings. Make a time line to show where these events fit in with other Old Testament and New Testament events.
3. Make a list of famous people who have stood firm (perhaps even alone) for what they believe. Say what they fought for and find out more about them. There are many examples in the Bible e.g. Noah, Elijah, Stephen (Acts 6,7), Apostle Paul (2Timothy 4:16), Jesus (Matthew 26:56).
4. When it was decided that the law Darius had made must be kept, describe how Daniel; King Darius; the counsellors, must have felt.
5. Write a story about someone who had to stand alone, when no one else would, but in the end they were proved to be right in the stand they took.

Teacher's Notes

Summary: Daniel was intelligent, handsome and healthy, and was chosen and trained to work in the king's palace. When the king saw Daniel's wisdom, he made him ruler over Babylon. When he was an old man, Daniel was the trusted Prime Minister for King Darius. He had many enemies who wanted to get rid of him. Daniel continued to pray even if it meant he would be thrown to the lions. God protected Daniel and shut the lions' mouths so they could not harm him. We should stand firm for what we know is right and good.

Point of Contact
Dependable Helpers
- If you were a king or queen, what sort of helpers would you choose to help you?
- What type of people would you want around you?
- Why?

Off To Babylon!
The people and the kings of Israel had grown more and more sinful in the things that they were doing. Instead of worshipping God they had turned away to worship idols. God was angry with them and warned them on many occasions to turn from their bad

ways. However, the people did not listen and eventually God punished them by sending King Nebuchadnezzar and the Babylonian army to conquer them. Thousands of Jews were carried away as captives to Babylon (show map). The beautiful temple that King Solomon had built was robbed and ruined. The city of Jerusalem was destroyed and burnt down.

Daniel Is Chosen

King Nebuchadnezzar chose young men, probably about 14 or 15 years old, from among the Jews who had been taken captive. He wanted to train them up to look after his affairs and help run his empire. Nebuchadnezzar wanted the most intelligent, handsome, healthiest and fittest young men that could be found. Among those chosen were Daniel, Shadrach, Meshach and Abednego.

Good Progress

For three years these boys received a special education studying every subject including the Babylonian language. At the end of three years the king questioned the boys. Nebuchadnezzar was very pleased with Daniel and his three friends. Some time later God helped Daniel to interpret one of the king's dreams. Nebuchadnezzar was so impressed by Daniel's wisdom that he made him ruler over the whole province of Babylon, and head over all the wise men in the palace.

Prime Minister

Many years went by and Daniel grew to be an old man. Many changes had taken place. King Nebuchadnezzar had died and there was a new king on the throne called Darius. King Darius chose 120 counsellors to help him to rule the kingdom. In charge of these counsellors were three men called governors. King Darius admired Daniel, because he was wise, reliable and trustworthy. He asked him to be the chief ruler. He would then be in charge of the three governors as well. He would be the king's Prime Minister.

Jealousy

The other counsellors and governors became jealous of Daniel. They hated the fact that he now had authority over them and could tell them what to do. They also disliked the fact that being a Jew, he was a foreigner. They wanted to get rid of him.

At first they watched Daniel closely, hoping they would be able to find some fault in him, which they could report to the king. However, this did not work, because Daniel was honest and trustworthy and always did his work well.

Finally they said, "We will never have anything against Daniel, which we can tell to the king, unless it is something to do with the way he worships God." They all knew that Daniel prayed to God every day.

A New Law

So these evil men went to the king and greeted him, "King Darius, live forever! We have written a new law and want you to sign it. If, during the next thirty days, anyone prays to any god or man except you, King Darius, they shall be thrown into the lions' den."

King Darius was a proud man and was very flattered by this idea. So he agreed and gladly signed the law, not realising that this was all a plot to kill his Prime Minister, Daniel. The counsellors were happy thinking they had Daniel trapped.

Daniel Still Prays
When Daniel heard about the new law, he went straight to his house to pray. He went upstairs to his room and knelt down before the open window as he always did. Daniel prayed three times a day, giving thanks to God and asking for his help. This new law made no difference. He knew that it was most important to obey God.

A Sad King
The jealous counsellors watched Daniel carefully. When they saw him praying to God they immediately went to the king and said, "This Daniel gives no attention to your new law! He still prays to God three times a day."

When the king heard these words he was deeply upset. He liked and admired Daniel very much. He did not want any harm to come to him. He did all that he could to find a way of saving Daniel's life. But it was no use. The cruel men insisted that the law could not be changed and had to be kept. Daniel must be put into the lions' den!

To The Lions!
Finally the king gave the order and Daniel was lowered into the lions' den. This was a dark dungeon where hungry lions were kept to punish people who had broken the law. King Darius called out to Daniel, "Daniel, the God who you serve, he will rescue you." After this a stone was rolled over the entrance to the den, the king sealed the stone with his own ring and then returned to his palace.

A Sleepless Night
King Darius was so miserable that he could not sleep. He did not want to eat, drink or listen to his favourite music. Very early the next morning, as soon as it was dawn, he rushed to the lions' den. In a sad voice he called out, "Daniel, servant of the living God, has your God kept you from the lions?"

He heard Daniel's voice loud and clear in reply, "O king, live forever. My God has sent his angel and shut the mouths of the lions, so that they have not hurt me!"

The Tables Are Turned!
The king was amazed and so glad that Daniel had not been harmed. He commanded that Daniel should be brought out of the lions' den. Daniel did not have a mark on him. God had kept him safe.

The king ordered that the men who had accused Daniel should now be put in the lions' den. In moments they were torn to pieces by the fierce lions. Then King Darius made a proclamation throughout the whole of his kingdom, saying that everyone must honour Daniel's God, the living God, who saved Daniel from the lions.

How thankful Daniel must have been, that he stood firm and did what was right. The king and the whole empire would be affected by this miracle.

Illustration: The Martyrs - Willing To Stand Alone & Stand Firm For What Is Right
Nicholas Ridley and Hugh Latimer were Christians who served as ministers in the Church of England. They taught the people from the Bible and told them about Jesus Christ.

In 1553 Mary, Henry VIII's daughter, came to the throne of England. She did not want the Bible to be taught to the people and so she had Latimer and Ridley thrown into prison. They were tried and sentenced to be burned at the stake. Though they faced such a painful death, neither would give in or agree to stop teaching the Bible. They knew what they were standing for was true and right. They believed that though they may have to die, God would strengthen them and help them through their ordeal.

In 1555 at Oxford, in front of Balliol College, Latimer and Ridley were taken out, chained to a pole and wood was piled around them. Both men were able to show the confidence and trust they had in God even at this time. They still refused to change their minds. As the fire was lit, Latimer uttered his famous words, "Be of good cheer, Master Ridley, and play the man; we shall this day, by God's grace, light such a candle in England, that shall never be put out."

Ridley was right. Their willingness to stand firm and suffer for what they believed, along with over three hundred other men, women, boy and girls, had a great impact upon people who saw them die. The whole country was moved. As a result the Bible was read by many and had a great influence on the people and history of Great Britain.
(* The story of 'Bilney, Tyndale & Latimer' can be found in "Men of Destiny" by P. Masters, published by the Wakeman Trust, ISBN 1 870855 03 5 - available from most Christian Bookshops)

Things To Learn:
- Daniel was an honest, wise and trustworthy man.
- He was not afraid to stand firm for God.
- God protected Daniel in the lions' den and shut their mouths.
- We should not be afraid to stand firm for what we know is right.

Discuss
- Have you ever had to stand firm for something you knew was right?
- What makes people do this?
- What do Christians use as their guide to what is right and wrong?

Daniel in the Lions' Den

The King of Babylon wanted some young men to help him. He chose Daniel and three of his friends who had been taken as prisoners by his army. The boys went to good schools and learned quickly. It was not long before the king made Daniel ruler over the whole of Babylon.

King Darius made Daniel his Prime Minister. The other men who worked for the king became jealous of Daniel. They began to plot together to get rid of him. They watched him carefully, but they could not find Daniel doing anything wrong.

So the men decided to catch Daniel another way. They knew that he prayed to God three times a day. So they went to King Darius and told him to sign a new law. This new law said that everyone in Babylon must pray only to the king. If anyone prayed to any other man or god, they would be thrown into a den of lions.

King Darius thought this was a good idea and signed the new law. He did not realise that it was all a plot to kill Daniel. When Daniel heard about the new law, he went straight to his house to pray to God. He always prayed three times a day and this new law would not change this.

When the king's men saw Daniel praying to God, they went to King Darius and demanded that Daniel be put into the lions' den. King Darius liked Daniel very much and was sad. But the new law could not be changed. So Daniel was put into the lions' den.

The next morning, King Darius went to the lions' den. He called out, "Daniel, has God kept you safe from the lions?". Daniel shouted back, "O King, my God has shut the mouths of the lions, so they have not hurt me!" The king was amazed and so glad that Daniel had not been hurt. Daniel was brought out of the den.

King Darius made a new law saying that everyone must worship Daniel's God, who had saved him from the lions.

DANIEL IN THE LIONS' DEN

Draw a line to match up the right endings for these sentences.

1. King Darius made Daniel the most ....keep him safe from the lions.
2. The other rulers were.....   .....tell the king that Daniel had broken the law.
3. They made the king agree to.....   .....important ruler in his kingdom.
4. The new law said that.....   .....punish Daniel.
5. If anyone broke the law they would be.....   .....no one must pray to God.
6. Daniel did not stop.....   .....praying to God.
7. The other rulers went to.....   .....a new law.
8. The king did not want to.....   .....put in the lions' den.
9. Daniel knew that God would.....   .....jealous of Daniel.

Fill in the spaces with the words in the pictures to find out what the King said to Daniel, and Daniel's reply.

Daniel ch. 6

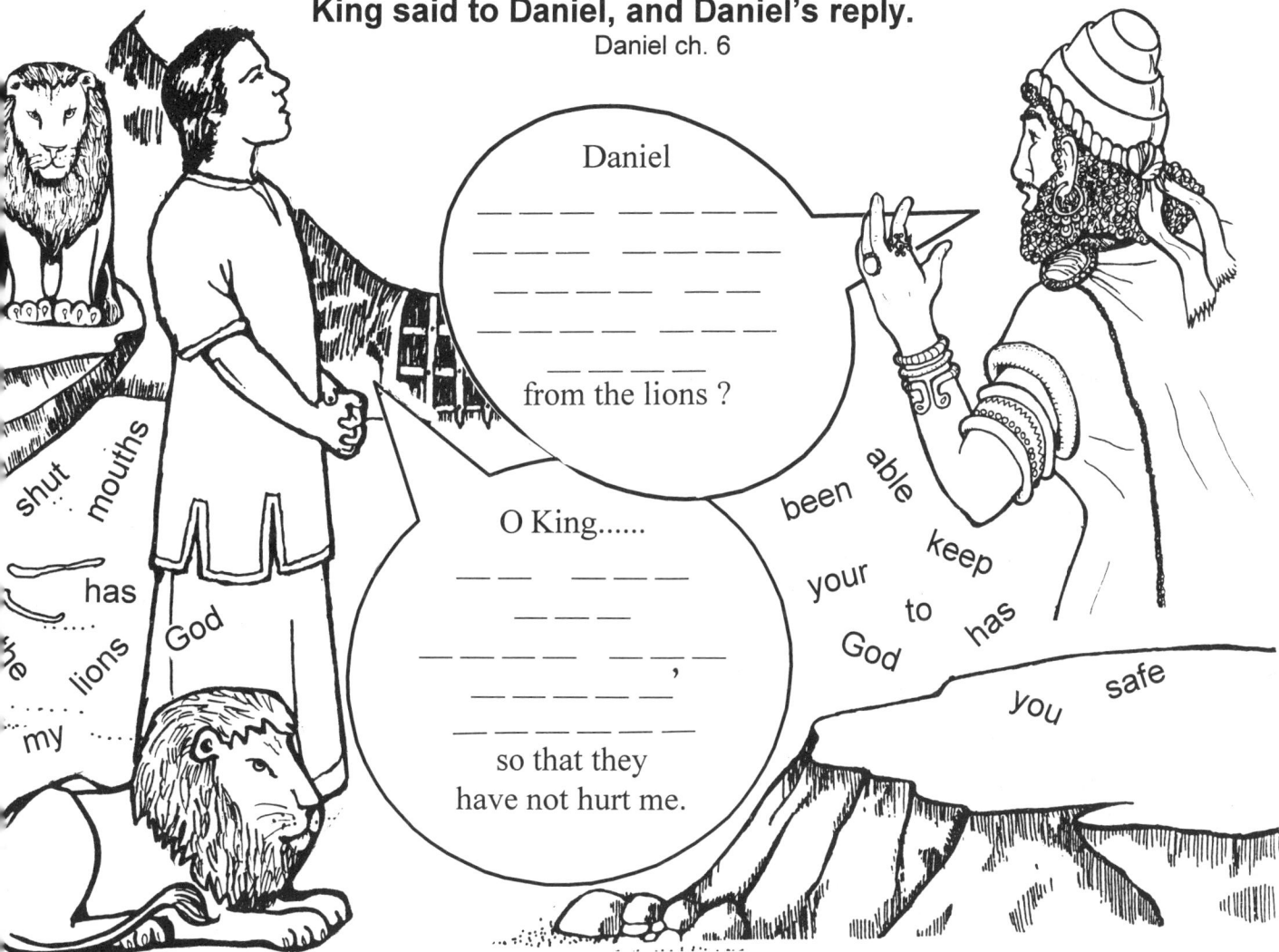

Daniel

_ _ _ _ _ _ _ _ _
_ _ _ _ _ _ _ _ _
_ _ _ _ _ _ _ _
_ _ _ _ _

from the lions ?

O King......

_ _ _ _ _ _
_ _ _ _
_ _ _ _ _ _ _ _ ,
_ _ _ _ _ _

so that they
have not hurt me.

shut   mouths   has   lions   God   my   the   been   able   keep   your   to   God   has   you   safe

Daniel

_ _ _ _ _ _ _ _

to God every day.

**Colour in the letters
with a dot in to find the
missing word.**

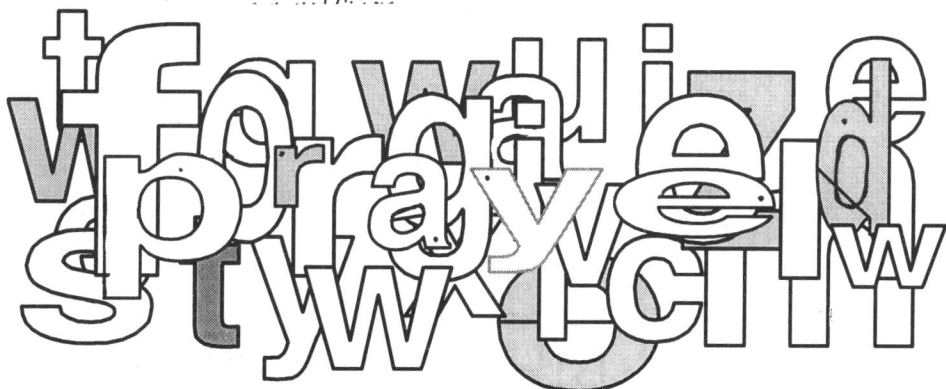

God kept the lions from hurting Daniel because he was obedient.

Dan. ch.6

back view lion

front view lion

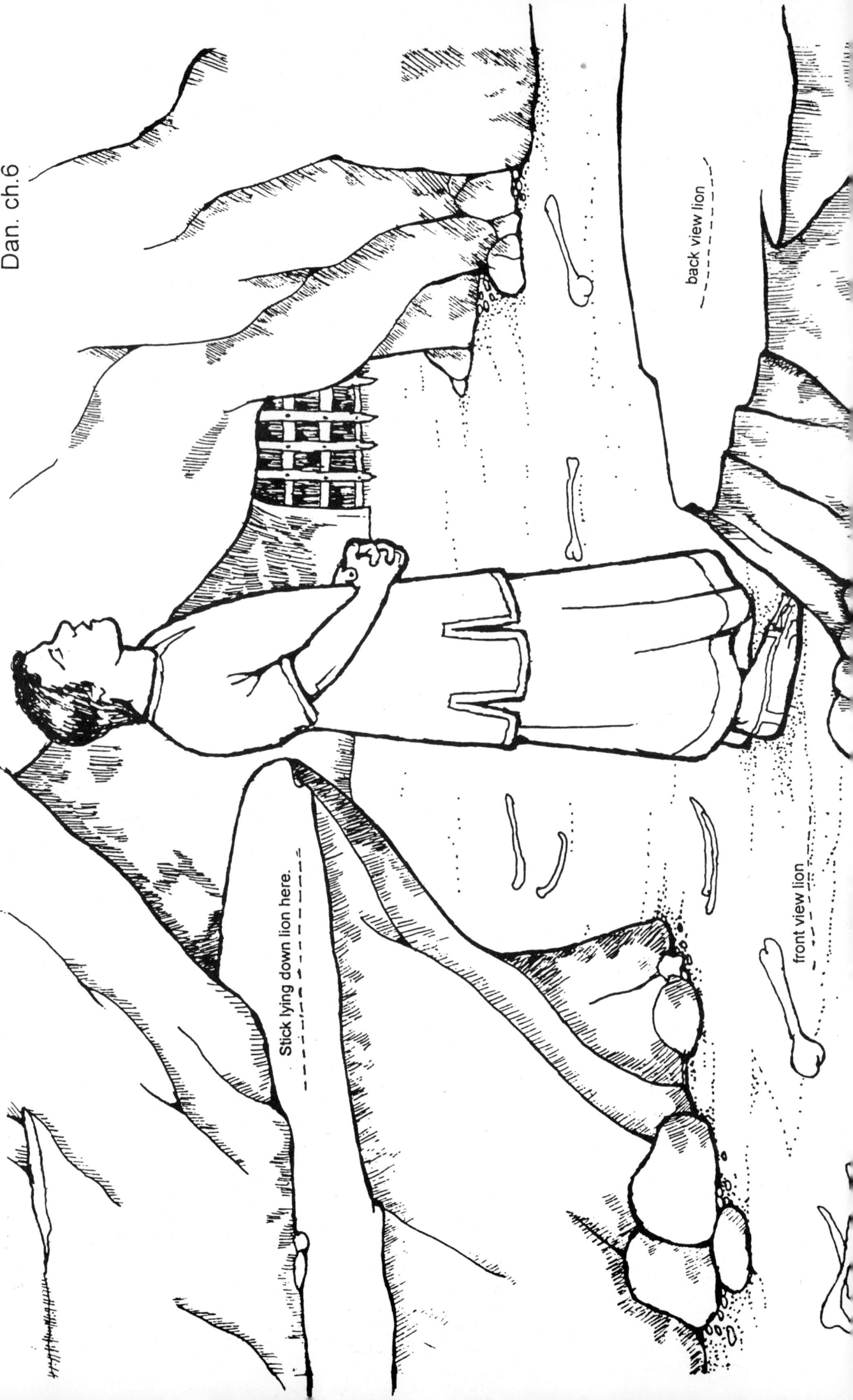

Stick lying down lion here.

DANIEL IN THE LIONS' DEN – ACTIVITY SHEET (2)

Cut out lions and stick to picture where indicated (3 per child).
Cut small lengths of orange/brown/gold wool and stick to
lions' manes.

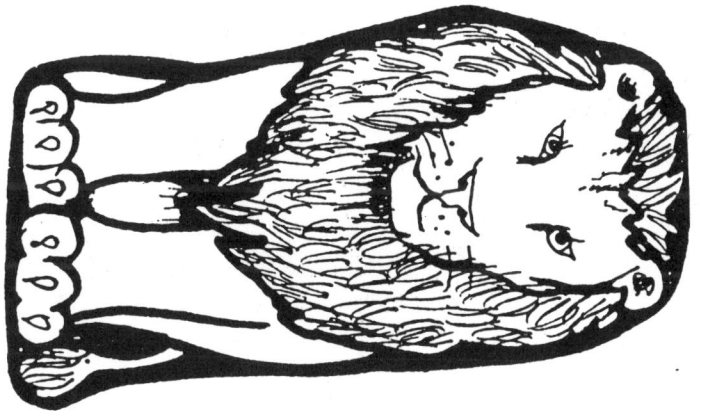

Esther Saves Her People

Esther 1 - 10

Themes	Taking Opportunities, Gifts & Talents

Aims	To teach how God protected the Jewish nation through Esther. To consider how we should make the most of God given opportunities and abilities.

Resources	Bibles, Children's Story Sheet, Puzzle Page, Activity Sheet, Map.

Other Ideas & Activities

1. Activity Sheet needs gold card/paper for crowns and sceptre.
2. Write a series of letters or notes between Esther and Mordecai explaining the events in the court, their plans and feelings.
3. Write a diary for Esther recording her feelings and thoughts throughout the story.
4. Esther was afraid when she first went to the king. She got the courage to go by asking the Jews to fast and pray for her. Are there times when we are afraid/worried about something we have to do? How can we get courage for this? Who can support us or help us?
5. Look at the hymn "Take my life, and let it be," by Frances Ridley Havergal. List all the things that the hymn writer is willing to let God use. How does she want each thing to be used?
6. Draw a picture of yourself doing what you are good at. Write down underneath your picture how you can use your talents to help/give pleasure to others.

Teacher's Notes

Summary: An ordinary Jewish girl called Esther become Queen to the most powerful man in the world - King Ahasuerus. Wicked Haman wanted to destroy the Jewish people. Mordecai, Esther's cousin, encouraged her to do all she could to stop Haman's plan. Esther needed great courage, tact and wisdom to approach the king and tell him of the intended destruction of the Jews. She used her position to save God's people. The Jews still remember this deliverance when they annually celebrate the feast of Purim. Christians believe that they should use what God has given them - their energy, time, money, position, etc - in a way that pleases God.

Point of Contact
What Is Beauty?
- How do you judge if someone is beautiful?
- Is true beauty on the inside or the outside?

A New Queen

King Ahasuerus was the King of Persia (Iran). He had great power and could do as he pleased. He became angry when his Queen did not obey him and he had told her to leave. His counselors suggested that they should bring to the Palace in Susa (show map) all the most beautiful girls in the land so that he could choose another queen. The king chose a Jewish girl, called Esther, to be the new Queen and a crown was put on her head.

Esther's Secret

Esther's parents had died when she was young. She was brought up by her older cousin Mordecai, who treated her like his own daughter. Many years before this, a large number of Jews had been forcibly taken away from their own country of Israel. Some had now returned to Jerusalem, but many others like Mordecai and Esther still lived in Persia. They were looked down on and despised for being Jews. Because of this, Mordecai thought it wiser if Esther kept it a secret that she was a Jew.

Wicked Haman

The most important man in the king's service was a proud man called Haman. Everyone in the Palace and in Susa, had to bow down to him, every time he passed by. Mordecai refused to do this because he knew Haman was an evil man. Mordecai knew that it could never be right to praise and respect a bad person. Haman was very angry that Mordecai would not give him the respect he felt he should have, so he thought up an evil plan, which would not only destroy Mordecai, but all the Jews as well.

A New Law

Haman made up a new law, which said that on a certain day, all the Jews in Persia were to be killed. He lied to the king, telling him that these people were disobedient citizens, and that they were dangerous and could cause great trouble. They deserved to be put to death. He did not tell the king that it was the Jews he was talking about. However, because the king trusted Haman and thought that these people were enemies of the king, he agreed that this law should be sent to every part of the Persian Empire. Haman rejoiced that he could now get back at Mordecai and his people. He immediately ordered men to start building a gallows, on which Mordecai could be hung.

Devastating News!

When the Jews heard this dreadful news they were terrified. Mordecai dressed himself in sackcloth and poured ashes over his head. This was the custom of those who were truly upset. Queen Esther's maids saw Mordecai and told her what was wrong. She sent messengers to Mordecai to find out what was wrong. Mordecai told her about Haman's plot. He also sent her a copy of the law so she could read it for herself.

Esther's Responsibility

Mordecai sent a message to Esther, suggesting that she should go to the king and plead for the lives of her people. Esther was afraid. She sent a message back to Mordecai that said, "No one dare go into the king's presence without being invited. He can get angry and even have them killed! It is only safe to go and talk with him, if he first holds out his golden sceptre as a sign." Esther was really saying that she was too frightened to go.

Mordecai replied to her. "Don't forget that you are also a Jew and you will be killed too!

Who knows, perhaps God has made you Queen just for this reason, so you can save your people?"

Esther Decides
Finally Esther replied to Mordecai. "I will go to the king. If I die, I die! Tell all the Jews in the city of Susa to meet together for three days and neither eat or drink, but give themselves to prayer." Esther wanted the people to ask God to help her when she went in to see King Ahasuerus.

In To See The King!
Esther put on her royal clothes and came towards the king as he sat on his throne. When the king saw her standing in the courtyard of the Palace, he held out his royal sceptre to her. How relieved she must have been as she went forward to touch the sceptre and to speak to the king. She didn't speak to the king straightaway about the Jews, but immediately invited the king to come and join her at a banquet she was giving.

Esther Pleads
Esther held a banquet to which she invited the king and Haman. The king was in a very good mood, and pleased with Esther's hospitality. He turned to Esther and said, "Do you have any request Queen Esther? Whatever you ask I will give you."

Here was Esther's opportunity. "Oh king," she said, "A law has been made to kill all the Jewish people in the Empire, which will include me! Please spare my life and the life of my people."

The king was surprised! "Who is the man that dares to do this thing?" he asked.

"It is Haman!" Esther replied. The king was furious. Having learnt that Haman had built a gallows to hang Mordecai on, he commanded that the evil man Haman should be hung upon them instead. Then the king cancelled the orders given by Haman. Instead, he sent out a new law, which made sure that the Jews would be safe from attack from any one in the Empire.

A Great Victory
Haman's plot was an attempt to destroy all of the Jewish people. If it had succeeded, there may well have been no Jews left, and no Jewish nation. This would have meant that the promises that God had made to Abraham, which said, that eventually, Jesus would be born, as a Jew, in the country of Israel, could not have come true. However, Esther was courageous and used her position to help God's people. Not only was the whole Jewish nation saved, but also God was able to fulfill the promise he had made.

God used an ordinary girl - Esther - to save his people. The Jews still remember this great victory, when each year they celebrate the feast of Purim on the 13th -15th of the month of Adar (our March). Christians believe that they, like Esther, should use what God has given them - their energy, time, money, position - in a way that pleases God.

Illustration: Using Your Position For Good
Lord Radstock (1833-1913) was a remarkable man, not just because he had outstanding natural gifts, but because of his desire to use his gifts and position in the service of God.

He enjoyed the privileges of wealth and status, being a Lord, with a large estate and mansion at Mayfield in Southampton. Today if you go to Mayfield Park in Southampton there is an obelisk there, which was put up by Radstock. On it is written, "The earth is the Lord's and the fullness thereof," a quotation from Psalm 24. Radstock believed that all he had been given by way of privilege and position, should be used for God. He didn't believe in wasting his abilities and gifts. Often he would live in third class accommodation, rather than waste vast sums in luxurious hotels.

He gave large sums to relieving the poor in London and India. His status as a Lord meant that he was able to work amongst the royal family and nobles in Denmark and Russia. He had a great effect upon Princess Louise, who became Queen of Denmark in 1906. He also influenced many at the Czar's court in Russia, telling them about Jesus Christ and the teaching of the Bible.

Like Queen Esther, in the Bible, Radstock used his privileged position to do good works for God.

(* "Lord Radstock and the Russian Awakening" by David Fountain, published by Mayflower Christian Books, ISBN 0 907821 04 9 - available from most Christian Bookshops or direct from Mayflower Christian Books, 114, Spring Road, Southampton, SO19 2QB.)

Things To Learn
- A Jewish girl Esther became Queen of Persia.
- Haman plotted to kill all the Jews, but Esther bravely goes to the king and asks him to save her people.
- The Jews were saved and Haman executed.
- Jews remember this great deliverance each year with the feast of Purim.
- Christians want to use all God gives them to please him.

Discuss
- Did Esther think only of herself or others?
- God has given us all gifts, abilities or opportunities.
- What are you good at?
- How can you use your abilities to help others?
- How do Christians use their abilities to please God?

Esther Saves Her People

King Ahasuerus was the king of Persia. One day he chose a new queen. Her name was Esther. She was a Jewess who lived with her cousin Mordecai.

Haman was one of the king's helpers. He was a very proud man and wanted everyone to bow down to him as he walked past. Mordecai would not do this as he knew that Haman was an evil man. Haman was angry that Mordecai did not bow down to him, and he thought up a plot to kill Mordecai and all the Jews in Persia.

Haman went to the king and asked him to pass a new law. The law said that all the Jews were disobedient and must be killed. The king believed Haman's lies and agreed to the new law.

When the Jews heard about the new law they were afraid. Mordecai told Queen Esther about the new law and advised her to go to the king and ask him to save the Jews. Esther was afraid of the king and did not want to go, but Mordecai reminded her that she was a Jew and would be killed as well. So Esther agreed to go. She asked Mordecai to tell all the Jews to pray for her as she went in to the king.

Esther put on her royal clothes and went to see the king. As he saw her coming he held out his royal sceptre to her. This was a sign to Esther that she would be welcomed. Esther invited the king to a banquet.

At the banquet the king said to Esther, "Whatever you ask I will give you". Esther replied, "Oh King, a law has been made to kill all the Jewish people, which will include me! Please save my life and the life of my people!"

The king was surprised and very angry with Haman.
He ordered that Haman should be executed.
Then he cancelled the new law and made
sure that the Jews would always
be kept safe.

ESTHER SAVES HER PEOPLE

Link the speech bubbles to the correct person.

Haman

I wanted to kill all the Jews

I agreed to a law which said that all the Jews should be killed

Queen Esther

I went to the king and asked him to change the law

I looked after Esther when her parents died

I asked Esther to go to the king

I was afraid to go in to the king

I married a Jew called Esther

Mordecai

King Ahasuerus

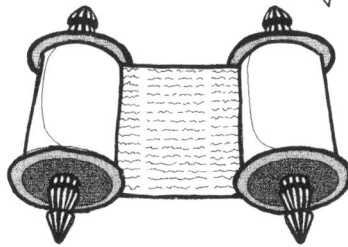

Find the words in boxes in the grid.

The King granted Esther her request and the

Jews were given their freedom. Esther was only an

ordinary girl but she was brave and God used her to

save the Jewish nation. The Jews celebrate this

victory every year at the Feast of Purim.

r	c	f	J	x	m	v
v	e	e	q	d	i	z
z	w	h	v	c	r	e
s	x	k	t	y	u	v
r	a	o	n	s	P	a
h	r	v	z	b	E	r
y	s	v	e	x	v	b
m	o	d	e	e	r	f

Find out how the Jews celebrated when they heard the good news. The words are written backwards.

t a e f

j o y

g l a d n e s s

h o n o u r

Esther ch.8 v 17

Only when the king held out his golden sceptre was Queen Esther allowed to speak.

Esther ch.5.

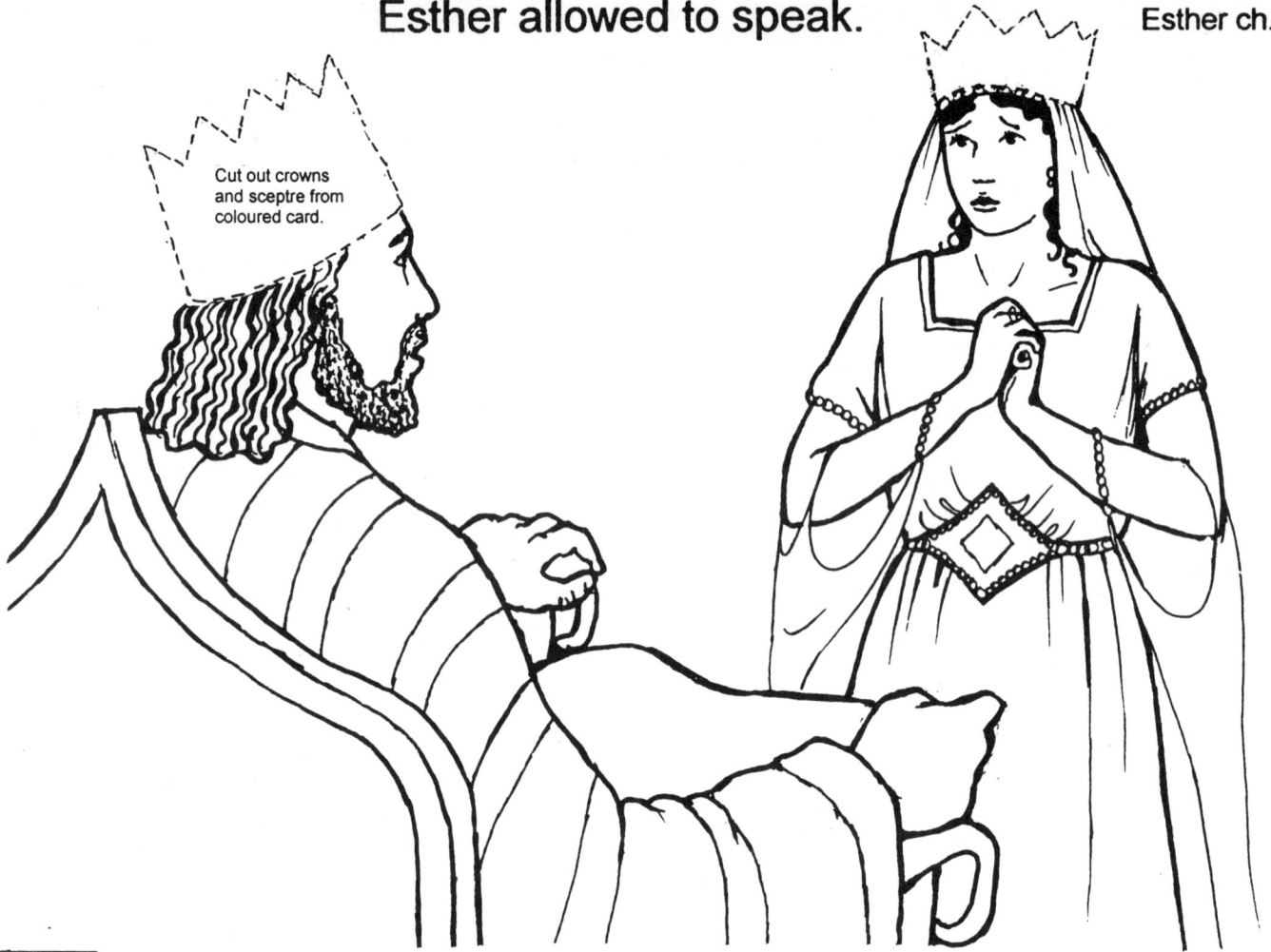

Cut out crowns and sceptre from coloured card.

Only when the king held out his golden sceptre was Queen Esther allowed to speak.

Esther ch.5.

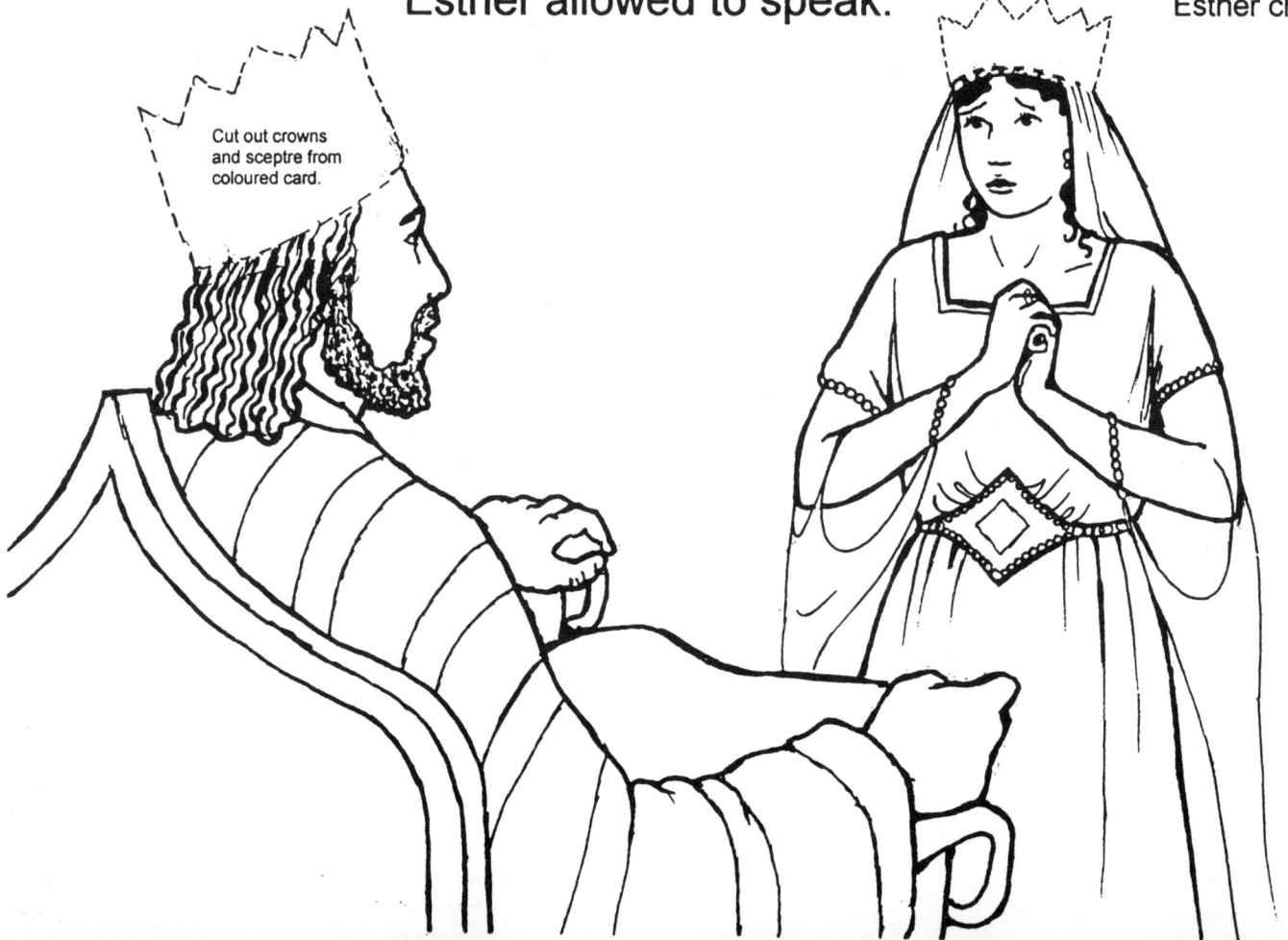

Cut out crowns and sceptre from coloured card.

Nehemiah Rebuilds Jerusalem

Nehemiah 1 - 4 & 6

Themes	Hard Work, Perseverance, God's Plan

Aims	To teach the Biblical account of the rebuilding of the walls of Jerusalem under Nehemiah. To emphasise the value of perseverance. To consider the role of Jerusalem with regard to God's promise to send Jesus into the world.

Resources	Bibles, Children's Story Sheet, Puzzle Page, Activity Sheet, Map.

Other Ideas & Activities

1. Activity Sheet needs buff/grey card/paper.
2. Look at maps of Jerusalem as it was during the time of King David, before the exile (under Solomon) and after Nehemiah had rebuilt it. (These are sometimes found at the back of Bibles.) Make drawings to show the expansion of the city, using a key and colours to show the various boundaries. (A helpful resource here is 'The Student Bible Guide to Jerusalem', published by Candle Books, ISBN 1 85985 082 0 available from most Christian Bookshops.)
3. Research the modern day Jerusalem. Find out about notable landmarks, such as the temple mount, the wailing wall, the Kidron Valley, the dung gate, etc. (A helpful resource here is 'The Student Bible Guide to Jerusalem', published by Candle Books, ISBN 1 85985 082 0 available from most Christian Bookshops.)
4. Why are city walls important? Look at local or famous ones like York. Why were they built? How were they built? What is left?
5. The Jews completed the walls in 52 days. How many weeks/hours/minutes was this?
6. Jerusalem was a mass of rubble when Nehemiah arrived. He had to plan carefully for the task. Write/draw Nehemiah's plans for the job to be done.
7. Draw before/after pictures of Jerusalem.
8. What qualities did Nehemiah and his helpers need in order to be successful? Make a list.

Teacher's Notes

Summary: Nehemiah was deeply upset when he heard that the walls of Jerusalem were in ruins. He asked King Cyrus if he could return and rebuild the walls. Permission was granted. Nehemiah faced an enormous task. There was a great deal of work to be done and opposition from Sanballat and Tobiah. However, God gave the builders wisdom, strength and courage. After 52 days the walls were complete. Nehemiah knew the city was very important. One day Jesus would walk its streets. Christians are willing to persevere, and with God's help achieve difficult things

Point of Contact

Perseverance

- Have you ever struggled to finish something where it seemed you would never get it done?
- How did you feel once it was finally finished?
- What made you keep going until it was done?

Seventy Years Captivity

God's people had refused to obey him and keep his commandments. Instead of loving and serving God, the Jews worshipped idols made of wood and stone. God warned them that if they continued to disobey him, then he would punish them. Still the Jews carried on in their disobedience.

Eventually God sent the King of Babylon, King Nebuchadnezzar, with his army to the city of Jerusalem. He captured thousands of Jews and took them back, on a journey of a thousand miles, to the city of Babylon. Jerusalem was burnt down and left in ruins. God had told the Jews that they would stay in captivity for seventy years.

There were many good people like Daniel and Esther who were captive in Babylon. They believed God's promise concerning the seventy years and longed for the time when the Jews would go back to Jerusalem.

A Change At The Top

The seventy years of captivity were almost complete. Many Jews were very excited because they believed that it would not now be long before God made it possible for his people to return to their own country.

Cyrus became king over Babylon (show map). The Bible says that God put it in his heart to allow the Jews to return to their own country. He made a proclamation, saying that those Jews, who wished to, should be free to return. About 50,000 Jews took the opportunity to go back.

They packed up their belongings and carried them with them as they made the long journey to Jerusalem. There must have been a great sense of excitement and expectancy as they travelled home.

A Great Shock

When they at last arrived, they saw the state that the city was in. Its walls lay in ruins and its gates had been burnt with fire. The great temple King Solomon had built had been completely destroyed. Quickly they made homes for themselves and then set about rebuilding the temple. At last, after many days of hard work, the temple was finished. The people sang for joy.

Nehemiah

There were still several Jews who had stayed behind in Babylon. One of them was a man called Nehemiah. He had a high position in the king's court. He was the king's cupbearer. His job was to serve food and drink to the king. He had to make sure that it wasn't poisoned.

One day some of Nehemiah's friends came from Jerusalem and told him how the walls and gates of the city were still in ruins. Nehemiah was very concerned. He knew how important it was that Jerusalem should be rebuilt and inhabited. He believed that it was God's special city, and that one day the Saviour (Jesus) promised to Abraham (Gen. 12:3 & Gen. 15:4,5) would be born in Israel.

Nehemiah's Request
When Nehemiah received the bad news he spent several days crying and praying to God. One day as he was serving wine to the king, the king noticed Nehemiah's sadness and said, "Why are you sad Nehemiah?" Nehemiah realised this was an opportunity God had given him. He prayed, asking God to help him, and he then told the king his concerns.

The king listened sympathetically and then asked Nehemiah what he would like to do. "Please may I go to Jerusalem and rebuild the ruined city, " Nehemiah asked. The king gave him permission and also supplied building materials that Nehemiah could use for the walls and gates.

Surveying The City
When Nehemiah arrived in Jerusalem he went all around the outside of the city walls, to assess what repairs were needed. He found the walls in a dreadful broken state with heaps of stones and rubble everywhere. The gates were all badly burnt.

A Tremendous Task
Nehemiah called the Jewish leaders and people together. "Come," he said, "Let us build the wall." He encouraged them to work hard, assuring them that God would help them. There was a great deal of rubble to clear away, before they could start building. The work on the walls was extremely hard, because the wall needed to be high and strong to defend the city.

Enemies!
When Nehemiah first arrived there were many enemies, who opposed the work of rebuilding. Sanballat and Tobiah were two of these men who wanted to stop the work of rebuilding. As they saw the walls being built, they were angry. They mocked the Jews saying, "Even a small animal like a fox could knock this wall down!" Nehemiah was concerned. He was worried that Sanballat and Tobiah might organise an attack on the city and stop the building work.

On Guard!
Nehemiah prayed to God and then made some very wise plans. He told the Jews that everyone working on the wall must be on their guard, looking out for any possible attack. Every worker must carry a sword. With one hand he must hold a tool to work with, and with the other hand he must hold a weapon to defend himself.

Nehemiah told the people that if there was an attack, the trumpet would be blown. When the people heard this they must run to the place of attack and defend the city. Nehemiah also made sure that the walls of the city were guarded both day and night. He encouraged the people saying, "Do not be afraid. Remember that God is great and powerful and he will protect us."

Finished!

The Jews worked night and day for 52 days. At last the walls were finished. Now God's special city was safe from any attack. Even Sanballat and Tobiah realised God had helped the Jews to rebuild the wall.

Rejoicing

Nehemiah and the people rejoiced at the completion of the wall. Though they had faced such difficulties and opposition, they thanked God for the wisdom, strength and protection he had given to them.

Nehemiah knew that God's blessing was upon the city. He also knew God's prophets had predicted that one day Jesus the Saviour would be born as a Jew, and would walk Jerusalem's streets.

Illustration: Overcoming Great Difficulties

William Wilberforce lived 200 years ago. He was a wealthy man and a member of Parliament. At 25 he became a Christian. Now rather than just think of himself, his own pleasures and his career, he decided to serve God by helping the under-privileged.

William soon became interested in the slave trade. At this time men, women and children were rounded up on the West coast of Africa and then shipped across the Atlantic Ocean in English ships, to be sold in the West Indies and the Americas. Hundreds of thousands of slaves were crowded into the lower holds of ships. They were treated in the most inhumane ways, being regarded as nothing more than animals. Many died on the long voyage. Wilberforce was horrified and began to expose the evils and horrors of the trade. He was determined to have the slave trade abolished.

His great crusade took over 40 years. At first Wilberforce was hindered by friends of the plantation owners in the Americas, who wanted slaves to work their land. Then the English shipping companies opposed him. It was a long and difficult struggle. In 1823 Parliament passed new laws which made the slave trade illegal.

Wilberforce, like Nehemiah, took on a project which was good and pleased God. They both worked hard and persevered against many difficulties. Their ambitions were accomplished and they were thankful to God who had given them courage and strength for their task.

Things to learn:
- Nehemiah returned to rebuild the ruined city of Jerusalem.
- Despite great difficulties and hostility, and with much perseverance, after 52 days the walls were rebuilt.
- Nehemiah knew God had a great plan for the city. God's prophets had said that one day Jesus would walk Jerusalem's streets.

Discuss
- Why was it so important for Jerusalem to have a city wall?
- What do you think would have happened if the Jews had given up building?
- If we think a project is important are we willing to work hard and not give up until it is completed?
- Are we the sort of person who will battle on to the end or do we give up easily?

Nehemiah Rebuilds Jerusalem

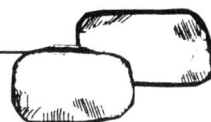

After their capture the Jews were in Babylon for seventy years. Now the king had let them go back to their home country.

As the Jews came to Jerusalem they saw that the tall strong walls were completely broken and the temple was destroyed. But the people were determined to rebuild the city. They quickly made homes for themselves and their families, and began work on rebuilding the temple. After many days of hard work the new temple was complete. The people were so happy that they sang for joy.

Some Jews were still in Babylon. One of these was a man called Nehemiah. He had an important job working as the king's cupbearer. One day he heard about the ruined walls of Jerusalem. This made him sad. The king noticed that Nehemiah was unhappy and asked him, "Why are you sad, Nehemiah?" When Nehemiah told the king about the ruined city, the king gave Nehemiah permission to go to Jerusalem and rebuild the walls.

When Nehemiah arrived in Jerusalem, he walked around the city to see what work needed to be done. Then he called the people together and told them that God would help them rebuild the city walls. So Nehemiah and the people began the hard work. There was a lot of rubble and stones to be cleared away before new stones and materials could be brought in for the walls. The walls needed to be very strong and high enough to keep out any enemies.

Sanballat and Tobiah, who stood nearby, were angry that the walls of Jerusalem were being rebuilt. They watched the workers and laughed at them. Nehemiah thought that Sanballat and Tobiah were planning to attack the city, so he prayed to God for help. He gave orders for every worker to carry a weapon as well as their tools when building the wall. The people would then always be ready for any possible attack. Nehemiah told the people that God would help them and protect them.

After 52 days of hard work, the walls were finished. Nehemiah and the people thanked God for helping them build the walls and keeping them safe.

NEHEMIAH REBUILDS JERUSALEM

**Which city did God help Nehemiah and the people to rebuild?
Take the first letter from each object on the road.**

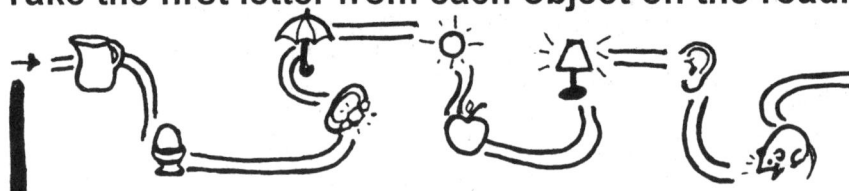

_ _ _ _ _ _ _ _ _

**Fit the words into the grid and
then put them in the story below.**

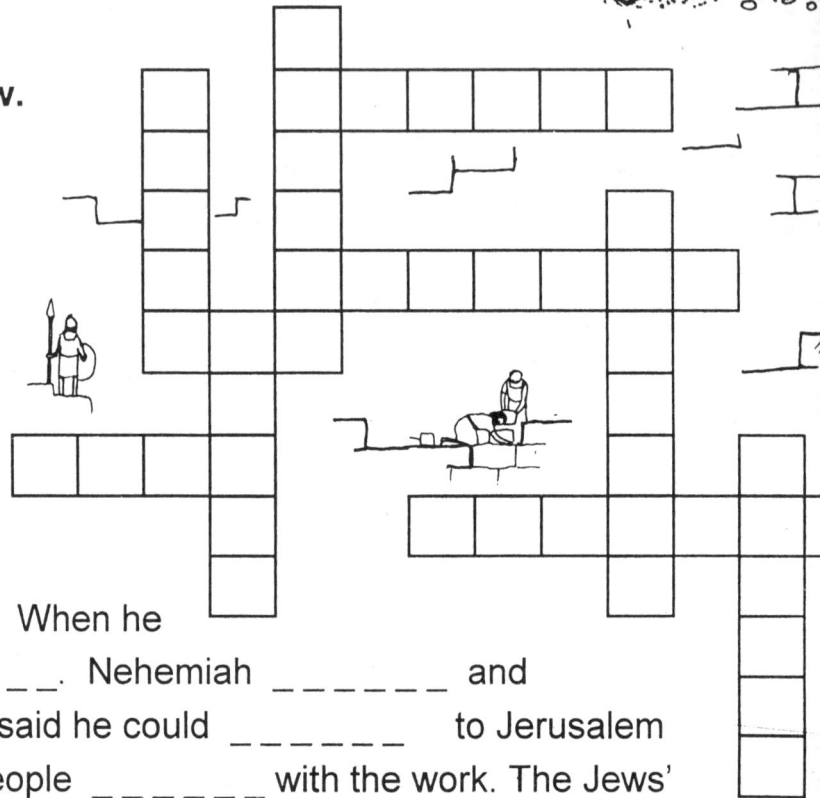

3 letters	4 letters	5 letters
sad	king	walls
		angry

6 letters	7 letters
prayed	enemies
return	weapons
helped	thanked

Nehemiah worked for the _ _ _ _. When he
heard about Jerusalem he was _ _ _. Nehemiah _ _ _ _ _ _ and
then spoke to the king. The king said he could _ _ _ _ _ _   to Jerusalem
to rebuild the _ _ _ _ _ . All the people _ _ _ _ _ _ with the work. The Jews'
_ _ _ _ _ _ _ were _ _ _ _ _ when they saw the work had started. The people carried
_ _ _ _ _ _ _ _ in case their enemies attacked. They _ _ _ _ _ _ _ God when the walls
were completed.

Use the code to find a verse from the Bible.

a b c d e f g h i n o r s t u w
■ ✓ ⌣ ⌢ ✢ ⌂ ● ? ◀ ▶ _ ▼ □ ✕ ⍀ ⌒

_ _ _ _ _ _ _ _ _ _ _ _ _ _

_ _ _ _ _ _ _ _ _ _ _ _ _ _ _ _ . Romans ch.8 v 31

Nehemiah and the people built the walls of Jerusalem again although their enemies tried to stop them.

Neh. ch.3

Glue stone here.

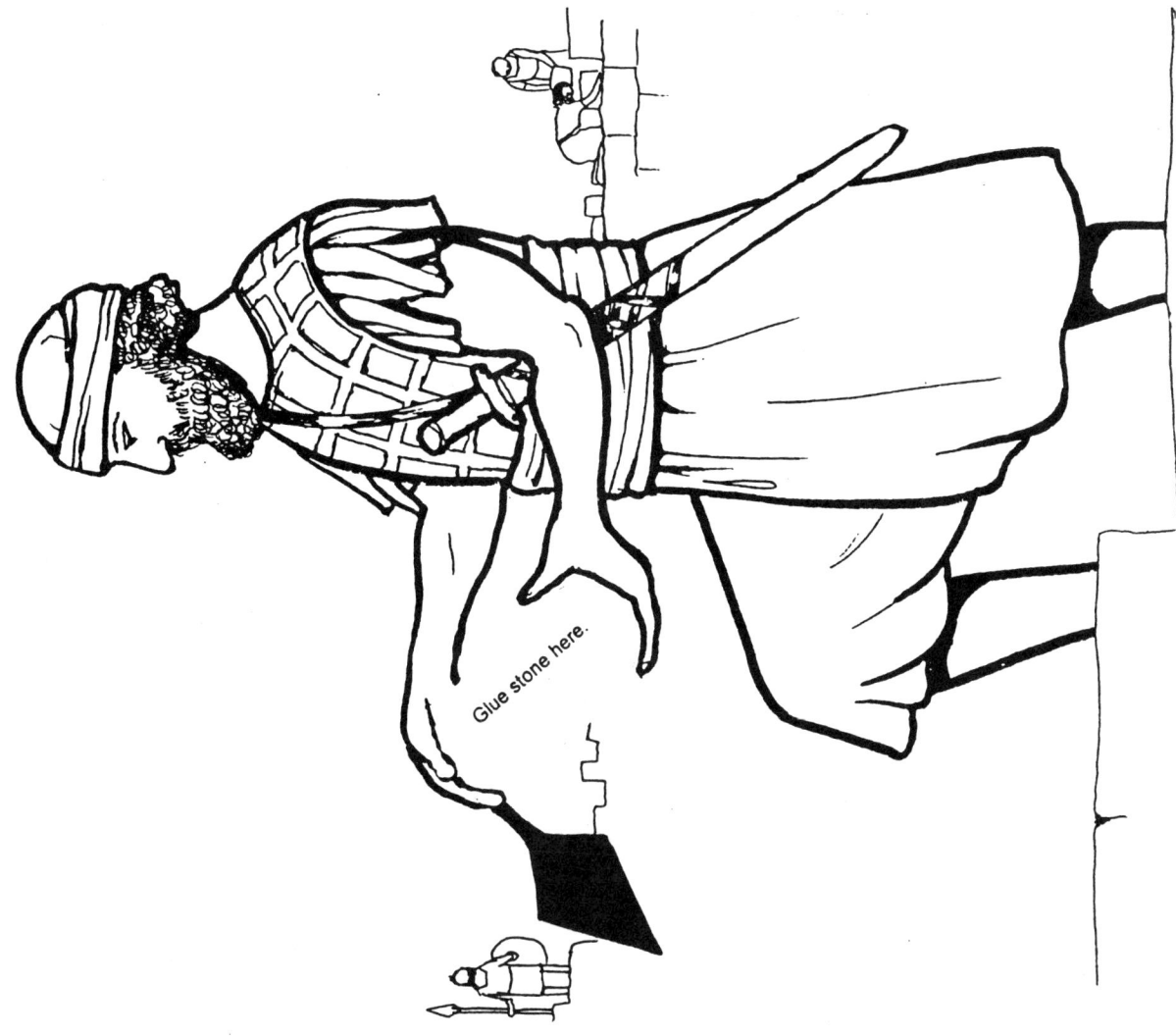

Cut out stones (4 x 3cm approx) from coloured card and build a wall.

Nehemiah and the people built the walls of Jerusalem again although their enemies tried to stop them.

Neh. ch.3

Glue stone here.

Cut out stones (4 x 3cm approx) from coloured card and build a wall.

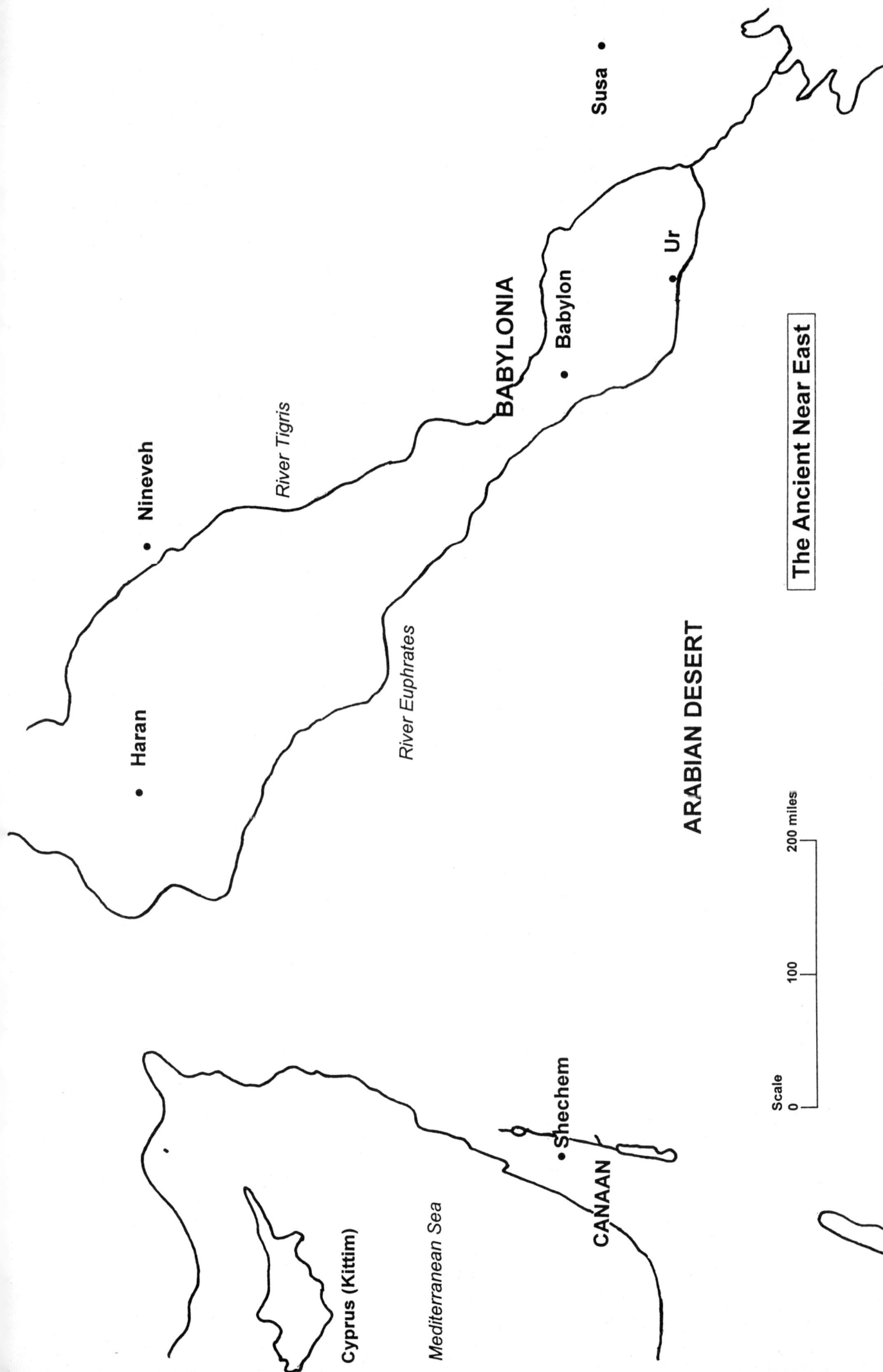

Susa

BABYLONIA

Babylon

Ur

River Tigris

Nineveh

River Euphrates

Haran

ARABIAN DESERT

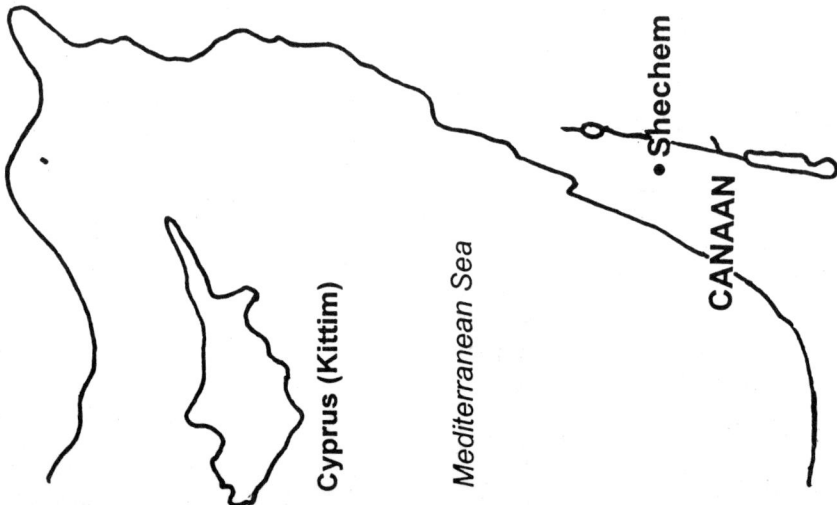

The Ancient Near East

Cyprus (Kittim)

Mediterranean Sea

Shechem

CANAAN

Scale

0

100

200 miles

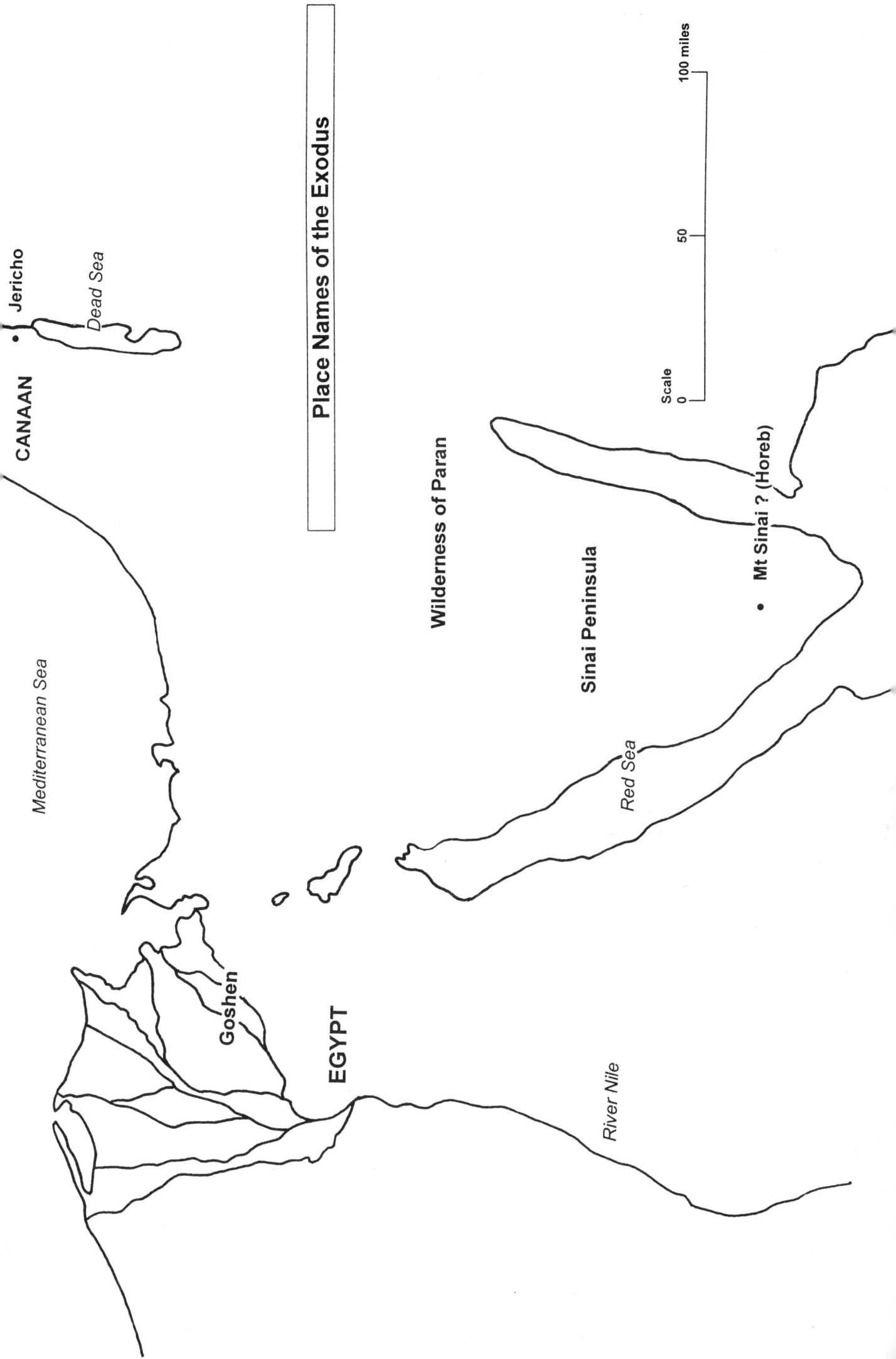

Place Names of the Exodus

Mediterranean Sea

CANAAN

Jericho

Dead Sea

Goshen

EGYPT

River Nile

Red Sea

Sinai Peninsula

Wilderness of Paran

Mt Sinai ? (Horeb)

Scale

0

50

100 miles

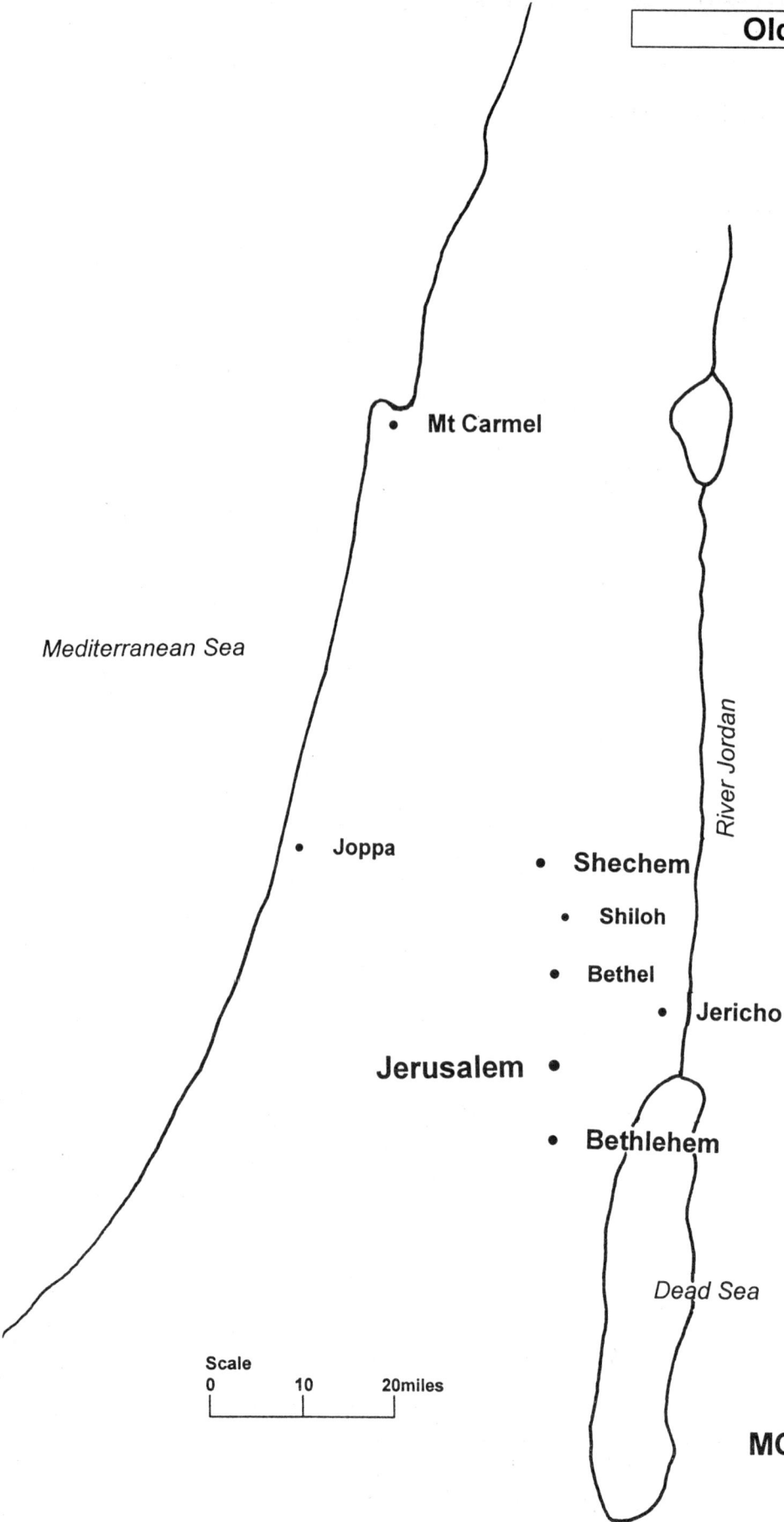

Old Testament Israel

Mediterranean Sea

• Mt Carmel

River Jordan

• Joppa

• **Shechem**

• **Shiloh**

• **Bethel**

• **Jericho**

Jerusalem •

• **Bethlehem**

Dead Sea

Scale

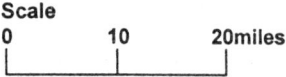

0   10   20miles

MOAB

Index of Lesson Themes

Theme	Lesson
Being Sorry	Joseph Forgives His Brothers
Bravery	David & Goliath
Change	Joseph - From Prison to Power
Character, God's	Elijah on Mount Carmel
Choices	Ruth - The Girl Who Put God First
Complaining	The Israelites in the Wilderness
Courage	Noah & the Flood
Creation of Man & Woman	Adam & Eve
Danger	David & Goliath
Deceit	Jacob - The Man God Changed
Deliverance	Crossing the Red Sea
	Noah & the Flood
	Passover, The
Design	Creation
Doing What Is Right	Daniel in the Lion's Den
Faith	Joshua & the Walls of Jericho
Faithfulness, God's	Abraham - The Man Who Trusted God
Favouritism	Joseph's Coat & Dreams
Forgiveness	Joseph Forgives His Brothers
Forgiveness, God's	Jonah - Preacher on the Run
	The Tabernacle & The Golden Calf
Freedom	The Passover
Gifts & Talents	Esther Saves Her People
Good Behaviour	Daniel in the Lion's Den
Goodness, God's	The Israelites in the Wilderness
Hard Work	Nehemiah Rebuilds Jerusalem
Hardship	Joseph - From Prison to Power
Hatred	Joseph's Coat & Dreams
Idols	The Tabernacle & The Golden Calf
Jealousy	David - The Man Who Loved His Enemy
	Joseph's Coat & Dreams
Loving Your Enemies	David - The Man Who Loved His Enemy
Judgement	Noah & the Flood
	The Passover
Kindness	Jacob - The Man God Changed
Law	The Ten Commandments

Mayflower Christian Resources Old Testament Manual

Mercy	Jacob - The Man God Changed
Obedience	Joshua & the Walls of Jericho
	Noah & the Flood
	Samuel Listens to God
Order	The Ten Commandments
Patience	Joseph - From Prison to Power
Perseverance	Nehemiah Rebuilds Jerusalem
Plan, God's	Moses' Birth & Call
	Nehemiah Rebuilds Jerusalem
Power, God's	Creation
	Crossing the Red Sea
	Elijah on Mount Carmel
	Pharaoh & The Plagues
Praise	Crossing the Red Sea
Prayer	Elijah on Mount Carmel
	Samuel Listens to God
Preparation	Moses' Birth & Call
Presence, God's	Jonah - Preacher on the Run
Promises, God's	Abraham - The Man Who Trusted God
Provision	The Israelites in the Wilderness
Putting God First	Solomon - The Wise King
Reconciliation	Joseph Forgives His Brothers
Reward	Ruth - The Girl Who Put God First
Riches	Solomon - The Wise King
Right & Wrong	The Ten Commandments
Salvation	Adam & Eve
Sin	Adam & Eve
Slavery	The Passover
Standing Firm	Daniel in the Lion's Den
Stubbornness	Pharaoh & The Plagues
Taking Opportunities	Esther Saves Her People
Temptation	Adam & Eve
Trust	Abraham - The Man Who Trusted God
	David & Goliath
	Joshua & the Walls of Jericho
Unselfishness	Joseph - From Prison to Power
	Ruth - The Girl Who Put God First
Wisdom	Solomon - The Wise King
Wonder	Creation
Worship	The Tabernacle & The Golden Calf

Timeline of Old Testament Events & Characters

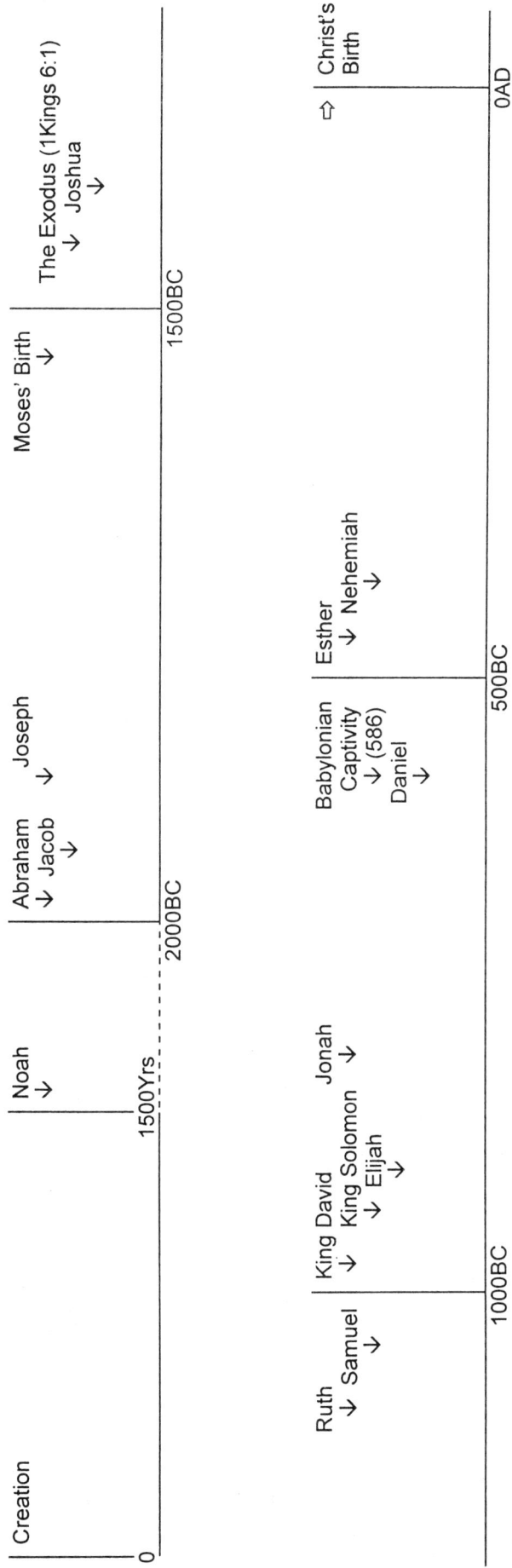

Creation

0

Noah
→

1500Yrs

2000BC

Abraham
→ Jacob
→

Joseph
→

Moses' Birth
→

1500BC

The Exodus (1Kings 6:1)
→ Joshua
→

Ruth
→ Samuel
→

King David
→ King Solomon
→ Elijah
→

Jonah
→

1000BC

Babylonian
Captivity
→ (586)
Daniel
→

Esther
→ Nehemiah
→

500BC

⇑ Christ's
Birth

0AD